NUNS

Marcelle Bernstein was born in Manchester in 1943. After finishing college she completed her education on the staff of the *Manchester Guardian*. She then worked for Britain's biggest-selling newspaper, the *Daily Mirror*, before moving to London to join the *Observer*. There she spent seven years as feature writer specializing in depth profiles of people and places. Since 1970 she has worked as a freelance, writing for major English and international newspapers and magazines. Among the publications in which her work has appeared are the *Daily Telegraph*, the *New Statesman*, the *Washington Post* and the *Melbourne Age*. She has always been fascinated by people's motivation and particularly their obsessions – one of the reasons she wanted to write this book. She is married to another writer, Eric Clark, and has a daughter.

NUNS

Marcelle Bernstein

Fount Paperbacks
COLLINS

First published by William Collins Sons & Co Ltd 1976
Published in Fount Paperbacks 1978

© Marcelle Bernstein 1976

Made and printed in Great Britain by
William Collins Sons & Co Ltd Glasgow

For Eric
and our red pavilions

CONTENTS

Acknowledgments

It would be impossible to thank individually all the nuns and sisters in so many countries who, by their co-operation, made this book possible. They will know who I mean and, I hope, realize how grateful I am. But there are some I must single out. First, Sister Morag Michael of the Community of St Mary the Virgin. As the first sister I ever met, her tremendous enthusiasm for the religious life really caught my imagination. I owe a great debt to Father Gilbert Volery, secretary to the Conference of Major Religious Superiors, who gave so freely of his time and knowledge. Sister Honor Basset of the Society of the Sacred Heart and Sister Mary Joseph of the Vocation Sisters were sources of invaluable guidance. Sister Margaret Moran of the Good Shepherd, Sister Madeleine of the Augustinian Sisters of Meaux, Sister Eileen Gielty of the Sisters of Notre Dame de Namur and Mother Joanna of the Deaconess Community of St Andrew gave much advice. David Miles Board and the Catholic Information Office did everything they could. My especial thanks for all the kindness shown to me by the many nuns I visited in Europe and America, particularly Sister Marie-Marthe of the Holy Child Convent in Neuilly and Sister Lorenzina Guidetti of the Daughters of St Paul. The Maryknoll sisters in New York, Sister Liz Thoman in Los Angeles and Sister Pearl McGivney in the Coachella valley all showed more hospitality than I can ever repay. I would like to acknowledge the help of the Catholic Central Library, and the British Museum for access to their private pornography files – a curious experience. Finally, and most deeply, I thank Mother Michael and the Carmelites of Llandovery for showing me what the religious life can be.

INTRODUCTION

My first contact with nuns was a revelation.

I had gone to visit the Community of St Mary the Virgin in Wantage, Berkshire, for a magazine article I was writing. I knew what they would be like: I had a vivid picture in my mind's eye acquired from books and films. At worst I expected formidable strictness and the stuffy aura of sanctity, at best sweet, unworldly women encased in black and white, hands folded in prayer, living in a convent out of *The Sound of Music*.

What I found could not have been more different. Here were chatty, intellectual women perfectly prepared to discuss not only their reasons for entering but the difficulties they encounter; not only what it means to sacrifice much emotional and all sexual satisfaction, but where they buy their underwear – in bulk from a well-known chain store under the brand name 'St Michael'.

I left wanting to know more. Surprisingly, most books on the subject seemed intended for the knowledgeable insider: they were written by academics and theologians, by nuns for other nuns, or by ex-nuns seeking to justify themselves. None of them answered the questions I wanted to ask. I decided that the best way to learn what I wanted to know was to write a book myself.

My qualifications were, to say the least, unlikely. I could hardly have a less Christian background – I am a Jew. I am in no sense a religious person. Neither, I confess, did I have much sympathy for the idea of such a way of life. Celibacy, which more than any other single factor marks the nun out from other women, may be regarded by Christians as understandable, or even as a state of perfection, but Jews are likely to see it as sterility and view it with disfavour.

On the other hand I am a journalist, used to submerging

my own opinions. I could be objective because I had no axe to grind. I also felt real interest for two reasons. First, my husband is – nominally at least – a Christian. The second was growing fascination; fanaticism is a compelling force and there is no doubt that nuns are, in our terms, fanatics. 'No one is going to be a successful nun,' one novice mistress told me, 'unless she's touched with fire.'

So I embarked on *Nuns*. There are approaching a million of them. In precise religious terms those in active orders – teaching, perhaps, or nursing – are sisters. Only those in contemplative communities, for ever enclosed, are, strictly speaking, nuns. But 'nun' is generally held to mean both.

In addition to those in Roman Catholic orders, there is a much smaller number of Protestant sisters. Some are included in the book, but I have concentrated on the Catholic majority. Deciding which orders to cover in detail and which to glance at briefly posed a major problem. In America alone there are 359 different orders and convents beyond number. The Sisters of Mercy, largest of all the orders, has 192 convents in Ireland alone, not to mention schools, colleges, hospitals and homes, and it is an order which spreads world-wide. Ultimately the choice was of course haphazard. Some orders – the Carmelites and Cistercians, for instance – I found particularly intriguing: the Carmelites because of the character of their extraordinary Spanish foundress, the Cistercians because of their extreme asceticism.

Others I chose for their unlikely work, such as the French Sisters of Marie Joseph who nurse in prisons. Others were chosen because they are in some way experimental, like the Deaconess Community of St Andrew who have sisters in the only permanent mixed sex community in Britain. Then there were communities which had undergone extraordinary change, in particular the American Immaculate Heart Sisters in California, all of whom have been officially 'reduced' to lay people. Finally, there were individuals who stood out from the rest, women attracting attention because of what they were saying or doing.

Nuns at this moment are in an unprecedented position, literally caught between two worlds. Many still cling to the rules and standards of the Middle Ages, unable to wash their clothes in anything but soda, encouraged to scourge themselves with whips, sleeping fully dressed upon pallets of straw and rising at night to pray for a world they will never see again.

For others there has been a revolution as they move out of their medieval chrysalis into the modern world. These nuns are today among the most highly trained professional women in the West: doctors and economists, scientists and policewomen. There are nuns working on the factory floor, staffing ghetto schools and running homes for unmarried mothers. Nuns nurse alcoholics and lepers, drug addicts and the destitute of city slums. They are to be found in the most remote corners of the world: as missionaries they work in the mountains of Peru and the forests of the Amazon, in the deserts of Australia and the Arctic wastes of Canada. They are politically aware and active on issues as diverse as the rights of Jews in Russia and the equality of women.

This process of modernization was brought about partly by increased awareness and a growing sense of responsibility among the nuns themselves, and partly by the need for change pressed upon them by Vatican II, the great meeting of bishops in Rome in 1965. Yet desirable as this process may seem, there are those who question the need for it. Certainly it has brought nuns to a crisis point. Coming out of their enclosures, abandoning their habits, rethinking their rules – these changes have made many nuns question their relevance for the first time and thousands have walked out of their convents. Others have left not because of uncertainty about their new roles but because of disgust with a system which legally classes women with children and idiots. With eyes opened by their realization of the growing social importance of women, they find it totally unacceptable that the male hierarchy retains power over matters which vitally concern them – and even denies them a voice. Nuns outnumber men in religious life by more than two to one – but they are forced to remain a silent majority.

During the last four years I have talked at length to more than 500 nuns tackling work as diverse as helping handicapped children in France to picketing with the grapepickers on the Mexican border; from publishing books in Italy to living in the ghettoes of Harlem and Chicago – where they still walk in pairs, but now for protection rather than from modesty. I have met nuns nursing people dying of cancer, listened as they advised pregnant schoolgirls and helped battered wives. I saw architects and artists, university professors and poets; nuns who won the Croix de Guerre for their bravery during the German occupation of France, and missionaries who survived prisoner-of-war conditions in the Philippines.

I have been deeply moved and greatly impressed. For some of the nuns I now feel immense and lasting affection. If my ignorance about so much of their lives amused them, they did not let it show. They were painstaking in answering my questions and did so with an honesty and openness for which I had hardly dared to hope. I was treated with unfailing kindness and hospitality. They let me share their own cells. They drove me around. (Nuns, incidentally, are perhaps the world's worst drivers. They seem to have the touching belief that if they point the car in roughly the right direction, God will take care of everything else.) I have shared their silent meals on wooden tables in European refectories, and warmed-up TV dinners in the apartments of liberated American sisters.

Out of all the nuns and sisters to whom I have talked, only one or two older women clearly found me hard to take on religious grounds. 'I don't think,' one told me sharply, 'that a Jew can really understand Christianity.' So perhaps I should point out that I have not tried to do so. This book is not an attempt to justify or vilify, to 'explain' Christianity, Catholicism, or any particular point of view.

The constant question in my mind was why should any woman choose to live the life of a nun. I believe I understand a little better now. But I still cannot totally comprehend it. It is, I am reluctantly convinced, incomprehensible. A mystery of the human spirit that cannot be completely explained.

I wanted to make this book objective but I think that finally it has become very personal: this is how I see the nuns I have met. What I really wanted to do was to listen to what they have to say on all aspects of their lives, and give them the voice they still do not have. They discussed their work and their superiors, their relationships with the outside world and their need for more freedom. I asked how they feel about the vows they have taken, whether they miss the company of men, or regret the children they will never bear.

'Nuns,' declared an irate sister at a recent convention, 'have remained a mystery for far too long.' This book is an attempt to unravel that mystery.

I

INSIDE THE ENCLOSURE

Turn left out of Llandovery station and walk along the wet
Welsh road up into the hills, where on the right there is a
long winding drive, with a one-room lodge spouting smoke
at the gate. A great round sign reads LLAN CARMEL. It used
to read CARMELITE MONASTERY but the Welsh Nationalists
started painting it out at night.

The heavy piece of wood on which the words are written
was once inside the monastery. It used to be the 'turn', the
revolving cupboard which was the only communication the
nuns had with the world outside. The extern sisters, who
lived outside and could never enter, would put on it provisions
and letters, and the nun within would swing it round: it
was so designed that they never even saw each other's faces.

The turn has gone now – but only just. Life here continues
as it has always done, exactly as it is lived in every Carmelite
monastery in Europe. The Carmelites are one of the oldest
orders, following the rule of life as it was laid down by Teresa
of Avila in sixteenth-century Spain. Together with the
Cistercians, Benedictines and Poor Clares, they are among the
grandes dames, the aristocrats of the religious world. The
Carmelite life is contemplative and penitential; the divine
office is recited daily and enclosure is complete and constant.
The way they look and the way they live has not changed in
four hundred years: this is the way people imagine nuns and
convents to be.

This particular Carmel is a solid, foursquare house standing high in its thirteen acres of ground surrounded by a ramble of rhododendrons, looking out across a gentle triple-rivered valley causing one of the nuns to nickname it 'Llanduckery'. It is the last of three foundations made in Wales in the 1930s by Mother Mary of Jesus, the French-born prioress who first brought the Carmelites to London in 1878 and established thirty-three monasteries in Britain. Bishop Vaughan invited the Carmelites to Wales – scarcely a Catholic stronghold – and on October 15, 1934, he performed the enclosure ceremony in the open and a deluge of rain that cost him a week in bed afterwards. As with all Carmel houses, the local population was invited in to see round before the enclosure door was shut for ever.

Today, a visitor arriving at the house across the gravelly drive rings a bell and enters the hallway. The only furniture in it is a dark wood dresser which contains Christmas cards even in May, and notelets designed and printed by the nuns, with bluebells on them and: 'May your prayers ascend to God this happy day and draw upon you the blessings of heaven.' And a large printed card: 'PLEASE would any kind caller POST THESE LETTERS. THANK YOU!' At the end of the hall a heavy door is set with a massive lock and key, and a panel which slides back to reveal a grey-painted wire grille. Sister Rosalie, the turn sister, opens the panel cautiously when the bell is rung, and only her pretty round face is visible through the crack. She directs all visitors to the parlour, on the right of the hall, whether they are family, priest or friend. No one may enter the enclosure except, in emergencies, the doctor, though the Holy See does permit exceptions in the case of cardinals, bishops, and reigning heads of state.

The parlour is a small room, with one comfortable chair and one upright, a table with a little bunch of blue flowers clearly gathered by a child, and an electric fire. The end of the room is partitioned off by a low wall, with a pelmet above it. Beyond this, another upright chair is for the nun. This fitment is all that is now left at Llandovery of the formidable double grilles of Carmel. The nuns still keep, as they always will, the sturdy outer enclosure door with its massive double keys. But the grille itself used to consist of an iron grid fitted with spikes several inches long, then a wooden screen of heavy slats, and finally black shutters which could be closed and locked. These not only reached from floor to ceiling, but were hung with black veiling, as were the nuns who went to the grille even to see their parents. In addition, they had to be accompanied by two other sisters. The mother prioress is delighted the grille has gone: 'We took it for granted, but it was medieval. It didn't mean anything.'

It is to this parlour that many visitors come. Not only relatives and other religious, and students in their summer vacations, but men and women who over the years have built up close friendships with the enclosed through their visits. And there are 'souls', as the nuns call them: women who need a day or two away from demanding families; people in all kinds of distress. They come in such numbers that the nuns tell you they are 'very booked up in the summer' and they recently built a bungalow to accommodate their guests.

That they come in the numbers they do is a tribute to the mother prioress, a woman of marvellous warmth and wisdom. Now seventy-two, she had her golden jubilee in 1971 – fifty years a professed Carmelite. Like so many nuns, she looks years younger, her face comfortable and benign beneath the soft headdress. She is a woman of considerable intellectual power, who in her youth corresponded with Jung about her dreams. It is undoubtedly her personality, her deep quiet voice, and her energy which hold the community so firmly together. Her religious career has been by any standards extraordinary: she has been prioress almost continuously since 1938. A Carmelite prioress is elected by the community every three years, and can be re-elected once. After that the father general of the order in Rome must be approached for permission to elect her yet again; it is done only when qualities of leadership are quite outstanding.

It is under Mother Michael's guidance that the Llandovery Carmelites have begun, in accordance with the obligations put upon religious by the Second Vatican Council, to renew and revitalize Carmel. They have, for example, relaxed their rules sufficiently to allow a nun out into the world briefly if perhaps a close relative is ill and there is no one else to nurse.

But these women have chosen to follow that chilling decree of Pope Boniface VIII in 1298: 'We command by this present constitution, whose validity is eternal and can never be questioned, that all nuns, collectively and individually, present and to come, of whatsoever order of religion, in whatever part of the world they may be, shall henceforth remain in their monasteries in perpetual enclosure.'

Perpetual enclosure. The words ring heavy with drama and denial. As well they might. Any woman who cuts herself off from her family and forfeits her freedom has made a most complete sacrifice. And yet the nuns of Llandovery go into great giggles at the idea that they are in any way heroic. For them, this choice was as inevitable and irresistible and undeniable as a great love affair, only their love is not for any man. One nun, over eighty now and nearly blind, says of her entry into Carmel that 'it was wonderful to give up everything to God.'

For Carmel is, above all things, a giving of the self to God. As Mother Michael says, 'People who think that we're wasting our time and ought to be doing good in the world have not recognized that God has his needs.' She acknowledges, however, the perils of Carmel's physical and mental isolation from the world. 'The danger of enclosed nuns is to become an island, used to being on your own. It's terribly important to remember that we're not.'

Just behind the heavy enclosure door lies a small, whitewashed courtyard. Carefully tended, with daffodils and the blue stars of forget-me-nots round a central rockery, it has a Spanish air. Round three sides of it the house stretches, providing shelter under which, in bad weather, the nuns move from office to office, their feet in great big wellingtons with their habits tucked up into their belts revealing their heavy tweed underskirts, plastic pixie hoods topping their headdresses.

The interior is that of any large underfurnished English country house, remarkable chiefly for an abundance of religious statues, like the white St Joseph dear to the Carmelites, standing as a protection to the home. In a long stone-flagged corridor a sign reads: 'PLEASE NO SPEAKING IN

THIS PASSAGE. THE CELLAR STEPS FOR A QUICK WORD, FOR LONGER SPEECH THE LAMP OFFICE OR THE COMMUNITY ROOM.' This corridor leads to the heart of the community, to the chapel where the nuns gather for prayer seven times a day in the pattern of homage which has continued unbroken in religious houses since the sixth century.

The day begins when the nuns rise just after five o'clock to go straight to an hour of silent prayer and meditation in choir. They enter through the ante-choir, with its polished wooden floors and little pots of garden flowers offered before a carved figure of Our Lady of Walsingham. The chapel is modernized, with big windows and reading lights which the nuns switch on in the dawn darkness. Their side of the chapel is cool and empty, with rows of seats down the sides and high-backed chairs at the head for the mother prioress and the mother sub-prioress. A wide-meshed grille divides the nuns' choir from the public side of the chapel, which is used by visitors to the monastery and the local Catholic population. This grille has a square opening cut in it through which the nuns are given Communion by the priest, and through which they reach to light the great Paschal candle in its brass and copper holder, made for them by a Caldey Island monk. Just to the right there is a relic cupboard, covered in damask, containing what they believe to be a piece of the True Cross and slivers of bone from various saints; tiny portraits of St Teresa and St John of the Cross are enclosed inside crucifixes.

This chapel is the hub of their lives. Aromatic from the incense and the pine branches with which the walls are decorated, hushed except for the slip of sandalled feet on wood, the only music the high and unaccompanied voices of the nuns, it is simple and austere, as functional as a workroom. And that is in fact very much its atmosphere. The nuns make formal and measured prayer, but they are as matter-of-fact about it as women in a kitchen: this is their home.

For these nuns of Carmel can do nothing themselves for the world but pray. And through prayer, they believe they become instruments through which strength can flow. It is a contract with God which brings down love into the world. 'It is a very mysterious thing.'

The purpose and aim of the enclosed life of prayer is perfectly defined by Mother Michael: 'A few should have their lives centred on God, on worship.' A woman who wants to live so, leaving everything else in search of God, must have sufficient mental and physical health to withstand so arduous an existence. 'Many people,' explains Mother Michael, 'long for this kind of life, yet psychologically may be unfitted for it. Enclosure is very strict and if they weren't really suited everything would go wrong.' Out of the million women in religious life, there are just sixty thousand contemplatives. The six per cent return on capital, they have been called, which God reserves to himself. And so to these women prayer comes as easily as breathing. Mother Mary of Jesus of Carmel, the nineteenth-century French prioress and foundress, would ask for any guidance or help she might need: for the best way of altering a building, or the removal of obstacles; that the Carmels would be supported, and that some tiny salad plants might thrive. No nun of Carmel ever asks for proof of the efficacy of her prayer. They are praying for the world, and they are quite certain they are helping. Proof is unnecessary. 'We don't need it. We know.'

After that first silent hour in choir the nuns breakfast in the refectory on tea and the crusty brown bread they bake weekly. Until religious orders of women were ordered to undertake revitalization in 1965, the only hot drink they ever tasted was sugared water. One sister remembers that: 'My first cup of tea sent me into *raptures*.' The refectory is a new extension of the old house, a modern wide room with wooden floors. Six long tables are set with benches, and before each place there is bread in a polythene bag, basic cutlery and a napkin. There is a pat of butter on a plate, a handle-less cup called a godet, and a platter. At one end of the room there is a hot-plate. Before the mother prioress's place there is a little bell, which she rings for the meal to commence.

Sub-Prioress Mother Imelda is the cook. At thirty-two she is one of the youngest sisters, serious and shy, and until three years ago she had never cooked at all: in those days she would start dinner at 9.30 a.m. in case anything went wrong. Now she is highly organized in her huge, high-ceilinged kitchen, with rows of cereal laid out ready for the next meal in brown earthenware bowls. These days she orders from Llandovery by telephone and food is delivered in bulk, but the nuns provide for themselves as much as possible. In the larder there are two dustbins full of preserved eggs laid by Sister Mary's hens at the rate of forty a day. Fruit and vegetables grown in the kitchen garden are stored in the deep freeze. 'I don't know how we managed without it. We wouldn't have this luxury, but a sister had a legacy.' Everyone in turn helps to prepare the vegetables for the day, working in silence. At the end of the meal washing-up is communal; one nun wrapped in a huge oilcloth apron stands on a box to reach the high sink with its teak washing-up bowl, while another dries and puts away.

Fifteen minutes is allowed for breakfast before Matins at 7.0, then the nuns do odd chores and make their beds until Lauds at 8.0, followed by Mass and Tierce, for which the priest from the village has dressed in one of the hand-made vestments which hang, glowing with the subdued colours of stained glass, in the sacristy. Then just after 9.0 the nuns begin work.

To live 'a life of prayer' sounds easy. It conjures up a vision of calm and candlelight, of slow hours in silent gardens, hands clasped in tranquillity, mind bent on the spiritual. Hard on the knees, perhaps, but scarcely arduous. Such imaginings could not be further from the truth. All the Carmelite nuns have the lined, stubby hands of good workmen, which is exactly what they are. 'People think,' comments one on certain aspirants, 'that they're going to sit and pray. Well, we haven't much time for that: we don't think much of that sort of prayer.'

Much of their day is spent in hard physical labour, repetitive work deliberately chosen for the community so that it can be done mechanically. For what they do, the exterior, is not important. They regard it merely as an outer shell. What matters is that their minds are free for God. So their work must not encourage them to worry and bustle, which is against the prayer life. None the less, Teresa of Avila herself laid down that they must support themselves, not living on alms, nor eating of the bread of the poor unearned.

Sister Antonia Maria of Jesus is one of several nuns who has as part of her work the making of altar breads. This work was chosen for the community as being reasonably rewarding financially. They can work on it alone, it is not too absorbing but simple enough to leave the mind free for contemplation.

In the stone-floored cooking office overlooking the little courtyard stands the cooking machine, which works on the principle of a giant waffle iron. It needs to be regularly greased with the wax collected from the monastery candles to keep the surfaces smooth. The upper plate provides a number of designs. White flour and water are then mixed by hand to a soft paste and a dollop – it must be exactly the right amount and practice, says Sister Antonia, makes perfect – is placed on the square, baking-hot metal plate. Then the top plate is brought down by hand, pressing the dough out flat, so that it oozes out round the edges and is rapidly trimmed with a knife. (The edges of the sheets are given to the local farmers for pig food.) After a few minutes the machine is reopened and there is an almost opaque white sheet of altar bread, stamped on the back with the chosen design, incredibly smooth and perfect. At the end of the day, the sheets which by then have cooled are taken on enormous trays down the steep stone steps to the cellar, where they are stored on racks under cloths until they are taken up to the room where they will be cut. This is on the first floor (and tied to the pipes there is a rope ladder which is the community fire escape: the nuns have practised shinning down it once or twice, which they rather enjoyed).

The cutting machine stamps out four thousand breads a day, all fed through by hand. They are then packed into tins for the various religious retailers and individual churches who have ordered them: the Anglicans insist that theirs have crucifixes on the back, the Catholics prefer a waffle finish. When there is a rush on, for Christmas or Easter, all the nuns sit round the table and help pack them, three hundred to a tin.

The work is done in silence. It is the profound quiet of enclosure that strikes the outsider most forcibly, the peace that wraps itself round the monastery like a cloak. It is a contemplative silence which one Carmelite has called 'the wordless understanding between two lovers'. Except at mealtimes, when one of the nuns will read, or during the occasional hours of recreation, they rarely speak to each other. The only exception would be when speech is necessary sometimes for their work, or in an emergency, such as illness or the breakdown of a piece of machinery. And special permission for speech can be asked of the mother prioress if it might help one nun spiritually to talk to another. But when they do talk they are so articulate it is hard to realize how little conversation they have. 'No one,' says a particularly quiet woman with a wide smile, 'enjoys talking so much as an enclosed nun.'

Although most of the day is spent working, their tasks are well balanced and they do not feel they do too much at a stretch. Each day is broken several times by the bell ringing high above the convent for prayer. But occasionally there is so much to do that they have 'work days' at times of pressure. 'Sometimes it can be a break to have a day free for working.'

Sister Antonia stops the exhausting altar bread work after an hour – the heavy top plate is an effort to raise and lower – and goes up to her old-fashioned sewing-machine in the robe room on the first floor, where the bulky habits are stored. Each nun has two for summer, one for winter, and Sister Antonia makes these for each nun, to a strict pattern set out under the rules of the order in which it is specified that 'before a new habit is given to a Sister, the Sister in charge of the Robe Room must ask permission to have it blessed by a priest.' Every little detail must be observed, to the exact length of the points at the side of the habit.

There is a story the nuns tell with glee about two nuns and a postulant who had lately entered, at the time when the same heavy habit was worn winter and summer, regardless of extremes of temperature. The postulant said she did not know if she would like it. One of the nuns told her: 'Oh, that's all right, Sister, don't you worry. In summer it's loose and cool and in winter it's thick and warm.' But the other said: 'It's very penitential, our habit. In winter it's very draughty and in summer it's very hot.' The nuns use this to illustrate that what you get out of life depends on what you are looking for, but the fact is the habit does look as if it could be something of a mixed blessing. The Carmelites wear a comfortable, monkish, dark brown habit which reaches to the ground, and their hair is covered by a white band and a heavy black veil. It gives them a timeless look, like figures from a medieval manuscript, and they certainly need the warmth and comfort of the robes during cold winters in a huge old house. But the robes have none of the advantages of instant-wash synthetics, and even the relatively light summer habit must make gardening, for instance, singularly difficult. And anyway, as Sister Antonia points out, 'It's only since we got not so terribly penitential that we have summer clothing. When I entered, everything was thick. I was clothed on June 2 and it was a sweltering hot day.'

Originally, the only thing that changed from summer to winter was the bodice, which in cold weather was double wool, hand-seamed. Each was given this and two separate long sleeves, which she had to sew in. 'And it was hard lines if, once you got into this, you had a spell of hot weather.' This was changed every ten days. Sister Antonia remembers that 'when I first entered, I used to wear soft flannel vest and pants. You didn't have new ones till your profession. And when I was first clothed, I had a rather rough tunic.' There is an underskirt of thick tweed with a hem which can be let down: the width of this must be exactly five inches. There is a big pocket at the front of the underskirt in which the nuns keep their enormous white handkerchiefs and any oddments they might need with them. Over it all goes the scapular, the sleeveless coat that slips over the head, covers the robe and reaches the ground back and front. This is held to the robe with scapular pins, a sort of primitive safety-pin. Sister Antonia makes these out of berries which she collects in the garden and keeps in a tin till they harden. They are soaked in water, and strung on to cords. The nuns all wear a headdress, which they call a torque, wrapped round the head under the veil. When a girl is clothed as a postulant, the mother prioress will trim her hair to fit neatly under it.

Sister Antonia herself entered Carmel in 1954 when she

was twenty-eight. A gentle woman with the melancholy dark eyes of her Italian ancestry, she found she had 'great doubts' in those early days but felt strongly that life is short 'like the grain of sand and the seashore. And it wasn't worth giving your love to that.'

It is this attitude more than any other which marks out the contemplatives. They believe that love of the world, of ease and comfort, do actually come between themselves and the love of God. God has called them to something which is, in Sister Antonia's words 'more pleasant – but less pleasing'. He is calling them to Himself. 'You just know that God is there, that good things are prepared. So it's worth giving up the joys of the world: there's something more lasting at the end of this.'

Like all the other Carmelites, she knows well how unnoticed they are by the mass of the world outside. She folds the tunic she is stitching, and pats it smooth. 'We're doing little things, we're completely tucked away, forgotten, of no importance. Yet we're accomplishing a great missionary work by putting love into every little action.'

Just along the corridor, Mother Michael is working in the prioress's office. There is a picture of the Good Shepherd on the door, and on the desk the typewriter with which she was presented on her golden jubilee. Next to it, the *Church Etymological Dictionary* and *The Anathemata* by David Jones. There is also a list of names: 'We're all going to sign the Mary Whitehouse petition for public decency. Though as we don't see television we can't say we know about that from experience.'

There is also a book on wood carving and another on anatomy for artists: Mother Michael is an accomplished artist and is now working on the headstone of her mother's grave. 'I hoped very much to do a carving, but it's taken me three years to do a very small inscription.' The grave is within the enclosure. A special dispensation from the bishop allowed this, for normally none but the Carmelites lie here. But Mother Michael's sister, Mildred, is in the Carmel at Falkirk in Scotland. 'She was my novice at one time: she was a worldly little miss but she realized this was her call.' When their mother died alone at ninety the rules had not been relaxed and neither daughter was with her. 'My mother wouldn't have wanted us to come to her. She would have felt we were breaking something. She'd given us to God – she didn't want to take us back.'

Yet Mother Michael herself was at first reluctant to see her destiny in a convent. 'I remember thinking, how ghastly to shut myself up with a lot of women for the rest of my life.' She entered at twenty-one – the same age as another unwilling nun, Teresa of Avila. Teresa was as flirtatious and romantic as it was possible for a well-born and well-chaperoned Spanish girl to be in sixteenth-century Spain. She felt she should become a nun, yet the idea of religious life repelled her. Even so, she went into the convent of the Incarnation in Avila believing that if the cloister was purgatory, there would be heaven at the end of it.

Mother Michael, who has been more than fifty years in Carmel, affirms that the life can be 'terribly hard', and the natural things which are renounced and sacrificed and done without 'can be a pull. After all, this is against our natural desires and longings. Naturally one wants to marry and have children. Naturally we want to have friends. Naturally we want to have a career.'

Even now, she finds that faith cannot be put into words. 'It's alive and real, it's an assurance of truth.' She knows that this life is the direct search for God. 'And yet the paradoxical truth is that if you hadn't already found Him, you wouldn't be searching for Him.'

Mother Michael, like every nun, knows God's silences. 'When there's no response from God, that's hard. If you have a very positive awareness of God's presence as love, you can stand anything. When you haven't got God – or anything else – things are pretty grim.' It is a feeling to which contemplatives are perhaps more subject than those in active orders for they cannot bury themselves for a while in outside work, or in the problems of others. 'You just feel hours of great despondence,' explains Sister Antonia, 'when you sense that He is not pleased. But you know that deep down nothing is going to pull you away from God.' Mother Michael has, however, a piece of advice culled from Thomas Aquinas which in just such a situation she particularly treasures. 'If you're in a stew there are four things to do: you can have a hot bath; talk to a friend; have a good cry; contemplate truth.' And this, she feels, improves matters. 'Even in bad times, God sends compensation. He'll send you a special friend, or you'll find the community is very fond of you.'

The Llandovery community is clearly not only very fond of Mother Michael, but it also relies on her. For the Carmelites, as for other contemplative orders, the personality of the superior is vitally important to the happiness of all. Because the community is small – it is laid down that there should always be twelve nuns and the prioress – and carefully regulated, there is no area in which her influence is not felt. For even the smallest thing – an aspirin to relieve a headache – the nuns will ask a 'permission' from 'Our Mother' before going to the well-stocked infirmary.

It is, though, with some relief that Mother Michael is now serving her final term: 'I shall be enormously glad to be an ordinary member of the community, not to have to make decisions.' The Llandovery Carmel at present comes under the authority of the bishop of the diocese, in their case Menevia, and under the laws written by the Carmelite Fathers. 'But now we're all being asked to say what we want, to change that.' It would, she feels, be better to have government by the nuns themselves, which Teresa herself would surely have wanted, 'though we ought to have regional authority of some kind'. She feels that if everything were left to the individual Carmel prioresses, 'you might get somebody too rigid. And left to each prioress, it might put too much strain on her.'

It was in the early 1960s that Mother Michael first arrived at Llandovery, brought in to revitalize a community literally dying on its feet, since the nuns were all elderly and there were no novices. There are several young nuns now: the turn sister, Sister Rosalie, is twenty-two and the new novice, Sister Ann Patrice, is twenty-eight. There are a couple in their thirties and forties, but 'four of us are in our seventies.' Nor is it easy for the Carmelites to attract new entrants.

Mother Michael has advertised twice in the Catholic press, to no avail. 'It's so much a special vocation that just asking people won't do.'

Several nuns have come to Llandovery from the main Welsh Carmel of Presteigne, where Mother Michael spent so much of her life. One is Sister Mary of Carmel, whose tasks include looking after the tunic office where the woollen nightshirts for winter are stored, and the flannelette or cotton ones for summer. There are great piles of thick sheets ('I'm afraid they only get washed once a year') and more piles of long-sleeved, round-necked petticoats made out of scratchy, hopsacky material. 'Ten years ago no one wore pants. For more than half my religious life I didn't have them.'

Sister Mary is a vigorous woman with a strong face. When she was considering the religious life, she says: 'I thought to myself, I'm a very active person, my attraction would be to action. But even in an active order, one can do so little, and there's so much to be achieved. It wasn't enough, somehow.'

But Sister Mary has been very happy. Her one regret is that she did not see more of the world before entering, though she did manage to visit Rome three times. She does think that 'going about might cheapen this life.' It is not that she feels contaminated by the world, like Thomas à Kempis, but 'I feel I've been given something else.' Rather wistfully, she says it might be nice to go for a walk, but adds realistically: 'Each day I pray for the grace and perseverance to continue. I'm signed on for a Carmelite, and that's the finish of it.' And she closes the door of the linen cupboard firmly.

Somewhere in the distance a bell tolls for Sext, and every nun immediately stops whatever she is doing to make her way to choir. This is in obedience to the rule that the work of God comes first, and obedience is important to the Carmelites. Twenty minutes later, everyone troops to the refectory for dinner.

Meals are taken without speech, but from the wooden reading-desk the reader for the week will first go through the rules for the month, for, said Teresa, 'without this foundation everything will go wrong.' They are also reading the Book of Daniel which they think is 'gorgeous', and the refectory book.

At the moment this is Cardinal Heenan's autobiography.

Carmelite meals used to be less heartening affairs than they are now. Mother Michael remembers all too vividly the food they used to have. 'I can remember being given for dinner soup, then cold fish with oil and vinegar, then just a plate of cabbage. And that wasn't nearly enough for me. In those days you were trained to the kind of appetite that needed a lot of food at one go. But no luxuries, no meat.' Teresa of Avila, despite the poverty of her Carmels, saw no harm in enjoying food when she got the chance: when a comment was passed as she ate a juicy bird she retorted: 'There is a time for partridge and a time for penance.' Though the Carmels still do not serve meat, fish appears once a week, perhaps baked, and eggs most days – in salad, with sardine, with rice in fritters, baked in custard. There is always, dinner and supper, Carmelite soup, absolutely delicious and made with anything left over from the day before. The day I was there it was followed by cheese dreams, roast potatoes and sprouts, then junket and fresh fruit cake. In the evening there were nutmeat noodles, carrots, then apricots and hot milk. For half the year, from the Feast of the Exaltation of the Holy Cross in September until Easter, the nuns fast. This means taking a cold collation in the evenings, which might be plain ginger-bread with cherry jam at six o'clock.

After dinner there is the washing-up, and more peeling of vegetables. Then, for an hour, they are free to read until None at two. They have a library in the monastery, well stocked under various sections: Classics, Language, Poetry, Church and Secular, Popes, Memoirs of Lay Women, Women Religious, General Lives of Saints, Spiritual, and General. There is a lot of Teresa of Avila and a study of Cardinal Newman over which Mother Michael enthuses: 'Oh, he's one of my greatest friends in heaven. I'll go great walks with him when I get there, over hills and mountains.' Thomas Aquinas is there, a review for religious called *Cistercian Studies*, but few periodicals: one thing Mother Michael 'can't abide' is 'religious literary trash'. There is a healthy amount of fiction including a well-read copy of *The Borrowers* and C. S. Lewis's 'Narnia' books.

The nuns of Carmel are encouraged to read: when a prioress complained to Teresa that one of her nuns read too much, Teresa flashed back 'Better a bookworm than a fool.' Even so, their sources of information are limited, mostly by choice. They used to take *The Times*, but stopped it because Mother Michael felt that 'except for the big things, at a shilling a time it didn't seem worth all that money'. They had a transistor radio at one time, but found they did not care for the 'tittle-tattle' so it disappeared. Not long afterwards, in July 1971, the Holy See, through the Sacred Congregation for Religious, the body which ultimately governs the affairs of all religious orders, approved a new statute for the next ten years which emphasized their enclosure. One paragraph specifically stated that the radio must be used by the community only for 'special occasions of a religious nature' and must be kept under lock and key.

Now they just take the Catholic newspaper, the *Tablet*. Not that they believe any of the papers outright, 'but it gives us a good sense of what is going on in the world'. They rely on the housekeeper who runs their guest bungalow for a précis of world events, 'and our relations tell us things. We have an ear for what is important and if anything blew up we'd take a paper – when the Irish thing began, we took *The Times*.' Despite the inadequacies of such a system, they really do seem to have some kind of special antennae going. They asked with great concern, for instance, about a South American earthquake which had received only the scantiest of news coverage.

But the nuns of Carmel are remote from the seamy side of life. 'I don't take in all the happenings of the world,' says one. 'I know there are great tragedies and people suffering in a way we don't suffer in Carmel. We are kept safe from so much that is sordid.' Even so, they do not feel remote. 'We can help by loving God and loving people in God, having that tremendous compassion for people.' They do believe that in this way they are closely in touch with the unhappiness in the world. Through their way of life, they believe they have a more intense sympathy and understanding, a closeness with people in concentration camps, and displaced people in the third world: 'We're more intensely united with the people who suffer.'

It is because of their consciousness of suffering that they are in Carmel. 'That,' says one seventy-year-old nun, 'is just what we're here for.' They know that love is needed – and so they give love. And though they are religious living under vows, they do not see themselves as any different from the people outside. 'There's the thought that people in the world are sinners,' says Sister Antonia, 'and I'm helping: I'm a sinner with them, and what I experience in myself is part of their suffering.' The nuns do what they can to offer practical help. On Fridays they do without milk and send off the money they have saved to various charities.

They have little enough to send. The huge old house and the attached grounds are all the property they own, and are common possessions. They have no capital at all, and their income of around £3000 a year comes mainly from the altar breads they make for religious suppliers all over the country. They own the machinery needed to make the breads, and also such things as the mini-tractor for the market garden. Even so, says Mother Michael, 'we only just manage. There's nothing to fall back on.' She firmly believes, however, that they are given security. 'Oh yes. In Providence of course we're secure, knowing we'll always be provided for, not being alone with no one to care.' The nuns do not give in to anxiety on questions of money, even though they could not quite live on what they earn. 'God does make it up quite inexplicably. It's Divine Providence. We get something like a tax return, or a grant. Or once someone sent us a cheque for £100 out of the blue. It just keeps about right.'

The Depositrix, the accountant of the order, is Sister Mary of the Holy Child, short and round and bespectacled, who sits in her office and admits that it is 'not my cup of tea at all, but if you've got to do a thing, you've got to do it.' Before her, great accounts books sit in daunting piles. *Analysis of all Expenditure* and *Withan and Wells on Concessional Relief*, a breakdown of the amount each nun is allowed free of tax. In the corner cupboard there are the toys Sister Mary makes for Teresa's feast-day, which she either gives away or sells, like the little cribs made out of foam plastic. She also paints cards for children. 'When I sit down and paint, I forget everything.' Also in her cupboards are some of the stores — neat piles of vests, O.S. Next door to her office is more evidence of thrift: a lavatory papered by the nuns laboriously and economically with sample squares of wallpaper cut from the pattern book.

Apart from the altar breads, there are other ways for the Carmelites to make money. Sister Theresa, for instance, has her own cottage industry going. On a sturdy table that she made herself she operates a large knitting-machine, making not only garments for the nuns but private orders for friends of the convent, like the blue and white cardigan she is currently working on for the dentist's wife. She is enormously proud of what she can produce, showing off the intricate patterns the machine will follow. And outside the wafer-cutting room there is a beautiful old spinning-wheel, which the nuns used in Presteigne for spinning the creamy undyed wool to knit their stockings and the long white cloaks they wear for Mass. They will be using it again here soon, when they get the sheep they are planning to buy, and the prospect delights them: 'The grease in the wool is terribly good for your hands.'

They are going to keep the sheep in the garden, a plan of which the gardener, Sister Mary of Carmel, vastly approves. It was her idea, but the decision as always was made by the community. Some sisters objected at first, but eventually they came round. They are starting with a ewe, and she will be put in the brambly wood behind the kitchen garden, after Sister Mary has hacked down the undergrowth with a billhook. Sister Mary is in charge of all the 13-acre garden, apart from the kitchen section and the lawn ('Our Mother does the mowing with the automatic machine'). She keeps several hives of bees. She has the touch for them: at Presteigne she could produce 150 lbs of honey from one hive if the weather was good. And there are also the 60 hens, who have to be fed and cleaned out, and their eggs collected daily. When they get broody, she puts them in a shed and feeds them well. And she wrings the necks of the old ones herself. 'You hold them for a minute and they don't struggle. I was shown that by a butcher, and very thankful I am to know it.'

In a quiet walk near the hen-run the nuns are about to build a hermitage, facing the flowering cherries. Flourishing a wicked-looking gooseberry pruner, Sister Mary says she has moved a baby azalea and a baby wistaria already to make way for it. The hermitage will actually be a hut with an asbestos roof, but Sister Mary is going to put withies of willow branches tied with wire in the grooves so that it looks more countrified. She contemplates the prospect with satisfaction. 'It's extremely nice, you know, how good the Lord is to us. We just wait and wait and eventually it comes.' There is already one hermitage at the front of the monastery, a garden house with nothing but a table and a chair, a cross with a fresh piece of greenery behind it, a statuette and an icon. It looks out on to the rather weedy herbaceous borders: 'We don't have time for them.' The two hermitages are for the nuns when, once every month, they have a day of recollection: desert days, when they do no work and need attend no prayers except Divine Office. Even their meals can be taken in solitude, and they can read or think or pray as they wish. 'It's a wonderful help to our life of prayer,' says Sister Mary, 'to have these surroundings. And those days are marvellous. It's one of our penances, you see – oh dear, that bell – and you want to go on and finish the job.'

Mother Michael particularly would love a chance to lead an even more solitary life than she does now. As a child she used to draw pictures of caves in a desert, with a hole in the roof for light, 'and a bird's nest outside so I could eat the eggs'. This has been her great longing for years, though she fears that perhaps now she might be too old physically to support a solitary life. 'But I should love it. Perhaps it will come in my extreme old age.' Such longings are very much part of the pattern of Carmelite thinking. Teresa of Avila was forty-three when she decided to found a convent where the rules of the Carmelites were to be more strictly observed than they were in the then rather lax and easy life-style of the Calced Carmelites. She would return to the primitive rule of Mount Carmel, the eremitical order founded on the mountain itself in 1209 when Albert, the Patriarch of Jerusalem, gave the rule to a group of hermits. Teresa's convent of the Reform was to be a return to that simplicity, that devotion to prayer. In 1562 she settled in the convent of St Joseph overlooking the plain and the mountains. Behind the great walls of the garden there are still four tiny hermitages hidden. And the French prioress, Mother Mary of Jesus, would beg her beloved daughters: 'For the love of God, live on the mountain, the love and eye of your prayer fixed upon God, not upon the news of the plain.'

The Carmelites of the Reform were called the Discalced, the barefooted, to differentiate them from the Calced (literally, those of the boots) who did not accept her reform. (Though, as the Calced Carmelite prioress in Bolton today points out, 'We're all discalced at night.') At first, Teresa's friars and their students went barefoot, even in the snow, though she herself forbade it. The nuns always wore alpargatas, sandals with leather tops and thickly plaited hemp soles which they made themselves. They still do, pinning and sewing the hemp, then washing and heating them two or three times until the shape and texture are right. They last for about a year, and are worn with 'choses', as they call the inner bootee of linen cut like a pair of moccasins and coming up the leg. Teresa's nuns did not originally wear stockings, until she began to expand her order and was forced to travel. Venerable Anne of Jesus inadvertently displayed a shapely leg when climbing into a mule cart and the driver passed an admiring comment, causing Teresa to decide that that would be the last time anyone saw the legs or ankles of one of her daughters.

The footwear is not only extremely picturesque but very quiet. On the other hand, those who wear them stand a good chance of getting wet feet and also of developing severe foot trouble. Some older nuns have badly deformed toes as a result. But it is not inconvenience so much as cost which is causing this footwear gradually to disappear, giving way to comfortable leather sandals. As Mother Michael drily observes, 'Old-fashioned poverty is so expensive today.' All the materials the nuns use, their footwear, their mattresses, the habits which in Teresa's time were made out of the coarse wool used for horse blankets, were of the poorest available to her. 'But to have them specially made for us costs a fortune and would be quite out of the question.' The nuns themselves regret the change. Mother Imelda remembers when she got her first pair, and how 'incredibly privileged' she felt. 'To be a real Carmelite at last was marvellous, whatever it involved.'

When Mother Imelda is not in choir or her kitchen, she is out in the kitchen garden, which is her special territory. Most of the nuns have a good sense of time, living as they do by the hours of the day, but she works so far away from the priory that she tends to forget herself, and she does not always hear the bell for prayer the first time, and has to dash back breathless. The kitchen garden is vital for the community, providing all their vegetables and fruit throughout the year. In the greenhouses there are over a hundred tomato plants, and in frames grow strawberries, peas and beans, cauliflowers, lettuce and brussels sprouts. There are apple trees, gooseberry and blackcurrant bushes, and in the distance the hunched figure of Mr Davies is working on the cabbages. He has been gardener here for many years, living quietly in his lodge at the gates. He is a great source of information, although until Mother Michael arrived at Llandovery he was only allowed to talk to the nuns when strictly necessary, and then only if there were two of them – one alone could not address him. Mother Michael went out to introduce herself and he backed away nervously and held up two fingers. He does some of the heavy work three days a week, but not all of it. Mother Imelda, slight as she is, does a large part. Wearing thick gloves, with her habit looped up with two hooks and a lackey – a strap to hold the hem of the scapular up above the inner skirt – she ploughs with the little tractor, or pulls the truck heaped with manure. 'When the tractor arrived I was nervous of just sitting in it. I couldn't drive and I had to go off in the slowest gear. But I gradually gained confidence, and we occasionally ride on the back for fun.'

Sub-Prioress Mother Imelda is one of those nuns who make their decision about a vocation young and stick to it: she has been quite sure since she was fifteen and first visited Presteigne. Restricted as she is in many ways, she has never felt frustrated within the regime. 'I've chosen it freely. I could go freely if I still wanted to. And there's a terrific fulfilment in this life: it's all for love.'

Mother Imelda, like all the Carmelites, is insistent that their leaving the world is in no way a flight from it. They are concerned only that they do not become 'a slave of the world', as they put it. And the world they envisage beyond the boundary of their stone walls is mysterious and enticing. Mother Imelda feels that 'there are so many pleasures, and we could become enamoured of them. Standing back from it, we can keep it in focus not only for ourselves but for other people.'

The contemplative life may perhaps be a flight from the world in one sense – a woman in an active teaching order suggested that such a choice might be influenced by a woman's need for solitude and tranquillity, intensified by the stress of modern living. But they go to a life of such introspection that there is nothing in themselves from which they escape, no thought they do not examine, no desire they do not question. As Sister Antonia says: 'You pray to God that He will reveal yourself to yourself.' Mother Imelda knows that: 'If you didn't have a vocation, it wouldn't be possible. Looking at it, humanly speaking, we're denying all human values, all things we have a right to, like a husband and children. But it's only occasionally, when my nieces visit, that I feel the want of children.'

In the distance, the bell peals seven times for Vespers at 4.30. Mother Imelda strips off her gardening gloves and rushes back through the gardens to chapel and, later, supper. After the community has eaten, they can go to the recreation room for an hour on some evenings. 'The real, ancient, old-fashioned Carmelite custom at recreation,' according to Mother Michael, 'was sitting in two rows with a workbasket and only talking to your neighbour. And you always sat in the same place, year after year. Now we just try not to talk shop. Some people love talking about their friends and their childhood, which can be an awful bore. And we do not gossip. If we did, this could be a little hell.'

The community room, on the second floor, is the social

gathering place for the monastery. High and sunny, with again the polished wooden floors, it is almost bare: only a few chairs around the walls and a heavy wooden sideboard almost lost in the space. 'We always try to buy second-hand and cheap things. We must try to avoid any kind of luxury.' There is, however, a large modern painting called 'Easter Candles,' and the focal point of the room is an enormous table-tennis table which Mother Michael acquired when she had permission to go to an auction for furniture, and got it as part of a job lot. It is so big the whole community can sit round it together. But usually they do play table tennis at it, and occasionally football, which is harder to imagine. When there are feast days they may have 'extraordinary recreation' which can go on all day if they like, and then they might do Scottish folk dances, or the novices might do some Irish reels, and Mother Imelda occasionally gives an impromptu ballet performance. They have a record-player now, a recent present. Until it arrived they had no way of listening to music at all. The first record they played was religious, the psalms, and they now have a small collection ranging from Your Hundred Best Tunes to Chopin, from Gregorian chant to Rawicz and Landauer. My Fair Lady is a particular favourite.

Most of all they enjoy the simplicity of making their own entertainment. The Carmelites delight in excuses for self-expression: Teresa herself played a drum and little Spanish pipes, and made up verses. 'We need all this,' she told her daughters, 'to make life liveable.' The Llandovery Carmelites sometimes mime scenes from the Bible, and recently they did the Resurrection with a tin bath for the tomb, Sister Antonia of the beautiful voice hidden away as an angel, and Mother Michael speaking Christ's words from the scullery.

If there are visitors the nuns will hold a Noson Lawen, Welsh for a happy evening. This will not be in the community room, forbidden as the interior of the monastery is to visitors, but in a small additional sitting-room on the ground floor, which has a waist-high wooden partition dividing it into two, half for the visitors, the inner half for the nuns. They squeeze into the little space, crowded in their heavy brown robes, and sit perched on tables and cupboards. Amid chatter, song books are handed round and the mother prioress is begged for a certain song – 'Oh, let Sister Antonia sing!' She does, unaccompanied, 'The Falcon hath borne my love away', her voice soaring through the falls and cadences, the words heart-breakingly poignant. And when she finishes, there is a remembering silence.

Then they sing together – 'Whoops, we've gone a bit flat' – the 23rd psalm, *The Lord's My Shepherd*, and then into *Morning has Broken*. They enjoy themselves enormously, particularly when Mother Michael does her justly famous recitation about the priest and the potato, with much wagging of an admonitory finger.

Each other's friendship is understandably important to these women, even while they are well aware of the problems and boredom of being in such close proximity all the time. 'But that means we have so many opportunities of practising love with the sisters, giving the same love and attention to those you don't like as to those you do.' They regard the community as their family, and that is certainly how it feels: the Carmelites are rather like all the Victorian daughters spending their chaperoned days at home. But the feeling of family goes even deeper than that. Mother Imelda states, quite simply, 'God is my husband. That is how I think of Him. Normally your husband would do anything for you. Well, I feel that about God. I talk to Him about my family, and I feel He really does care. He's so real to me, so alive. I know I've given some things up, yet I'm enclosed within a greater love.'

Teresa of Avila would have liked that. A formidable mixture of practicality and mysticism, with her raptures, her visions and her careful advice, heaven and earth for her were not separate. And John of the Cross, Juan de Matias, her first friar, that persecuted scholar of whom she said, 'Small in stature though he is, I believe he is great in the sight of God' – there is much in the Carmelites that comes from him. Acknowledged now as one of the greatest of religious poets, in his lifetime he was hounded by the Inquisition and at his death recognized as a saint by the people who tore off his fingernails and bit off his big toe for relics. It was he who explained the melancholy that comes sometimes in religious life in that famous phrase, 'the dark night of the soul'. And it was he, too, who said of the nuns of Carmel, that they should be 'like mirrors, shining lamps, glowing torches, brilliant stars'. In his day, of course, the life of the nuns of Carmel was more rigorous even than it is now. Yet wherever they are – America, Britain, France – the Carmels with their long hard hours, their flashes of joy ('I never laughed so much in the world') and their intense asceticism keep still the flavour and atmosphere of Spain. They are wholly Spanish. Teresa and Carmel could have been forged by no other country.

'Yet we don't have as pentitential a life as some people think. You'd think it was much more austere.' In some ways, though, there are the remanants still of more extreme discomforts: on Friday, after Compline, the nuns say the *Miserere*, a long psalm, standing with their arms stretched out in the shape of a crucifix. It is all that is left of the severe penances which continued until less than ten years ago. One nun, elderly now, remembers 'losing my head in my cell at the idea of taking the discipline for the first time. We used to have it together at five in the morning. You slipped your robe off your shoulders and beat yourself with a little whip with lots of straps: you had to do it to offer up suffering for Our Lord in the world. Other people suffered in prison, so why shouldn't we suffer? But I must say you got awfully used to it.'

The woman who is talking is Mother Gabriel of the Resurrection. Over eighty now, with the garrulous frailty of the old, the thick lenses over her near-blind eyes cannot quite hide their blue beauty, and she still keeps much of the manner and vocabulary of the girl she was at the turn of the century. One of a family of fourteen, she remembers asking to be a nun when she was seven so that she could go and help the lepers. For her, Carmel was like going to heaven. 'Everything I'd always wanted and more.'

It must be difficult to remain vividly aware of a world you will scarcely see again. The nuns of Carmel used to have two extern sisters who lived outside the enclosure, doing the shopping and other business, spending their days in a little sitting-room outside the enclosure. Their only contact with the nuns was when their tray of food came through the turn three times a day. They wore long skirts, little capes and squared-off black bonnets, prim as Victorian governesses. The extern sisters were the women who entered Carmel without any educational qualifications, while the better-educated choir nuns not only brought a dowry, but needed to be able to follow and make music, and read the Latin prayers. In 1965, in response to the Vatican's call for change within religious orders, Mother Michael brought in Sister Maria and Sister Cecilia. After twenty years, they were much missed in Llandovery, where they appeared daily. Sister Maria, a neat birdlike woman, says she could not believe it, she had wanted to enter fully for so long. 'But I knew that if God wanted me, He would arrange it.'

The only other Carmelite who has spent much time outside the enclosure is Mother Gabriel: since 1945 the only thing she has really wanted is to found a Carmel in Russia.

There are now 780 Carmels in the world with 13,000 nuns. Teresa of Avila spent much of her life travelling Spain in a springless mule cart in all weathers making foundations, so that she saw the handful of nuns in the convent of St Joseph grow to seventeen monasteries for women and fourteen for men – these last founded with St John of the Cross. Teresa was still travelling three weeks before her death.

So Mother Gabriel's wish is in the best Teresan tradition. She was, oddly enough, in Alaska with a woman friend on a special permission when the friend suggested they visit Rome. Here she obtained permission from the Holy See to visit Russia for a year to try and get a group of nuns together there. So off she went as a tourist through Cook's (all paid for by the same woman friend). Filling out the form for her visa, she put 'spinster'. 'Not only was I, but I could spin.' She wore a long brown postulant's dress and coat with a little brown cap, not to look too noticeably a nun.

In Russia, travelling alone, she attempted to find convents, only to be told such places did not exist. Nevertheless, she found her way to two, where her reception was highly suspicious. 'I told one superior I wanted to live in Russia as a hermit, and asked if she would let me use one of their little white houses round the church. But she said the Kremlin would never agree.' Eventually, travelling home by train, she was hauled off it by uniformed men at a border village, and dumped unceremoniously in the guard's van protesting that she was nearly seventy. 'I was surrounded by Polish officers and I said, "You should be ashamed of yourselves, you're Catholics." Of course,' she adds reflectively, 'they were communists. So then I said, "Do you think I'm a spy?" "Yes," they said, "you're just the kind."' Tired and frightened, she was finally helped by an American doctor who was also stopped. 'But you know', she says, 'I'd like to have been sent off to a camp, actually. I love adventure.'

While she is talking the bell rings softly again, through the monastery, calling the Carmelites to Compline at eight, the last prayers before the Great Silence falls on the house, not to be broken before the first prayers of the morning. The chapel is darkening, and the lamps of the nuns gleam in pools, while the altar light glows red.

After Compline, the nuns retire for the night, along the stone corridor lined with neat rows of alpargatas that leads to the cells. The cells themselves are something of a feature, instigated – like so much else here – by Mother Michael. At Presteigne it was she who had a chapel specially designed so that the nuns could build much of it themselves for economy, with only minimal aid from local workmen. Twelve of them, doing 'gang labour' for two years, built the choir and even cast the windows in cement. But they found they could not manage the weight of the blocks of stone for the walls.

Many of the cells at Presteigne were also built by the nuns, when they had finished the chapel. 'Until then a lot of us had slept in hen huts.' For this job they used old wooden slats from disused railway tracks and stuffed the walls, for warmth, with nylon stockings: when Mother Michael made a phone call, she always asked, 'Would you mind my asking what you do with your old nylon stockings?' with the result that stockings arrived in bundles.

The cells at Llandovery were also acquired from the Welsh railways. They are old guards' vans, parked in a large square which is roofed in for shelter and minimal warmth. One had been used for transporting bananas – 'it smelt terrific when we got it.' The nuns have painted them all silver now and built little brick stairs up to the doorways. But the lavatories are as they were, and so are the signs reading: 'CAUTION. DO NOT LEAN OUT OF THE WINDOW.' The two pink-tiled bathrooms with their heating-lamps were once horse-boxes.

Inside each cell, cardboard shutters have been fitted across the windows at the ends of the coaches to keep out the worst Welsh draughts. The walls are white-painted, the floors bare. There is in each cell a black cross over a little bookshelf, a stool and a picture of St Teresa. There is a stoup of holy water, a bit of palm from Palm Sunday, and a piece of box from the garden. The cells are surprisingly warm. Sister Mary says she felt a little trepidation about coming to Llandovery because of her arthritis. 'I thought we'd be shivering all winter and sometimes it's certainly pretty cold, but the cells don't hold the damp. Compared to most Carmels, this is the warmest cell I've ever had. And you don't hear snores and snuffles from the sister next door.' The only heating necessary, in fact, is a small electric bar fire and the heavy sheets and blankets. The beds are divans – school beds, really, with flock mattresses. But Mother Michael felt these were a bit fancy after the straw mattresses that in the old days the nuns would have made themselves, so they put their old horsehair ones on top. Over each bed is a reading-light and beside it a table with an alarm clock, a bible, and across some of the cells a washing-line of string is slung with pegs. If there is a waste-bin it will probably be made from an old Snowcem tin. And each nun has a Thermos in her cell for hot drinks during the cold weather. 'It isn't the emphasis now to do without,' Mother Michael explains.

Even so, they live under the glance of God in an austerity few can match, confining the body in order to free the spirit. And the core and secret of the contentment they undoubtedly possess is their certainty of happiness to come. They have given their lives and their love to the glory of God, and in return they will know that glory themselves. As Mother

Michael points out: 'The afterlife is for ever. But this is only seventy or eighty years at most.'

She has a very positive approach to life, though. 'You should look for what is good and happy. You mustn't waste this life, but make the fullest use of your gifts.' Much of what she says is, in recollection, couched in religious clichés. But when she is actually speaking, it is all so wise and true, and said with such utter conviction, that she sweeps the listener along with her. Yet, acknowledging regularly and often man's physical end as the nuns do, their life would be hard to bear without certainty such as Mother Michael's that the spirit will eventually inhabit an eternity, which she sees as an endless sunny garden, where 'everything one wants is going to be happiness. One will be young, and everything will be marvellous. I simply long to have long, long walks and never be tired. And we'll have innocent friendships. On earth they're tremendous, but there, there will be no limitations. Oh, jolly times.'

'Look,' she says, leaning forward, 'you *must* believe in the afterworld. It's a great comfort, you see. Pray to know. It is a matter of faith, beyond anything we can argue and reason about. Beyond reason and yet reasonable, in that we can discuss it and show that there is more than can be known by the senses. And one of the greatest arguments for eternal life is that you can't do all the things you want to in life.'

Mother Michael has the serene, fulfilled look associated with happy marriage, with many children and grandchildren. Nothing of the elderly spinster there. It all becomes clear when she says, speaking of her belief in the afterlife, 'Nobody in love can believe it will end.'

So the nuns of Carmel go about their lives and their days pass quietly, quietly. And their eyes are turned inward, searching for that dim inner place where God and the soul meet. And their hearts are turned to the sorrows of the world beyond their walled acres.

And up in the kitchen garden, just before you come to the cabbages, there is a barred gate. It was once the heavy outer grille that kept them from the world. The inner, finer grille is against the wall of their little Spanish courtyard. The metal screen that once kept them from ever touching their mothers and fathers, or their sisters and brothers, is almost hidden now. Sister Mary is using it as a frame for a perfumed mass of golden Peace roses.

2

A STATE OF PERFECTION

If you are a foolish virgin – if indeed you are a virgin – you need the community. If you are a wise virgin, the community needs you.

BERNARD OF CLAIRVAUX

'Why on earth are you going into a convent?'

There must be very few young women entering religious communities in the twentieth century who have not heard that. It is the single most intriguing speculation about any nun. One American Poor Clare who took the decision to enter twenty years ago says that everyone asked her why. 'A priest said: "Don't expect the world in general to understand your way of life. But if anything in life is true, the truth will stand." '

It is of course the voice of God that takes women into religious life: a calling heard only in the heart, a need. But it is not enough to say they enter because they love God. Obviously they do – but so do other people, and most of them do not become nuns. The one remark that was made to me by almost every sister I talked to – and it was the only one they all made in common – was that this was not something they had decided for themselves.

The Belgian Jewess who converted and felt anything less was not giving enough; the slender American with honey-coloured hair living in a slum apartment in Rio de Janeiro; the elegant actress who became superior of an Anglican community – all of them felt what one put into words: 'It is less a question of choosing than of being chosen. It is a very strong conviction – I wouldn't even call it a feeling – that this is the life to which one is called.'

The religious life was described by Matthew as 'a city set on a mountain'. Canon law terms it 'a state of perfection' because, by living it under vows, the nun is removing the main obstacles to holiness, withdrawing from all that is against the habit of virtue. So a woman who has a religious vocation must be prepared to give herself to God. But it is not only what she can give, but what she can give *up* that matters. The less she has, the better she is. Like an English Channel swimmer, she will go further that way. Pope Pius XII summed up the *raison d'être* of religious life. It is, he said, 'intimately connected with the special purpose of the Church, namely to lead all men to the acquisition of holiness. Though every Christian is bound to attempt to reach that sacred pinnacle, the religious proceeds on a path which is entirely her own and relies upon help of a higher nature.'

A daunting prospect. St Bernard simplified it when he told his monks of Clairvaux more than seven hundred years ago: 'Brothers, the whole object of our lives is to love and to make ourselves lovable.' Basically a religious vocation is a mystery and perhaps to none will it remain so deep as to those favoured with it. They themselves find it fascinating and at least two orders of nuns run a series in their house magazines on the subject – one of them entitled 'How I came' and the other 'My call'.

The motives for entering are as different as the entrants. 'The varieties of call,' according to a superior who has seen many women choose convent life, 'are like the stones of the sea.' One woman, trying to explain it, says, 'You hear it. You know it.' Another adds, 'It's not so different from other things, from getting married, for example. You know you must marry a man, that this is right for you, that you are called to be joined with him and bring new life into the world. It is the same for us.'

It is material for newspaper headlines when young women in the news decide to enter convents – particularly since such people tend to go to the strictly enclosed contemplative orders. The most successful contemplatives, one mother superior says, are not those you would imagine, not the introspective, reflective people. 'You need an extrovert personality to cope with the life. The bubbly, tomboyish ones make the best contemplatives.'

In 1973 a former prima ballerina of the Paris Opéra, the twenty-seven-year-old Mireille Nègre, who had danced often with Nureyev, entered the Carmelite convent at Limoges as Sister Mireille, Heart of Jesus. She took with her pink tights and one pair of dancing slippers. About the same time an Australian beauty queen, Christine Francis, announced that she was joining the Cistercian nuns and had a last fling in London nightclubs. The *News of the World* immediately – and erroneously – announced that she would rise at 3.30 a.m. and start her day with five hours of prayer, but no one actually thought that a vivacious twenty-three-year-old from Brisbane would take such a step: the Cistercians are the most austere of all religious orders. But in fact, seven months later, Miss Francis returned to London and went straight from Heathrow to take the habit as a novice at Holy Cross Abbey, Dorset.

'Fear and desire,' according to Sister Marie Edmond of the Helpers of the Holy Souls, are nearly always the first signs of a vocation. She believes every woman, called at whatever age, invariably feels both. 'The first contact with God is disturbing and the conflict is natural: every woman wants to be loved by a man, to bear children.'

The experience of Sister Mary of Carmel mirrors this exactly. At convent school: 'I had a great idea of being married and having lots of children.' She was asked back to the order for retreats after leaving school and finally made one 'to get it off my chest'. To her surprise she suddenly realized how happy she felt. 'And I had this ghastly feeling, only God can give it, so perhaps I ought to give it back.' She really did not want to give up living in the country, 'hunting and all that sort of thing.' Finally, she told a priest she would like to be a Carmelite, and was accepted by the order, but asked to wait until she was twenty-one. 'I was delighted, I thought I should be married long before that. But no, it was meant for me.'

One deputy superior, Sister Morag Michael of the Anglican Community of St Mary the Virgin, confirms that in her experience many women struggle for years against the conviction that God wants them to enter a convent. 'I know a lot of my sisters would say they had fought hard against choosing this life. I think the majority of us came very reluctantly. Comparatively few said, "How marvellous," because it does mean you are turning your back on a lot of things that honestly are very desirable and great fun. But there is a feeling that one must *try*, at least, and see.'

Mother Joanna is superior of the Deaconess Community of St Andrew in Tavistock Road, Bayswater, London, an Anglican order founded by Elizabeth Ferard. She felt she should enter a convent, but at that time was not even aware that Anglican orders existed. 'I went to the vicar and hoped he would say, "Oh no, quite ridiculous, you're not the sort to be a nun." He didn't. He suggested an order.' The Mother Superior gave three dates to see her, and 'I chose the very last one. I felt the whole thing was too extreme, that I'd like a middle-of-the-road thing, a job and a nice flat. I didn't want to give up all these things. But I felt this compulsion.'

A member of Mother Joanna's community, Sister Denzil, was a medical worker at St Thomas's Hospital, London: 'I had this feeling when I was very young, and resisted it till I was thirty-eight. I was happy and fulfilled, and I knew that if I entered I wouldn't have marriage or children, which I should have loved to have at some point. But it seemed to me like God saying, "Look, I'm sorry, but this is the way you must work." I railed against it for years. At one convent where I was very unhappy, I don't know, looking back, why I didn't pack up and go. But you don't.'

No one seems to mind admitting their reluctance to enter. Sister Mary Victoria is a Franciscan Missionary of the Divine Motherhood, a missionary group based in a country house near the south coast of England. She said that she was in her first job when she read the *Life and Letters* of Mother Janet Erskine Stuart, a Sacred Heart nun. 'Every time I picked it up there was a vague uncomfortable feeling at the back of my mind. The ghastly truth dawned on me – perhaps I ought to be a nun, too?' Another sister in the same order, Sister Mary Simon Stock, remembers 'kneeling in church and listing mentally on one side all the reasons why I should become a nun, and I could think of only one reason why I should not –

I didn't want to And to me, that didn't sound like a very good reason.'

'God,' says an Episcopalian sister, more succinctly, 'just picked me up by the scruff of the neck.'

An American girl went to a clothing ceremony of a friend as a Poor Clare. 'I thought, that's beautiful, but not for me.' She laughs and looks a bit amazed at herself. 'Five years later, I was back.' She is not the only nun who found herself in a convent for the first time almost by accident. An Anglican novice of twenty-seven: 'I'd never been inside a convent or had anything to do with sisters till I went to college to read theology. At the end, I wanted to do some work, but I didn't want to go home. A tutor suggested I go to a convent as a quiet workplace. I wrote to one, but they didn't have room. And I thought, I'll have to go to that awful place in Paddington.' Two years later she entered there.

Even those who are certain of their vocation can be put off by the formidable exterior presented by some orders, particularly the contemplative ones. A woman who is now a Carmelite abbess had long realized she was going to be a nun: 'I never had love-affairs or anything like that, I wasn't interested.' So she went to a clothing ceremony at the Carmelite convent in St Charles Square in London's Notting Hill. 'It was a foggy November night, the building was vast and dark, and I saw these two young girls in this gloomy hole and my heart sank lower and lower: I'd wanted something that was absolutely *it*.'

Many women deliberately test themselves first before acknowledging their vocation.

An Anglican sister says that, having read maths at Oxford, she decided to teach for two years. 'I went to the worldliest, richest, most aristocratic school I could find to see if I was influenced away from the religious life.' Sometimes this is done at the insistence of parents. One young woman, who had wanted to enter as a contemplative from the time she was fifteen, spent eight months in an income-tax office first because her family wanted her to make some contact with the world before leaving it. 'I sat at an enormous desk and thought about the convent.'

Another enclosed contemplative, Sister Antonia Maria of Jesus, left school to work in Swansea as an accounts machine operator for the National Coal Board. Then she went to London as a receptionist in the busy Strand Palace Hotel, 'and it was in London that my vocation developed.' She felt a great longing for close living with God, but 'I wanted God to decide for me, I didn't want to get my own will entangled.' She returned to her family, went to Mass daily but said nothing to them lest by doing so she commit herself. 'I wanted to be free until the decision.' She had already received information about the order's life 'which I found very forbidding,' but there was nothing to draw her away from it. 'I didn't have the attraction for the married life, or for having children: I never was attracted enough to boys. I needed some purpose in life.' When, finally, she entered, 'I was very thankful: it was a tremendous relief when my life was settled, a feeling of great security.'

For most women who become nuns, the conviction that this is a choice they must make overrides their realization of loss.

Out of a group of novices in one convent, the first said, 'I don't think it's necessarily what you want: I think you're drawn to it anyway.' And another: 'It might not be your personal choice. It is in the end. But not in the first place.' And the third: 'It's not up to yourself, really. You've got to come.'

Many superiors and novice mistresses say they prefer entrants who talk like this. The famous Carmelite prioress, Mother Mary of Jesus, wrote in her private papers: 'Today, someone was asking to come in. I had to refuse. It is often so, when they want to come in. It is not we who choose, but He.' Not everyone would agree, however. Sister Madeleine, novice mistress of the French community of the Augustinian Sisters of Meaux, considers that since religious are 'easy prey for superficial psychologizing, they prefer the explanation "I have been called by God," since it shifts the initiative of their choice.'

There are some women to whom religious life comes so naturally that there is for them no question of hesitation.

'Everything in my life,' remembers a contemplative, 'seemed to lead to this.' To a Spanish superior, the desire for religious life came from 'just knowing *this* was what God meant you to be.'

It is rare that a woman will know exactly which order she wants from the very beginning of her desire to enter religious life, though it does happen: Mother Imelda remembers the moment when it became clear that 'God wanted me.' A sister at her convent school was explaining that solemnly enforced enclosure had replaced deserts for the hermit. 'I thought, this is for me, a life of total commitment.' It was not that she just wanted to be a nun – she wanted to be in Carmel.

Often the attitude of the family is the major influence on a vocation. Many nuns have brothers and sisters in the habit, and this is true not only in Catholic countries such as Ireland and Italy, where it is traditional for one or two members of a large family to enter the Church for reasons both of faith and finance. Few families, though, carry things to the extreme practised by the offspring of the Counts of Andeche and Meran, nobility in southern Germany in the early thirteenth century. So ascetic were they that all the sons became bishops, the daughters nuns, and the line completely disappeared. It is, however, an odd coincidence that contemplatives in particular seem often to come from big families: perhaps it has something to do with learning early to live as part of a group. Mother Imelda, for instance, left behind her a warm family life: she is one of seven boys and three girls, and it was 'terribly hard' to leave them. Yet she feels she can still reach and help them through her prayers. Because they can make the journey to her monastery only twice a year, she is allowed to spend as much time as possible with them for perhaps a week, though this would be more restricted if they visited regularly. 'I've cooked the dinner and popped in and out to my mother in the sitting-room in the middle of it.'

The influence of the mother particularly in encouraging vocations is acknowledged to be immense. At a recent meeting in London to discuss the subject of vocations, one of the tactics recommended to boost the diminishing numbers of entrants was that a mother should 'encourage her little ones to play at being nuns and priests'. An Episcopalian sister believes that: 'My mother's influence on my vocation was much stronger than either she or I realized. I resisted, but in the end I saw it was the most important thing there was.' A missionary, Sister Marguerite of the White Sisters, felt 'very aware that God was asking me. I remember saying to my mother when I was seven, "I'm going to be a nun but I'll enjoy myself first and then when I'm thirty-five I'll go in." My mother said, "Oh, so you'll give what is left over of your life to God?"'

Another woman who entered young remembers a superior telling her about the contemplative vocation. 'She said: Some of the sisters in this convent are in their eighties, and if you ask them to look back on their lives, the only regret they have is that they didn't give themselves to God earlier. Youth is a thing you only have a very short time and it's very precious. And if you can say, "I gave that to God," it becomes even more valuable.' This woman, Eileen Gielty, is a member of the Institute of the Sisters of Notre Dame de Namur, an educational congregation founded in France at the beginning of the nineteenth century. She, too, entered because of her mother. 'She was a very pious Irishwoman, and I knew that the greatest desire of her heart would be fulfilled if one of us became a religious. But I had no urge whatsoever to satisfy this desire. I was a bit of a rebel. If my mother suggested I went to church, it would be enough for me to decide I wasn't going. In fact, when I really thought seriously of becoming a sister, I had to face this, that I was going to please my mother in spite of myself.'

Eileen Gielty fully expected the thought to pass. 'But then, when I was seventeen, I went to the Ordination of three young men. They were in their early twenties, and they were giving their lives to God. It was just terrific. And I wept and wept and wept. And I came home and told my mother that night. I said, "I've been thinking about this for some time. I don't see how I can escape it now."'

At the other extreme, there are families who are horrified at the idea of their girls taking the veil. A superior who regularly gives talks on vocations says: 'Of course, we often find parents are not terribly anxious for their girls to become nuns. They prefer them to get married, and then there are possibly grandchildren.' A recent enquiry into the subject of vocations carried out in France showed that while a son becoming a priest was acceptable, a daughter choosing to be a nun was a calamity. A few months later a similar survey in Britain produced the same result.

Sometimes parents object only until the daughter convinces them of the validity of her choice. 'My father was a convert and he was opposed because of my youth. They wanted me to make some contact with the world before leaving it. So I spent eight months in an office. When I couldn't wait any longer, I wrote to my father – and he agreed.' Many parents never accept their daughter's decision. A thirty-year-old novice had desperately wanted to enter for ten years before her parents would consent. 'I told them I wanted to be a nun at sixteen. There was a terrible row and they thought I was mad. But really they thought three years at university would put paid to that. Mummy was very upset but prepared to try and understand. It was Daddy who still hasn't accepted it.'

Another sister remembers that: 'Every birthday from the age of nine I said, "Mummy, you know I'm going to be a nun when I'm eighteen." But when eighteen came she practically threw me out of the house, she really couldn't understand.'

Many nuns have had such intense opposition from their families when they entered that relationships with them are completely broken off. An Anglican and a Catholic novice mistress both agree that this is quite a common occurrence. 'It happens with a lot of my novices,' says the Catholic. 'Their parents have never spoken to them since the day they entered.'

Pat Drydyk is an American Franciscan, a calm and intelligent young woman. 'I went through five years of struggling with my parents on this. My mother has not spoken to me for thirteen years. When I go home, she speaks briefly, but she doesn't ever write. She told me that if I entered I'd not be a daughter of hers.' An Englishwoman from a Catholic family who has been a nun for thirty years admits that her mother never forgave her for becoming a nun. 'As for my father, he never spoke to me again.' For many women such reactions have caused terrible unhappiness, like the sister I met whose mother had died years before after a long illness – and she had only just learned of it through a letter from a friend: everyone assumed she already knew.

Almost all orders have their own stories of families bitterly resenting the entrance of their daughters: the mother who broke her umbrella on the spikes of the parlour grating; the father who threatened to abduct his daughter by main force on the day of her Clothing.

Parental opposition has been in part responsible for enclosure: convent walls were put up not to keep the nuns in, but intruders out. In the thirteenth century an Italian girl called Diana d'Andolo determined against her family's wishes to enter the community of St Dominic. Her brothers forcibly removed her from the convent of Augustinian canonesses to whom she had gone for protection, breaking her ribs in the process. She did eventually start a Dominican community at Bologna and St Dominic afterwards put stout walls and metal grilles around his nuns; he even, in times of danger, provided special guards.

It is hard not to sympathize with parents who reluctantly lose their daughters to religion. It must have been even worse when girls were able to enter early in their teens. Few, though, made the decision as early as St Catherine of Parc-aux-Dames is reputed to have done. She was a Jewish child born in Louvain in the early thirteenth century and when she was five a priest visited her parents' house. Afterwards she somehow got away from home to the priest, who took her to the Cistercian nuns at the abbey of Parc-aux-Dames where she was baptized and dressed in the habit. Her distraught parents begged the Bishop of Louvain and the Pope that she might be released, at least until she was twelve years old. But the Archbishop of Cologne and the abbot of Clairvaux approved her entry and there she remained, noted for her visions, until her death.

A more recent case of parental obstruction was a *cause célèbre* which involved the Pope, five cardinals, two papal nuncios, an auxiliary bishop and a *grand-vicaire* as well as the French ambassador to the Vatican and a premier English duke It was at the end of the last century that Marie Ambaud, a twenty-two-year-old French girl, left her home secretly to enter Carmel in London. Her father, inspector general of Customs, objected on the grounds that public opinion would henceforth be against him – anti-clericalism was rife in France at that time. He turned up in London to offer the prioress large sums of money if his daughter could leave. When this failed, he next contacted Cardinal Manning, and then the Pope. When newspapers took up his story and started attacking the Church for the detention of the girl in a foreign convent, the Holy See undertook an enquiry. Marie wrote to the Pope begging to be allowed to stay, but was told to stay temporarily in another convent to 'demonstrate her freedom'. The night before she was due to leave she developed heart trouble. 'It is,' wrote the prioress, 'the greatest grace of her life.' It caused more scandal: her mother could not enter the enclosure to nurse her, and her father declared he would have her out alive or dead. 'And if she dies, so much the worse for you.' He even visited the father of the prioress to protest. But Marie was finally allowed by the Pope to be professed a Carmelite, and died not long afterwards.

Often, girls educated at convent schools are influenced towards the religious life. Though as one superior pointed out, 'While I think a great number of girls come to a particular teaching order because of the nuns they were at school with, sometimes the nuns who taught them actually put them off that order.' Another sister does not think the nuns at her convent school put the idea directly into her head. 'Example was always a very important factor. They certainly did impress us as women who had all the gifts. Not in terms of looks – though some were very good-looking. But they weren't cast-offs of society, they were intellectually very able, and they were good personalities; I can remember in my last year at school having a realization of what their lives were about. It wasn't just teaching and encouraging people to go as far as they could: there was something else behind it, and that's what really first attracted me.'

For many sisters, an outside event influenced the decision. Mother Joanna of the Deaconess Community of St Andrew: 'It was the war that made me think what life was about. I came back to the truth of Christianity.' For another, the turning-point was highly emotional. 'I never believed in anything, I hated scripture at school. When I was fifteen the death of President Kennedy started a search for something. I entered here to get to know God.'

One of the most famous of all saints, Thérèse of Lisieux, the little Carmelite who entered at fifteen and died of consumption at twenty-four, was one of five sisters all in the order: Agnes, Céline, Léonie and Marie de Sacré-Cœur. They all lived in Lisieux, where the convent still has twenty-four nuns, double the normal complement, to cope with the letters that come to the place of pilgrimage. It was this last sister, Marie de Sacré-Cœur, who was responsible for the entrance of at least one nun, though she never knew it. Sister Marie-Marthe is a fragile, fluttery Frenchwoman of great kindness who is a member of the Convent of the Holy Child in the Paris suburb of Neuilly. She originally entered as a Carmelite, and it was a decision she took when she was eleven years old. 'I wanted to give my answer to God.' But it was not until she was twenty-three that she decided which order to choose. In January 1940, in the Lisieux convent church, she saw the body of Marie de Sacré-Cœur. 'She was exposed behind the grille on a sort of bed in the choir, dressed in the full habit. When I saw the face of that nun, radiant and beautiful, and I knew how she had suffered, paralysed with rheumatism, and yet in spite of all her suffering she died like that. Then I knew: That is where I should enter. Where I could find such peace.'

In view of the efforts so many women make to enter it is strange that one of the false impressions outsiders have of convents is that they represent for the inmates an escape, an evasion of responsibility, an easy way out if life does not offer the conventional happinesses of a husband, a career, children.

This is a myth one Episcopalian sister, a former PT instructor, demolishes. 'So many people think this life is a rejection, an escape from the physical. But that's not part of the pattern. If you marry one man, you're rejecting thousands – but people don't see *that* as a rejection.' And: 'Would a life in common,' asks a French sister, 'of obedience, and poverty, make up for the lack of a husband, beauty, intelligence?' Nuns cannot simply be dismissed as women no one wanted. Even if charming and intelligent people do not deserve more credit for the strength of the emotions which drive them to give their lives to God, their sheer numbers must prove something. Christianity has approximately a million nuns and sisters – and they cannot all be suffering from disappointments in love.

'I could have married,' explains an Anglican. 'I still think of the men I knew and loved. But I don't regret my step into the convent. I knew, somehow, that one man wasn't for me, that God's love for me was so strong that I had to respond to the whole world.' The reason, according to Mother Claire Bernes, an Algerian-born Daughter of Charity of St Vincent de Paul who was awarded the freedom of Israel for her work with children, is that: 'We don't join the Church in order to be happy, but to give to others. That is what we mean by love.'

One Good Shepherd novice actually became engaged three months before entering. 'I think I did it just to show I *could* have married.' This, she admits, was partly for the benefit of her parents, who are deeply unhappy about her choice. 'They feel it's a life against nature. They imagine I'm not going to have anything – no married life, no young family. They don't consider that I've had any fun, or that this life has any possibilities of happiness.' For a long time she was torn between feeling she should become a religious and her emotions for her boy-friend. But having made the decision to marry, 'I found I couldn't go on with my engagement. I had at least to give this a try. He couldn't understand, but then it's not the kind of thing you can explain so easily.'

Another myth about nuns is that they are driven into convents by unhappy love-affairs. As one very pretty young Anglican of twenty-seven said rather tartly, 'It's much more likely that they're driven in by no affairs at all.' A fairly typical comment – from a middle-aged Spanish sister – is this: 'I never thought of marrying. I was always disappointed by my acquaintances. I did not find enough in them. And then the urge of God's command became stronger.'

There must be a great many women in convents today who entered because they felt they could not marry for one reason or another, like the middle-aged sister who admitted: 'My mother said, "You haven't got many offers of marriage because we've got no money." I was very young and I entered because I couldn't meet men very well. I'd have lost my soul and maybe done low things: I was all for the stage and dancing and ruin.'

It is true that some girls, afraid of their own sexuality, can by entering avoid contact with men and at the same time ensure their own holiness. But someone who is not capable of good relationships with people in the world is going to be no better off inside a convent. She is not, after all, living a hermit's life but a community one.

Some women undoubtedly do still decide to enter for less than positive reasons: because they promised a parent they would do so, or to please a teaching sister they admired at school. Many are first attracted to the idea of religious life by what one nun calls the 'rubbishy romanticism' of films and novels. But as one nun/theologian points out: 'If you enter for the wrong reasons, it's certainly possible to be a religious, but not possible to be a *happy* religious. To do that you have really to make a success of your life, I don't mean professionally, but personally.' And she adds wryly that: 'You can, of course, delude yourself that you are carrying the cross.'

There was a time when thousands upon thousands of women totally unsuited for convent life none the less entered, not of their own free will but through compulsion. In the early days of religious life, when European kingdoms were small and kings many, it was in the interests of royal families that their daughters remain in convents in preference to contracting matrimonial alliances which might involve their relatives in political difficulties. Numerous princesses of ruling dynasties remained unmarried in their convents – one

German duke sent all nine of his daughters – but since their dowries were given them, they were able to make their own foundations and rule over them alone: they were powerful women. Margaret, daughter of a medieval king in what is now Hungary, was promised to a convent in return for victory over her father's enemies: the ruins of the foundation he made for her still stand on the island between Buda and Pest. And a seventh-century king of Northumbria made a vow that the Christian religion should profit if God granted him victory. His daughter Aelflaed he then gave to the Abbess Hilda at Hartlepool when the child 'had scarcely completed the age of one year, to be consecrated to God in perpetual virginity, besides bestowing on the Church twelve estates.'

The convent was a useful place to put women who became politically inconvenient, and several of the dynamic Romanov women ended up in Russian communities. One was Sophia, sister of Peter the Great, who was said to have a man's brain and clarity of judgement, and was made regent while Peter was a child of ten. When he was seventeen he had a trained army guarding his three palaces, and it was not long before Sophia was arrested and taken to a convent outside the walls of the Kremlin. No one from outside ever saw her again. She lived as Sister Suzanna, and to ensure her silence Peter had hideously mutilated bodies hung outside her windows. Later, he dealt with his wife, Tsarina Eudoxia, in the same way. This time he wanted a divorce, which the bishops told him was out of the question so long as she remained a laywoman. But a woman who entered a convent rendered her marriage void – an important political consideration for a husband who wished to be rid of her. So Peter had their son taken from Eudoxia and imprisoned her in a convent where, perforce, she became Sister Elena.

One of the saddest of such stories is that of Marguerite Farnese of Parma, the fourteen-year-old girl who was married in 1581 to a prince of Mantua, Vincenzo Gonzaga. Descended from Maria of Portugal, niece of Margaret of Austria, granddaughter of Charles V, she brought to her new husband 300,000 crowns, jewels and rich garments. But she was unable to consummate her marriage because, said the most famous surgeon of the day, 'May has not yet flowered for her.'

It never was to flower. She was sent back to her family and her father advised her to retire to a convent. Horrified, and loving her husband, she wrote a letter of supplication to the Pope which caused an uproar in Rome. Her father was summoned to report on the affair and asked why he wished to force the vocation of a soul. Nuns and friars prayed for a right outcome, there were medical examinations and discussions with lawyers. Finally her parents told her that if she promised to withdraw from the world she would be allowed to live not as a cloistered nun, but in her own house, in princely apartments, attended by pages. She agreed, withdrew her appeal to the Pope and asked permission to retire from the world and lead a life of chastity: only then did she discover that such a life would be impossible, since her marriage to Vincenzo would not be considered dissolved by canon law until the convent gate was barred behind her. Despite her bitter protests, in October 1583 she took the veil and made her vows as Sister Maura Lucenia in the convent of San Paolo. She was sixteen years old, and she was to remain there for more than sixty years.

The convent was also a convenient way to dispose of widows, particularly royal ones who would otherwise have retained vast amounts of money and land, and this goes right back to the earliest days of monasticism: in Arthurian legend Guinevere takes the veil at Amesbury on the death of Arthur and remains there until her death. Some royal women considered such enforced cloistering as unthinkable as suttee. When, for instance, Elisabeth Charlotte, Princess Palatine, came to France to marry the Duc d'Orléans (Monsieur, younger brother of Louis XIV), her marriage contract – drawn up by the French – stated that she had to choose between spending her widowhood at a convent of her choice or at her dower house. 'I am not,' she commented, 'such a fool as to shut myself up in a convent. That is not my way at all.' And sure enough, after Monsieur's death the distraught Liselotte was heard to shriek at the top of her voice, 'No convent for me, I'll go to no convent. Let no one speak to me of convents!'

There were other reasons, too, for placing a young woman

in a convent. If a girl had tarnished her reputation, or even borne an illegitimate child, it hushed scandal. And the Duc de Saint-Simon, the great French memoir-writer who lived at the court of Louis XIV, mentions often that it was perfectly acceptable for an elder, less attractive daughter to be sent to a convent to increase the dowry and desirability of a younger child. He even refers to a convent providing a solution in an embarrassing situation. The Duchesse de Piney remarried and her new husband, with an eye on the inheritance, had her son by her first marriage ordained a priest, the daughter made a nun. After twenty years the daughter started to grumble publicly from her convent near Paris, and the Pope made her a dispensation: she returned to court with a title.

For some, the convent was a place to hide illegitimate offspring. Cardinal Wolsey himself had an illegitimate daughter at the convent of Shaftesbury. Ex-mistresses, too, found their way there, though sometimes through their own choice. Two of the women involved with Louis XIV ended as nuns. Louise de la Vallière, his shy and gentle mistress, obtained pensions from him for her family and servants, begged the Queen's forgiveness and entered the Carmelite convent in Paris. The last years of her life were so edifying that there was a movement to have her canonized: thirty years of reparation after so few of love. Her successor, Madame de Montespan, whose grand passion with Louis lasted twelve years and produced seven children, did exactly the same, spending sixteen years in prayer and good works. Her penance, said society with satisfaction, equalled La Vallière's.

Ironically enough, the only woman in Louis's life who had always wanted to enter a convent was denied the privilege. His wife, Marie-Thérèse, Infanta of Spain, must have been a most unhappy woman. Married young to a grossly unfaithful husband, it was said that her apartment was like a cloister. She received the habit of the Third Order of St Francis with 'profound humility' and always signed herself Sœur Thérèse to indicate her devotion to religion. When she died at forty-five, her body was clothed in the habit of a Franciscan nun.

There were women who entered to expiate their own sins. The sister-in-law of the Marquis de Sade, Anne-Prospère de

Launay, fell in love with him and they fled to Italy. She entered a convent at twenty-seven and died there of smallpox nine years later. Some entered to expiate the sins of others. Princess Louise, daughter of Louis XV and Marie Leczinska of France, believed that only a princess of the blood royal could atone for her father's sins, and entered the monastery of St Denis as Teresa of St Augustine.

Perhaps the most unlikely nun of all was Heloïse, the beautiful pupil of Peter Abelard, the philosopher and theologian. Their love-affair was one of the most poignant ever, and it lives still through the letters they wrote each other. She bore him a son, but would not marry him lest she hinder his career. When her uncle in vengeance had Abelard castrated, the only future he could envisage was in a monastery and he begged Heloïse to enter also. She ended her life an abbess, but it was a sham, for to Abelard she wrote, 'I have no God but you.'

What concerns religious orders now is recognizing the true vocations. This is made all the more difficult because a woman may have not only good, adequate and conscious motives for wishing to enter – but also unrealized subconscious motives; minor inadequacies, even personality disorders.

Girls who want to enter usually contact a parish priest. He may advise her to contact a local order, or one to which she is particularly suited. He may advise her against the life: one woman was told by a priest that she had too affectionate a nature to become a nun, and should marry. She is now in her eighties, a completely fulfilled member of a strictly enclosed order since she was twenty.

Alternatively the girl might go to someone like Mother Mary Joseph. She is a short, imperious woman in her sixties with an awe-inspiring manner, and her sisters treat her with due deference. She founded the Sisters of Our Lady of Good Counsel and St Paul of the Cross, better known as the Vocation Sisters, whose headquarters is a manor house in Leicester. The main entrance hall is seventeenth-century and when one comments on the atmosphere, 'I hope,' she replies, 'that it is one of prayer.'

Together with a companion, Mother Mary Joseph started the Vocation Sisters to guide girls into the most suitable orders. 'Until 1939, there were no places like this where you could come and get information about orders. They were unknown, often to each other. Nuns didn't even know other nuns who lived down the road. In those days you just couldn't obtain information about an order unless you happened to know one, or unless a priest told you where to go. So we realized there was a need for a place where girls could go to be quiet, to think, to be away from any influence towards any particular order, to find out about religious life, what it meant, what it was, what the vows meant and what kinds of orders there were.'

Their early days were a struggle. They got together £200 for a house, spent their weekends on their knees scrubbing it, and collected leaflets of the various orders. 'There were enough then to cover a card table – now there are racks of them.'

Many girls come across Mother Mary Joseph in the course of her work. Talking in a school perhaps, or at vocations exhibitions at churches in different parts of the country. She tells them that the most important thing for a girl who wants to enter is that she must 'want to give herself whole-heartedly to God to use in whatever way he wants. You don't join to be a typist or a book-keeper, nor to nurse or teach, but to do exactly what is needed.' Mother Mary Joseph finds that few of them know what form of religious life they want. 'They don't feel called to marry or to remain single in the world, but they don't know if they want to teach or nurse, go to the missions or be contemplatives.' To advise them, she discovers their interests and talents. She explains the qualifications they will need, and describes the life-style of various convents. She lends them books and gives them pamphlets: often they spend a few days with her to get the feel of community life.

As early as this, clever guidance will often discourage an obviously unsuitable or immature girl. For convents now are far more concerned with quality than with quantity. Much as they want entrants, they realize as never before the problems the wrong recruits can bring. 'Do not,' wrote a foundress to a young superior, 'receive too easily. It is much wiser to wait.'

They do not want those who come into the category one Belgian novice mistress dismissed as 'pious Girl Guides'. And they might even be chary of over-encouraging suitable applicants. One Sacred Heart sister remembers the woman who later became her superior urging her to go to college. 'I wrote to her from Leeds, saying I was happy and busy, but there was a deep-down loneliness. She wrote back, "This is perfectly normal at twenty-two – you haven't met the one you'll probably marry." I was terribly indignant.'

'Prospective entrants might,' says Sister Margaret Moran, who handles admissions to the Sisters of the Good Shepherd, 'be the girl who writes from school, or a widow of fifty with a grown-up family.' She gets twelve-year-olds writing in to say they are interested in becoming nuns. 'I've got one girl at school who writes very philosophically, telling me she knows she has a very long time to go. I've told her, if God wants her to be a nun He'll let her know, but in the meantime to be a good girl. She'll very likely be the kind of girl to come. I don't deliberately keep in touch, but I sent her the Life of our Foundress.'

The American missionary order of Maryknoll Sisters of St Dominic has two of the order running their admissions department to handle the 1400 enquiries a year they get from eighth-graders alone. The order sends them letters about the work and the prayer life in the community. Out of this number, many will continue writing for years, then some might start doing lay missionary work. 'And out of that 1400 we'll have perhaps half a dozen left.'

Most of their contacts come through *Maryknoll*, the magazine produced by their brother community, the Maryknoll Fathers, which has a vast circulation. And the admissions sisters also go round the country doing promotions work for the community with films and tapes, although they are quick to point out, 'We're not yet beating bushes for girls: we have all the work we can do keeping in contact with those who write in.' Their job is to see the girls get to know the community – and vice versa. The sisters travel anywhere to meet prospective entrants: Philadelphia, Chicago, St Louis. 'We write and say we'll be in the area. We find it better not to go to the home, because sometimes they haven't told their families.' The meetings take place in the parents' home only by invitation. Usually they are in hotel lobbies, or the girl's apartment, "a neutral place, not threatening to the girl." ' Alternatively, the interested applicants might follow the European pattern of spending a weekend at the convent. With American distances, the English habit of asking the girls to tea is on the impractical side.

At this stage the applicant will usually go into the pre-entrance programme – that means she is in regular touch with the order, which gives her an abbreviated rule of life to follow, as well as some reading and a certain amount of prayer.

When a Good Shepherd applicant has spent some time at one of the convents, and if both sides are happy with what they find, she will be asked to join the staff, perhaps of one of the schools the order runs for maladjusted girls. During that time – usually about nine months – she is invited to spend part of her holidays with them at the house of formation, as they now call the novitiate.

The orders themselves have a very clear idea of the entrants they want, and their perfect applicant varies depending on many factors: their country of origin, their work, the ideals of the community. Teresa of Avila asked of a hopeful novice merely: 'Has she good sense?' but there would seem to be no place for such simplicity today. The constitutions of one new English community, the Sisters of Our Lady of Grace and Compassion, state that they look 'for women of sixteen to forty with a spirit of generosity, common sense, reasonable health, stability and a desire to give themselves utterly and unconditionally to God. The ability to get on with others is, of course, essential.'

The foundress of the American Maryknoll sisters declared that her ideal entrant would be 'distinguished by Christlike charity, a limpid simplicity of soul, heroic generosity, selflessness, unswerving loyalty, prudent zeal, an orderly mind, gracious courtesy, an adaptable disposition, solid piety, and the saving grace of a sense of humour.' And the Anglican Sisters of St Mary the Virgin feel that 'the best people we get are those who have been most active in life. And of course, the most important test is whether you can stay put.'

In order to be considered suitable, the entrant must not only be emotionally attracted by but attractive to the order she chooses; there are a great many qualifications which she must, in canon law, fulfil. (Though to one superior who showed signs of being too exacting, a foundress once wrote, 'It is not my intention to receive only postulants descended from Jupiter.') In their constitutions, under the section on 'admission of subjects', every order stresses that 'a candidate must not be debarred by any impediment.' The impediments make up a considerable list, though in some cases special dispensations may be made under particular circumstances. Some 'impediments' seem unlikely, but have evolved over the years – and not without cause. Among those women who cannot be validly admitted to the novitiate are those who are still married, or who 'are liable for punishment on account of some grave crime of which they have been or could be accused'. Another group excluded are 'any who are entering under the influence of violence, great fear or fraud, or who are received by a Superior under the same influence'. Anyone who is in debt 'and unable to pay the same' cannot enter, nor can those 'bound to provide support for their parents, grandparents, or for their own children'. Many women who have a 'late vocation' have been eager to enter for years, but had to wait until their obligations in these directions were fulfilled.

Another prohibition for a prospective entrant is to have 'abandoned Catholicism to join a non-Catholic or atheistic sect'. Such people would need a dispensation from the Holy See before they could enter. The same applies to women belonging to an Eastern rite, who must obtain written permission from the Congregation of the Eastern Church Nor does the Catholic church beam upon those who have been converted less than two years before they attempt to enter religious life – but again, the bishop of the province can grant a dispensation so they can enter.

There are now, and always have been, a great many superb women who have changed their religious beliefs and then entered convents. Many orders will not accept those who have been members of another congregation, whether as postulants, novices, or fully professed sisters. This can be overcome in special cases and I met several sisters who had tried life in one order only to find they were not suited. Different orders vary enormously. Their charisma, their spiritual personality, is peculiar to themselves and a woman might be utterly miserable in one order and totally fulfilled in another, like the sister who died in America recently at the age of 101 after eighty-one years in the convent: before entering as an Immaculate Heart sister in California she had been in two communities in England, both of whom told her she had no vocation. Sometimes the problem is physical: two of the women to whom I talked, one English and the other French, had entered contemplative orders and found their health would not stand up to the rigours of the system: the frugal meals, the broken hours of sleep, the manual work and the cold. And sometimes the clash is mental, as one Italian woman found. The order she chose was too restrictive, not modern enough for her ideas and beliefs. 'It wasn't something I could have known until I entered.' She is now very much happier with a teaching order.

The difference between orders has been intensified now that the rigid superstructure of convent life has undergone the massive undermining of the last ten years. A Good Shepherd novice mistress remembers one entrant who 'was so obstinate, we thought she'd never fit into community life. But she came back, and back, and back. And now she has settled. But the type of life we lived before Vatican II, she could never have fitted into that.'

The age of the applicant is also considered. Until Vatican II, sixteen was considered a perfectly acceptable age for entrance and it was not unknown for girls to enter even earlier: an Italian Daughter of St Paul now in her late thirties entered when she was fourteen. Orders would specify that applicants were only acceptable between seventeen and twenty-five. But it is now generally considered that a girl who has not yet completed her fifteenth year is ineligible, while those under sixteen can be received only if the mother general and the council consider it wise. They would make an exception, one superior said, in cases of 'a very unhappy home, something like that'.

There is, of course, yet another route by which girls entered, though it is one which is now out of favour. A hundred and twenty years ago many orders had attached to them boarding-schools for girls from fourteen to sixteen who intended to enter. These young aspirants lived strange lives, half in and half out of the convent, subject to many of the rules, observing silence at certain times, changing into the black dress and stockings of the postulant when they got back from school at four o'clock. This method of recruitment lapsed as educational standards changed and religious orders became more enlightened: they would sooner their girls sowed their wild oats before entering, and came into religious life with no regrets.

The Anglican Sisters of St Mary the Virgin do not encourage entrants under twenty-two and prefer those between twenty-five and thirty-five. As deputy superior Sister Morag Michael puts it: 'We're much happier if they've been out in the world, had boy-friends, and training in something, so they know what life is about.' Another superior at the Deaconess Community of St Andrew says: 'I'm always pleased if they've had ordinary relationships with boy-friends, and started a career going.'

Out of a group of novices I talked to in one convent – a group made up mainly of girls in their twenties, though one was over thirty – there was a laboratory technician, a teacher, a civil servant, a clerk and a secretary, as well as one girl who had been working as a matron in an approved school.

There are strong arguments for not taking girls too young. An Italian superior, Sister Maria Lorenzina Guidetti, explains that: 'It's not that life has a big secret. But it can be frustrating if a girl comes very young to the convent. Life, it seems so long.' She feels, too, that 'those who are all their lives in a convent, they don't mature so well.' Father O'Doherty, an Irish priest/psychiatrist who has written a great deal about the recognition of vocations, believes that entering young was reasonable at the time when adolescence ended at about nineteen. But in these days of extended student life, he is certain that a girl does not have a clear 'self-image' or a clear-cut idea of her personality until she reaches her twenties.

There are, of course, those who still advocate entering young. An elderly sister of the Sacred Heart: 'I do thank God so very much for my early vocation, I pretty well live with Him now.' And Sister Madeleine, of the Augustinian Sisters of Meaux: 'I look askance at the eighteen-year-olds entering now – but I entered myself at eighteen. You're peculiarly receptive at that age. And I'm glad I stayed naïve – I didn't have time to become sceptical.'

At the other end of the scale, there is an upper age limit of acceptance which before Vatican II was in many orders fixed at twenty-five. Today several orders will not take those over forty-five without special permission from the mother general. On the other hand, Mother Alphonsa Lathrop, the daughter of Nathaniel Hawthorne, who founded her own nursing order, made her vows for life at fifty-four. And at this moment, one Episcopalian house has two novices in their fifties.

The great bar to religious life used to be illegitimacy. Today few orders would refuse such a girl. Others, however, would still reject her – though making sure to justify it on more pragmatic grounds. As one novice mistress says, 'She might well have an unstable family background.'

The constitutions of most communities contain a phrase that asks that the entrant 'have both the physical and mental capacity to understand and practise the spirit of the congregation'. And a girl is asked to produce a recent medical certificate, or takes a medical just before joining. Inherited illness, particularly insanity, is something that bothers the communities a good deal. 'We go into that really thoroughly. After all, our work is looking after lame ducks – we couldn't take in someone seeking refuge from the difficulties of life.' Epilepsy, for instance, does disbar a girl from entering.

There are, however, several orders which welcome those who are incapacitated. The Sisters of Jesus Crucified is one. They have a house in France, two in the United States, and

ight more in Europe: they are even in Japan. The order
egan in 1930 when a woman called Suzanne Wrotnowska
decided to make a genuine religious life possible for disabled
women. While they cannot take anyone with nervous or
mental illness, they accept all those who would be turned
down by most congregations. They claim that poor physical
health and handicap should not be an obstacle for someone
wanting to live the religious life – rather, they felt it logical
such women should be accepted. They might even take someone with an illness as serious as terminal cancer, though this
would be a risk. 'It would all depend on the localization, the
prognosis – and the person herself.'

Few superiors would go so far as one Sister of Mercy who
even insists that among the qualifications for new entrants
should be that they possess 'middling good looks'. Why?
'Because you can't send people out visiting if they have huge
birthmarks across their faces: they'd have to go to another
community.' Her argument for such discrimination was that
'we're representing the community when we go out.'

One of the qualifications may be financial. Until only the
last few years, it was not only customary but necessary for a
girl to bring to the convent her dowry, as she would have
brought it to her marriage. It was this that financed the
convent, and in the case of those taking girls of good birth
brought them land as well.

It was not until the First World War that this custom
began to decline, and indeed in many orders it is still accepted
as perfectly normal. The constitutions of an order founded in
the 1950s read: 'No dowry is required but each one, if her
means permit, should provide for her support during the
period of probation prior to the first profession. The amount
is to be fixed at the General Chapter. This money must be
returned in full should the aspirant return to the world. Also
to be returned to her, if still remaining, are any other effects
which she brought in with her and which must be carefully
listed on her entry.'

Supposing that the prospective sister is eligible for entry, she will then be asked to fill in an application form. Her family background, character and conduct are carefully investigated. She used to have to provide written references of good conduct from the bishop of her birthplace and from the parish priests of all other places in which she had lived for more than a year since she was fourteen. This practice has just been dropped, but references from a priest who has known her for over two years are still required. An employer or a school might also be asked for references.

Until recently, aspirants were not psychologically screened at all. It was all done, says a superior 'in a very superficial way'. Five years ago, a priest speaking to a group of Anglican religious joked that religious life was the only profession left 'in which it is not regarded as necessary to identify ink blobs in order to discover vocation'. He would not say that now. In enlightened communities the next step is 'taking their psychologicals'. In other words, the girl is sent at the community's expense to see a clinical psychologist, usually making at least two visits.

Some European orders still prefer not to use these advanced screening techniques. 'Psychiatrists with a list of questions,' as one English novice mistress said scathingly, 'very American.' Such orders believe 'there's a lot to be said for knowing people at a human level.' So they invite sisters who know the girl, perhaps from college, to write a report on her. But any system can fail. One sister who wrote such a report on a prospective candidate remembers: 'I said this girl wasn't suitable, or capable enough. She was highly strung and couldn't afford another failure in her life. Well, someone else wrote and strongly recommended her. So she was accepted. And she stayed one day.'

The sisters responsible for the Maryknoll admissions say: 'The main thing is to learn she's not pathological, to get to know her strengths and weaknesses. We need to know she's a normally sound, healthy girl, not entering for a refuge, not running away. We want to know how she relates to others, which is extremely important for this life. And she must also be mature enough to act independently.'

Another American community, the Immaculate Heart of

Mary, has a lengthy 'orientation' programme every summer. A girl interested in joining will be invited to attend three times in five years. They travel down to the Casa de Maria, an immense Spanish-style house on the California coast which was once the community's novitiate. The first three days take the form of a retreat. Then different members of the community, a number of them on the Board of Directors, will explain the ways of the group and its purpose. There are informal discussions, question-and-answer sessions. And most important, there is time for the aspirants to get to know those who are in the community already.

Occasionally, superiors with an infallible eye for a vocation emerge. One such was Mother Barbara of the Sisters of the Cross and Passion, an order founded to care for North Country mill girls in England. It was said of her that she had only to look at a new arrival to know if she would persevere. Gazing intently at the girl, she would say, 'No need to unpack that child's trunk.' She was, it is claimed, never wrong.

But those who are in favour of psychological tests, like Sister Madeleine of the Augustinian Sisters of Meaux, feel that 'untangling people's motives is too complex a business to be done casually.' She is well aware that an entrant with the very best of motives might also have problems, which only a trained counsellor could find: she might, for instance, have a compulsive need for order, or a fear of marriage; a desire for emotional or spiritual security amounting to arrested development. She might suffer from religious mania or neurotic timidity. Yet it is true that even negative-sounding reasons may none the less lead to genuine vocations. One woman, who would almost certainly have flunked stringent tests today, entered out of loneliness when her mother died thirty years ago. 'I was eighteen and bitterly upset. I thought I might find happiness in a convent. And once the doors closed behind me I felt at peace: I knew I was in the right place.'

In the United States, a number of clinical psychologists advertise in the religious press that they are available for community work. But in Europe there are perhaps only three or four in each country, and they are used by everyone. Once a year in Britain, at Spode House, candidates from many communities are assessed by a group of experts. These assessments take the form of a day and a half of tests as well as depth interviews.

The psychologists, while they cannot assure a novice mistress that a girl has a vocation, are expected to confirm that she is neither neurotic nor entering under some unhealthy compulsion. The prospective nuns themselves clearly appreciate the value of these tests. One said: 'It made me feel they were really accepting me.' But not all orders, even today, show this kind of restraint. One novice I met retailed with absolute horror what happened when she visited another order. 'In half an hour they were handing me forms and telling me what day to come in.'

Of course, these tests are not the decisive factor. 'I don't,' says Sister Madeleine 'base my decision just on what they say.'

In the past, convents would have received borderline cases, girls they thought might have a vocation but about whom they were uncertain. Not any more. Now, a girl who on the surface seems to have all the qualifications and qualities for the religious life, and who desperately wants to enter, may not be found acceptable.

This report – abbreviated from a much more exhaustive document – was compiled on a girl who was anxious to join the Good Shepherd sisters.

M.J. is a pleasant, open girl of 21. Her father works as a labourer, she is the eldest of a family of nine, left school and went to work in a factory for two years. After that, at 17, she tried her vocation at another order but at the end of the first month was advised to leave as she was not considered mature enough. Before taking up nursing she worked as a cashier in a supermarket for 18 months. She has now completed two years of her training. Her intellectual ability is in the normal range. School leaving age shows poor inclination for study, but should have passed her final examinations. Her interests are medical, the social services and clerical.

Personality test – good emotional balance, good self-confidence. Healthy ability to relate to others. Tends to be very austere in interpersonal relationships, has some leadership qualities but lacks self-discipline. During the interviews she was open and frank, a typical working-class girl who has still to make more use of her talents. Psychologically there is no reason why she should not make a very good religious.

The whole of this report was presented to a council of eight sisters, under the guidance of the provincial superior, who is in charge of all the houses in that particular province. The novice mistress herself, who prepares the report, has no vote.

This girl was turned down by the order, at which she was quite relieved but a bit hurt'. The order commented on her: Her motivation for the religious life is centred on emotional feeling, sacrificial worship and a seeking for self-fulfilment – that isn't terribly good. There are few signs of spiritual commitment, though the interviews provided an opportunity for her to think out the meaning of a vocation and the sort of behaviour expected of a religious. But she must give evidence of ability to make a sustained effort. She gave up nursing: she couldn't discipline herself in a very demanding situation.'

The novice mistress added that a few years ago, without the intensive detail available on this form and through the psychological tests, they would probably have accepted M.J. And the problems would have shown up in the novitiate.'

At this stage, orders will accept the girl as a postulant for a period. The idea is that each is on trial, getting to know each other without any commitment on either side. If the girl decides to leave, she does so with no slur on her character – it is in no sense a failure, and she need not even explain why she is going. Some communities, like the Good Shepherd, would leave the girl working at her job for at least six months. 'We ask her to be in contact with a sister once a week for a chat to help with her reading. We ask her to be a good Christian.' There are, too, more personal changes they ask the girl to make in her life. 'We would ask her to give up dating, if she's got a boy-friend. Not her social life, but steady dating. We tell her, look, it's not fair to lead a boy on to

think she's available if she's not: she might break someone
heart for nothing. Oh, and we'd ask her to give up smokir
and drinking.'

Some orders stipulate three months of postulancy, but si
is more usual, although recent Vatican decrees have extende
it up to two years. The concept of this period of testing h;
changed. The Augustinian Sisters of Meaux is one group whic
realizes that any girl needs 'a long time of testing or prepar;
tion. For the first year or two, it should be quite clear they'r
not even novices. They're learning, getting to know us, ou
ideals and aims – and we can get to know them.'

When all is said and done, the only way to test a vocation
to enter, and the only successful entrant is the one who stay;
Because the varieties of call are so different, there is no norr
against which they can be measured, no quick way to prov
their validity.

Sister Louis Gabriel of the Congregation of Our Lady
Sion is an impressive woman. A German Jewess by birth, sh
holds doctorates from German and American universitie
and is known again now by her worldly name: Dr Charlott
Klein. Practical and highly intellectual, she is the last possib'
person to fantasize over a religious vocation. And yet, sh
says, 'I certainly had the extremely strong experience that
call had come to me that was not manufactured by an exterio
force but which was definitely, objectively, asking for
response outside myself.' It is not as though she had been i
any way actively seeking change. 'I was completely happy
satisfied and fulfilled. I had a job in the British Intelligenc
service, monitoring secret wireless stations. And when
finally said what I planned to do, the head of my departmer
was amazed.

'There was nothing visionary about it. I wouldn't call it
mystical experience – I am against all such things. But I mu;
say it was the definite perception of something outside m
asking if I wanted this life.

'And the result, after all, after twenty years or so, has bee
for me wonderful beyond all expectation. It proves that th;
must have been a real experience.'

3

INITIATION:
RITES AND RITUALS

*We were told to emulate the angels — but the angels
don't have bodies.*

A SACRED HEART SISTER

On the day of her Clothing, when a Benedictine novice
makes her Simple Profession, she is a bride, a virgin crowned.

Dressed all in flowing white, veiled in gauze and carrying
flowers, she walks behind the monks and the priest into the
abbey church, to kneel there before the prelate conducting the
ceremony. Into the silence he turns to her. 'What do you
ask?'

'The mercy of God and the grace of the holy habit.'

'Do you ask it with your whole heart?'

'Yes, my lord, I do.'

'God grant you perseverance, my daughter.'

Then the choir sing, *Veni, Creator Spiritus*, and two matrons
of honour, young laywomen, take her hands and lead her
forward.

'O God,' prays the prelate, 'who has called us from the
vanity of this world to follow our vocation, keep Thy hand-
maid, our sister, always modest, sincere and peaceful.'

The girl kneels again before him and the choir sings as the
two matrons take off her headdress, strip her of the veil. The
bishop takes a pair of small silver scissors and cuts off a lock
of her hair. 'She shall receive a blessing from the Lord, and
mercy from God the saviour.' She rises and leaves the
sanctuary. In a small room she is helped off with her bridal
clothes, and puts on heavy black shoes and thick stockings,
dons a plain underslip and sits on a low stool while the abbess
runs clippers quickly over her head.

When the novice returns to the steps of the altar she is almost unrecognizable as the bride of a moment before. She stands in the long black habit, cap and wimple. The prelate hands her the leather girdle, which the matrons buckle round her waist. 'May the Lord gird you with justice and purity, so that you may be worthy to approach the divine bridal chamber.' Then the floor-length black scapular, the straight sleeveless garment, is passed over her head and settled round her shoulders. 'Receive the yoke of the Lord and bear his burden which is sweet and light.' Then she dons the white veil 'in token of chastity and obedience. May it be to you a pledge of God's grace, enabling you to run the course of your probation without stumbling.'

A lighted candle is placed in her hand. 'Grant her grace to persevere, so that with Thy protection and help she may accomplish the desire Thou has given her.'

The girl kneels on the prie-dieu, the candle in a silver candlestick beside her as the prelate speaks of the life she will lead; of the pleasures of the senses she is giving up for ever, of the hard work and obedience that face her; of the silence and loneliness that will be hers 'from now until death if all goes well.'

She leans forward, and kisses his hand to the music of the *Te Deum*, then she rises and leaves the sanctuary. This time, she and her matrons walk before the prelate, the priest and the monks. The chaplain carries the cross, and the parents and extern sisters make up the procession that winds now through the abbey grounds to the forecourt, through the front door, and so to the doors of the enclosure, where she knocks.

'Open to me the gates of justice,' she calls softly. And from inside many voices answer: 'This is the gate of the Lord, the just shall enter.' Then the door opens, and there stands the abbess, the great crook of the Benedictines in her hand, the entire community behind her. The clothed novice steps on to the threshold and kneels there. 'This is my last resting place for ever,' she sings, and as the final prayer is said, she rises and kisses her parents.

The prelate takes her hand, and gives her to the abbess.

'We hereby entrust to you our sister and pray that, under the guidance of the Holy Rule and through obedience, she may deserve to obtain perfect union with God. May the peace of the Lord be always with you.' Once more the novice is blessed. She passes over the threshold, into the enclosure. And the doors are closed and locked.

This devastating ritual takes place not immediately upon the entrance of a girl to religious life but two years later, when she has advanced from the novitiate, been accepted into the community, but still has not made her final, binding, solemn profession.

The first entry through that locked enclosure door has always been simpler but, for the girl herself, even more momentous. She is greeted at the door of the enclosure by the abbess and her councillors, who lead her down the cloister to the church. She kneels with the abbess on the step facing the sanctuary and, for the first time, the abbess presents her to her Lord. She genuflects at the burning lamp on the altar, then she is taken to the chapter house where the whole community waits. Here, the new entrant is given her new name in religion – her old name belonged to the old identity she has now surrendered.

The novice mistress then takes her ceremoniously round the community and each nun gives her the Pax, the formal kiss of peace. She sees for the first time the women among whom she may live for the rest of her life. They will be her family and her friends, and only for the rarest possible emergencies will she ever again leave them, even for a day.

Receiving her new name is one of the most traumatic acts of her new life. The name might approximate to her own, or it might not. The novice is expected to try to emulate the qualities and virtues of her namesake: though, as one sister given the name Humiliata remarked, she never really thought she made it. Other orders allow the sisters to choose their own dedication, which might be Sister So and So of the Passion, the Precious Blood, the Resurrection, the Ascension, the Agony of Christ, the Peace of God, or perhaps the Divine Silence. Many orders actually add to the confusion by prefacing each name with 'Mary'. The Sisters of the Divine Motherhood, for instance, have Sister Mary Marcellinus, Sister Mary Inviolata, Sister Mary Pulcherrima, Sister Mary Misericordiae, and Sister Mary Stigmata.

To an outsider, the process of going into a convent looks remarkably like that of being admitted to prison: the taking of the person's clothes, the removal of all personal items, the life in common, the taking on of a new identity – for a prisoner a number, for a nun, the title 'Sister'. One woman vividly describes how she hated the title; 'the black nonentity of sisterhood'. As a Jesuit priest comments, 'This business of naming is said to be because it's a new way of life altogether. But frankly, it's just a way of depersonalizing'. The process is carried even further when many new nuns are given men's names, largely because the huge number of women in religion rapidly get through the available well-known women's names. So there are Sister Mary Thomas à Becket and Sister John Bosco, Sister Anthony of Padua and Sister William Eugene, Sister Mary Cuthbert Mayne and Sister Mary Paul of Tarsus, while Sister Aelred is named after a Saxon bishop.

Current thinking, however, is moving away from the changing of names. 'Freud,' says one novice mistress, 'is now listened to. We realize the past is important.' The former Sister Godric, who has just gratefully reverted to her baptismal name of Sister Maire, remarked: 'Godric was a Saxon hermit, then a pedlar and a merchant and a saint, and he ended up living in a forest near Durham. I found it hard to identify with him.'

That first day provides a memory which no woman who has entered a convent ever forgets. They can all describe the journey to the door. 'I remember my last taxi ride, puffing away madly on a last cigarette.' A strictly enclosed nun who entered over sixty years ago recalls with a shudder how she felt. 'It was very dark and there were four gaunt figures before me, draped in black. One put out her hand towards me, and it seemed to be enormous.'

When an American entered the Poor Clare enclosed order,

she was shown to her cell, with its two holy pictures covered with Cellophane and the straw mattress on the bed. 'I thought of an early American bedroom. They left me there, telling me to learn where everything was quickly, because we don't use electric light, though I was allowed to for the first day.'

Margaret McConnell, who describes her convent life in *Open Then the Door* admits that: 'What I had expected the inside of the convent to be like I cannot say. It is impossible to imagine a convent. It is not the building and not the nuns, but the strange worldless atmosphere that pervades the place.'

Most entrants find the hardest thing to accept at first is the bareness, the simplicity, the fact that nowhere is there a single object which does not serve a purpose. 'My parents' home was full of pictures,' says an Italian girl, 'and we had three cats. I just wanted something pretty to look at – not a statue, an ornament.'

The period of postulancy is hard because it is a trial on both sides. It is what one novice mistress describes as a time 'for the possible riding on the crest of the wave effect to subside, and the impact of daily reality to help that seep away, so they can discern our conviction with greater reality, and we can discern theirs'.

In every order, there are funds of stories about the behaviour of postulants: the one who arrived with an armful of magazines to get her through the time till she could decently leave; and the prospective contemplative who had so little idea of the life that she turned up complete with her cosmetics. Postulants do leave in large numbers – which the orders fully expect. It might be because they find once inside that the life does not match up to their expectations. One girl assumed that, like St Catherine of Siena, the only nourishment she would need would be the communion wafer. When the rest of the community sat down to a large dinner she left the house in painful disillusionment. Some women go in meaning to stay only briefly. 'I eventually decided I would enter, though secretly I intended to stay only for the postulancy, thinking that after that I could with a clear conscience tell the Lord I had tried, and return to my own sweet life.' This woman did remain, 'maybe because for the first time in my life I was really happy'.

The postulancy is a break with the past. Until a few years ago it was a harsh one. No journeys home were allowed, although parents could visit every third Sunday for a couple of hours. Postulants came under all the novitiate rules, such as the one decreeing that letters must be handed unsealed to the superior, and return post would be handed to the owner with the envelope already slit. And the girl was already required to wear a uniform, though with a shorter dress than the full habit, and a smaller, white veil instead of the black.

The period of postulancy, however, has changed. During the early days of convent life, the postulant was shorn, and should, in the words of an early Franciscan ruling, 'leve the robis of the worlde'. Today, in some communities, up to two years is spent half in, half out of the community, during which time the newcomer lives and dresses as she has always done. In others, she will probably have the opportunity to live in several houses within the order, sharing different kinds of work. Enlightened novice mistresses now go to endless lengths to determine that postulants are really suited.

Before the postulant can be admitted to the novitiate, she must ask formally if she may join the community. A vote may be taken among the members of any house where she has spent a considerable time. On the basis of this, and their knowledge of her, the mother general and her council of sisters will formally decide whether to accept her. All orders mark this step with ceremony. The Benedictines clothe the new novice in a short version of the habit and a white veil. The Sisters of Our Lady of Grace and Compassion have a short initiation ceremony in church. There is an opening hymn, and then the postulant tells the superior: 'Reverend Mother, I wish to become a novice in this Congregation,' to which the reply is 'Thanks be to God. You are welcome to our family.' She then makes her act of consecration, promising to dedicate herself to the Virgin Mary, and she is then formally received into the congregation, and given her name in religion.

Until six years ago, the Good Shepherd order received its postulants with the full church ceremony complete with bridal dress. Now, after an eight-day preparation, the girls in their blue dresses enter the community room. The mother provincial – in a ceremony hopefully written for several postulants simultaneously – addresses them. 'Dear Sisters, what do you ask from us?'

'Drawn by God's merciful grace, we have come here to experience your way of life. We ask you to teach us to follow Christ the Good Shepherd, and to live in poverty, chastity and obedience and zeal for the salvation of souls.' They ask to be allowed to learn the rule, and the mother provincial responds: 'May our merciful God nourish you with his grace, and may Christ our divine teacher grant us his light.' She then gives them a copy of the constitutions of the society.

The year of novitiate must, under canon law, be spent within the enclosure 'devoted entirely to formation of character, study of the Constitutions, practice of prayer, instructions on the vows and virtues, and exercises suited to correcting defects, subduing passions, and acquiring virtues. Hence the novices are not to be applied to the study of letters, sciences and arts; nor to be employed in the exterior works of the Institute.' This is no longer strictly observed, particularly since the majority of young women will be taking some sort of higher education or professional training. But the purpose of the novitiate remains: to find, as Teresa of Avila put it, 'whether they are of the right temperament and have the other qualities for keeping our rule'

The novice mistress is the person with whom the new entrant has most contact. In the monastic orders she is still 'Mistress of Novices' and she should, in the words of St Benedict, be someone who 'loves and is careful about the divine office, and is obedient, humble and persevering'. Until recently, many also seem to have been veritable martinets. It was the novice mistress who trained the novices in the ways of the convent, teaching them to join the hands in a special position, to walk on the ball of the foot, to observe silence. In doing so, she was expected, if necessary, to 'break the spirit'; this was not regarded as cruelty since conformity was all.

Almost every nun I met had stories about their strictness. 'The novice mistress stood at the bottom of the stairs just before night prayers,' remembers a German sister. 'The novices, passing her, had to admit to any faults during the day and ask special permissions: 'I broke a glass.' 'I didn't finish my prayer at noon.' 'May I take a bath?' One Good Shepherd sister recalls: 'My novice mistress was very cold – repelling, almost. She was very much the superior and she felt it her job to turn out very humble and obedient souls.' Obedience had to be, quite literally, blind. 'It wasn't just teaching you what to do but the exact, precise way you always had to do it. You were taught to brush a corridor in a certain way and woe betide you if you attempted improvements.' While it was undeniably destructive – 'It was hardship at a psychological level, destroying me as a person. It took me years to get over it' – some can none the less look back and discover hard-earned benefits. Rita Hannon of La Sainte Union des Sacrés-Cœurs found: 'The discipline, as a background, meant I learnt of the possibilities within me. I learned what I could endure. And that has remained with me. I feel now I could be jailed, or I could be free and sitting on a halfpenny because of this experience.'

The novice mistress is also responsible for explaining the intentions of the life. As Francis de Sales wrote to one of his sisters in 1690: 'The victim must be consumed, you must strip your heart of self, cut back hard all the little shortcomings prompted by nature and by the world.' This, he admitted, was no easy task: 'It is not done in a day.'

All the little shortcomings were indeed cut back hard. The following is part of the Carmelite Manual for Novices on Mortification of the Exterior Senses:

Do not smell fragrant herbs, fruit or flowers, etc., much less bring them into your cell, or keep them for their pleasant odour.

When you eat or drink, think of something unsavoury in order to mortify the taste, especially if you take things agreeable to the palate.

Sometimes mingle a little water or bitter flavouring with your food.

At intervals put the body to some inconvenience, such as keeping one foot raised, etc., in order that the discomfort of the body may impede the gratification of the taste or moderate it, that so each morsel may be dipped in the gall and vinegar of Jesus Crucified.

The role of the novice mistress has changed since that manual was published in the 1920s, and it is symbolic that many communities now prefer to call her 'Novice Guardian' or 'Formation Director'. (Though perhaps her role has not changed that much: the sisters of one American order refer to their novitiate, Humility House, as 'Humble Hut'.)

In most communities, she is at least thirty-five years old and professed for at least ten years: unlike the superior, she can be re-elected as often as the community wishes.

The constitutions of one congregation, founded ten years ago, say that she must be 'a model of obedience to her Superiors and very exact in the religious life. She should be charitable and prudent, motherly, just and firm, kind but not weak. She must be approachable, but not be afraid to humble the proud and correct the negligent and disobedient.' She also must be knowledgeable about doctrine, scripture, and liturgy because she is also expected to teach the novices these subjects. 'A very simple yet thorough knowledge of Christianity' is what one novice mistress defines as her aim. Another says: 'We go according to what the girl can take in and what her interests are. Some are very interested in theology, others aren't. We teach scripture and how to read the Bible intelligently, and read well in public. They're expected to know dogma before they come, though some don't.'

Today it is accepted that a training period is needed for such a post, and there are now regular conferences and courses available. Today's novice mistress is aware of group dynamics and interpersonal relations; she worries lest she is not understanding enough: 'I feel, suppose I reprimand a novice because I'm in a bad temper. It would be dreadful,

I'd be an obstacle in her path. I often pray for inspiration, that I may do what is most helpful for them.'

Novice mistresses are very conscious of the responsibilities of their task: 'It's quite a moment to see a person come in the door to enter, and know they've got to be transformed into a religious, the point of view they've got to get.' Yet the role is not wholly encouraging. Sister Madeleine of the Augustinian Sisters of Meaux sees as part of her duty the job of exposing novices to the drawbacks of religious life as well as the advantages. She claims she is a devil's advocate: 'If they take their vows after me, they make their choice in full, total conviction.'

One of the first things the novice mistress teaches her pupils is the pattern of day. This usually begins around five a.m. with a knock on the door and a call from the sister ringing the handbell. The call varies from order to order. For some it is, 'May Mary's Heart Immaculate,' to which the response is, 'be for ever praised.' Or it might be, 'Blessed be God,' and the response, 'Blessed be His Holy name.' The first gesture of the day might be to kiss the ground in monastic fashion, or perhaps to stand for a moment 'religiously', before kneeling for prayer.

The novice's day used to be strictly divided. 'We had to make a list accounting for what we did every half-hour.' This custom has not entirely died out. One novice was so closely watched that 'in the dormitory and chapel someone used to come and check you were meditating'.

In the past, novices used to be separated from other members of the community in order that they should not be unduly influenced by them. This is now recognized as absurd, since the novice is there to learn about the community. But her day is still different from that of the established sister, because so much of her time is spent in study.

The most important thing for her to learn is the meaning of the vows, and what it will cost her to live them. The only measure of loving, said St Bernard, is to love without measure. The purpose of the three vows of poverty, chastity and obedience is to give the nun greater freedom to love, to achieve a sort of spiritual nudity by withdrawing her heart from this world. 'Contentment,' as one novice master described it, 'is the absence of creature satisfactions.' The reason for giving them up is not that they are bad, but that the nun loves God more than the best of other satisfactions. So the vows are described as a sort of death, because they represent a complete break with the ways of the world, and are felt in the body, heart and mind as a death to things normally valued.

Vows did not exist at the beginning of religious life. The first religious, the desert fathers, lived without vows or a rule. It was only when communities developed that it became necessary to order the members' lives more firmly: 'To safeguard stability,' as one priest puts it, 'and strengthen the wavering will during time of weakness or stress.'

Stability is particularly important to the contemplatives. The Benedictines, like some other orders, make their first vow of stability to the house so that, as St Benedict stated: 'Its members should have no need to go abroad, which can in no way be good for them.' Their second vow is peculiar to themselves, the 'conversion of manners,' which teaches the opposite way of thinking to that in the world. Poverty is included, so is self-effacement, and listening rather than talking.

The religious state is a subjection of the individual, and this is brought about by observing the vows. This is how the Anglican Deaconess Community of St Andrew defines them:

Poverty is 'forgoing the right to personal ownership so as to live in simplicity and be more carefree in the service of God and people'. Chastity is 'living without the particular relationships of marriage and parenthood in order to be free to respond with warm yet unpossessive love wherever and whenever it is asked'. And obedience means 'giving up the right to determine one's own path so as to be available to be used by God in the way He wants'.

Of the vows, the first, poverty, is something of a misnomer. The nun is to give up everything in order to identify with those who have little of their own. Yet to most women, going into a convent means an end to financial worry and strain. Everything is provided for them – clothes and shoes, food and heat. In their old age, the community looks after them. Certainly they practise simplicity of life, but that is a very different thing from poverty.

Outsiders might well expect the Poor Servants of the Mother of God to be just that. But visitors to their Somerset house would be rapidly disillusioned – the house stands amid beautiful grounds at the end of a long, winding drive. Inside, visitors are shown into a richly carpeted room with a magnificent conference-sized wooden table, a cocktail cabinet full of glasses and a television set in the corner.

Certainly we have reason to be grateful for the superb buildings put up by some religious orders to house their nuns. But that is, after all, to the glory of God. Rich carpets are harder to justify.

Sister Rita Hannon is a woman who feels badly about religious being 'women of property. I wouldn't mind this if I could say that in the vast majority of cases we used our property generously. But the inspiring words of Christ about leaving all to follow him seem to have lost their appeal. It's disconcerting to think that, for many of us, these were the very liberating words which brought us into religious life.'

Poverty means the absence of extravagance; it is not supposed to mean penury. Nuns are not expected to share in common their clothes or their teeth, or even – as in one lay community on the Canadian lakes – their handkerchiefs, which takes communal property a lot further than any religious community I encountered.

Mother Gabriel, Mother General of the Sisters of Mercy convent in central London, says she estimates poverty by 'what you could afford if you were a mother in a house with an ordinary family. We're supposed to be poor, not indigent.' She feels it is a false economy to buy too cheaply because 'fairly good things, like good shoes, last much longer. And "seeming to be poor" doesn't mean to be in rags.'

But nuns are endeavouring, as the Sacred Hearts nicely put it, 'to live a simple life, resisting the pressure of a consumer society'. And of course, real and grinding poverty is no stranger to many nuns. As Teresa of Avila said, when asked to make two foundations: 'I had no means for making either but that was no disadvantage as I generally began with less than nothing.' And in Toledo, she wrote with mock despair, 'We had not so much as a scrap of brushwood to broil a sardine on.'

The Little Sisters of Jesus in Montreal live in the dock area. One woman who visited, planning to join them, said: 'I asked them how they would heat their rooms during the sub-zero winter. They said they had no idea.'

Nuns are charmingly unworldly about money when they do have it, like the superior who travelled across England with £400 tucked into her habit and secured with a safety-pin. One of the touching characteristics of the poorer orders is their trust that money will be found. When the Little Sisters of the Poor wanted to open a house in Glasgow, they found one that seemed to be suitable and threw a statuette of St Joseph over the wall so he could take possession of it: they somehow found the money, mainly through a priest who donated it. A member of the same order, Sister Emmanuel, wrote a letter to the French industrialist to whom she owed £500 for the building of a convent. She was dying, and asked that she be released from half the debt. 'From the chapter here, with God's help, the other half will be paid back at the rate of £50 a month. For that we are going to arrange with the Blessed Virgin and St Joseph to send you the amount in the first fortnight of every month.'

The order of the Poor Clares must not have a fixed income, but must live on alms. It has no endowments, no revenues of any sort. 'We just depend on divine providence and whatever we can earn with our hands to pay our way: we can never be self-supporting if we are to fulfil our life, our time of prayer, what our life is primarily about.' 'When the bills come in,' says another Poor Clare superior, 'it's quite true that often I just don't know how I'm going to meet them. But I generally take them and show them to Our Lord and remind him of his promise. It's just as simple as that. And somehow, just before I'm due to be summonsed, the money comes in. Sometimes just small amounts from the poor, or sometimes the occasional benefactor has come forward and taken over the bill for us.'

All sorts of economies are practised: it was said of a Franciscan for the Home Missions that so keen was she on poverty, she used one toothbrush all her life. And the Oblates of the Eucharist, a French semi-contemplative order at Sceaux, outside Paris, built their own first house after World War II. They were desperate for accommodation for their incurable patients, and in two years they had built the three-storeyed building from their own plans, of dark-faced brick, complete even to the electricity which they installed themselves. Although an architect designed their cool white chapel, they built that too.

To keep down costs, the American Maryknoll Missionary Sisters have a co-op inside the convent to buy necessities in bulk and sell them cheaply — deodorants, soap and aspirin. It was such a success that the order went into the dress business. There a sister returning from duty in a hot country can buy warm clothing for the New York winter from a sister just leaving the States. Outsiders donate clothes as well, and the 'Nearly New' shop in a recent sale had only a 52-in. girdle left, 'which we're keeping just in case'.

One area where nuns do seem to economize is food, even in these days of nutrition and balanced diets. It is said that this is far from true of male communities, who are reputed to eat vast meals. But at one English house the sisters ate in a gloomy basement lit by harsh neon. Twice, on the day I was there, the meal consisted of packaged fish fingers, great wedges of bread and margarine, tinned fruit salad, and sponge cake out of a packet. If these women were treating their food with monastic disdain, the Daughters of Charity of St Vincent de Paul in Paris certainly were not. At their huge modern hospital in Neuilly, where they look after physically handicapped children, the sisters eat better than diners in many a restaurant: grapefruit or pâté, followed by slices of beef, cauliflower au gratin, fresh green salad with vinaigrette, then home-made fruit gâteau, an ample cheeseboard, with celery and fresh fruit. All this was served in a freshly painted dining-room in the sisters' quarters above the hospital. Wine was served with the meal, and coffee was brewed afterwards. It was a far cry from the contemplative order whose superior once told the sisters the bell would be rung for dinner – if there was any by that time.

The early founders of religious orders took their food very seriously. St Benedict, for instance, laid down that each day shall be provided two kinds of 'mete' so that he who will not eat of one kind will take of the other. And in 1400, a Barking convent's meticulous records mention twenty-two oxen, pigs and sheep, geese, fowls and fish. At St Aldburgh's feast every lady of the convent had half a goose, 'also one hen or else a cock'. At the other end of the culinary scale, the Poor Clares today eat soup, potatoes and a meat substitute for their one full meal a day: for the others they make do with dry bread and coffee with, occasionally, butter for the postulants.

Much of the income of religious orders was originally brought by the dowries of the novices. Today, if a novice brings a dowry, it is usually spent on a long and expensive training course. Plenty of orders do still ask for dowries: a postulant of the Sisters of the Holy Family of Louisiana, for instance, must have not only a dowry but must provide most of the clothes she will need over the next three years; like a bride, the nun speaks of her 'trousseau'. A Benedictine choir nun brings a minimum of £600 but this is kept on deposit for her until her Final Profession.

A woman bound by vows or promises 'cannot retain the administration, use or revenues of her goods'. So before profession the novice must formally arrange for one or more people to look after them on her behalf: the order may do this, if she wishes and they agree. But she is advised not to relinquish ownership in case she leaves the order. Once she 'renounces the right of in any way using it or disposing of it or of any other goods of financial value, except with permission from the proper superior' any interest is paid to the order. She can still be given property as a gift, or an inheritance, if it is 'of a personal nature'. And in Milwaukee in April 1974 an insurance salesman was ordered to keep paying his ex-wife $250 a month in alimony even though she is now Sister Mary, a Dominican novice. He has to keep up the payments until she has taken her final vows in about five years' time.

On Solemn Profession everything is given away. A will must be made disposing of the nun's possessions as she wishes If she then decides to leave, under canon law no remuneration is due to her for her services. 'You can't,' says one superior, 'have people deciding to leave and claiming back this and that. It's impossible.' Most orders now have organizations into which they pay funds for just such contingencies, because they feel responsible for those leaving, 'but they have no absolute right to anything'.

To earn a living, contemplative nuns in particular turn their hands to all sorts of things. In the fifteenth century the nuns of Antwerp and Malines were famous for the lace collars and embroidered shirts they made for men of the aristocracy. Today it tends to be lavender bags or polystyrene models of cells. They produce hand-bound books, like the Benedictines, on their own presses. They turn out Christmas cards, like those drawn for the American Immaculate Heart of Mary Community by their former sister, the famous artist Sister Corita Kent. Another American order, the Sisters of the Cross, produce ceramic cruet sets and even ponchos. They also make 'dressed Infants of Prague' and bridal dolls.

Whatever they do, religious communities tend to find themselves in financial difficulties. These days, indigence is regarded by the public as evidence of inefficiency rather than holiness. 'You can't,' says one superior, 'live on the fringe of existence. For one thing, the state doesn't allow it.' In Britain, nuns are in a particularly peculiar position. The orders which do charitable work with the poor, or teach, are actively proselytizing. They keep the income earned by their members tax free: they are regarded as legal charities and enjoy relief from tax under the Income and Corporation Taxes Act of 1970. But the contemplatives, with their 'cottage' industries, labour under the same massive burden of corporation tax as giant companies. This absurd situation came about because in 1949 the Law Lords decided that, in this modern age, saying prayers could not be considered a charity. Religious orders, enclosed and established for 'prayer and self-sanctification', are not charitable because they lack 'the essential quality of public benefit'. And because they are under vows of poverty, the income of contemplatives is treated as a common fund, so they are not even eligible for the full tax-free allowance that every other taxpayer gets.

In the past it was all too easy for a nun to have no idea of the value of money. If she needed a stamp or toothpaste, she asked for it. For a bus or train journey, the treasurer gave her a purse with the money and her ticket. If she taught at a local school, she was given a certain amount of money at the beginning of the week and had to give an exact account of it.

The years since the Second Vatican Council have changed this attitude. Now that nuns are moving out of their vast mother houses, money is becoming real to them. One German sister says that as housekeeper for a small group of sisters instead of a community of twenty, she really knows what poverty means. 'I can't buy apples because they've gone up a penny a pound: it's the first time this vow has come home to me.'

Today, a nun might be on a personal allowance, the amount to be decided by the community, depending on her job – a teacher in a convent school may need very little, a nurse or university lecturer a larger amount. As one professional woman says, 'You have to read the gospel and see what demands are made of you. I can't go around with my books in a rucksack, so for me a briefcase is not a luxury but a necessity.' The allowances may be quite small. The Holy Child Sisters in Neuilly have had fifteen francs a month for the last two years for such things as special books or postage, and between three and four hundred francs a year for clothes, though this is not really enough. Consequently they are glad of relatives' cast-offs. Medical needs and books for study are paid for by the order. A Belgian Lady of Mary gets the equivalent of £2 a week for clothes, holidays and the cost of attending retreats. Even such a small amount 'makes for an individual being very independent'.

Most active communities have a common fund which is perhaps the combined salaries of their teachers. Out of this come the communal bills – heating, light and food. Then they allot to each sister the equivalent of a small pension. And, of course, all religious communities are accustomed to make their needs known, like the order which puts notices in all their visitors' rooms reading: 'OUR DEBT FOR THE CENTRAL HEATING IS NOW £1250. WILL YOU HELP US TO REDUCE THIS? MAY GOD REWARD YOU.'

Poverty remains the hardest vow for the people of developing countries to accept as part of the Christian religious life. Sister Alma, black superior of the Little Sisters of St Francis in Africa, says the people see it as a contradiction. 'These people hardly get the necessities of life, and they become very confused when they see the life the sisters lead. It looks artificial and seems hypocritical, an escape for girls from real poverty at home into that which is a made-up story, where sisters enjoy a high standard of living and security.'

It is still true today that of the three vows, obedience and poverty are considered in absolute theological terms. Chastity, on the other hand, is passed over with what one sister calls, oddly, 'euphemism and polite refrain'.

By her vow of chastity, the nun is consecrating her life more perfectly to God. She must abstain – and these or very similar words are used by every congregation – 'from every act, internal or external, opposed to the virtue of chastity'. To ensure a proper development of this virtue, she must practise constant mortification of her mind and feelings, particularly avoiding 'exclusive and passionate friendships and observing a sensible modesty' in her appearance and behaviour. But she must not be 'coldly reserved, cheerless and abrupt to others', for this would be failing in charity. The nun is advised to acquire this particular virtue through 'fervent and persevering prayer'. A consciousness of the presence of the Most Holy Trinity in their souls, love for the daily communion, fervent and careful use of the sacrament of penance, 'and a tender devotion to Our Blessed Mother, Queen of Virgins, and to St Joseph, her Spouse most chaste', are also recommended.

In Christianity, virginity is seen as the consummation of love between God and the soul. The idea is that a woman, by forgoing any physical expression of sex, is achieving 'spiritual motherhood', and thus belonging not to one family but to all. Virginity is seen very much as a positive thing — 'a shining sword', one sister calls it. So a nun's chastity does not come merely from sexual continence. She is, in the words of one religious — a man — 'in a condition of higher fruitfulness designed by God to give supernatural power to the world'.

The view of the Church is that chastity and virginity do not estrange nuns from this world, but develop the energy needed for wider involvement. 'Chastity,' the Pope told the First International Congress of Religious Sisters in 1951, 'is not merely a bodily affair, but a means of self-giving, part of the love and service of others for which our sisters are chosen.' It is surely true that the religious life is designed to provide an atmosphere where chastity is possible, where it is what one French psychologist calls 'psychologically viable'. A community of busy women with a rigid routine and a day filled to its very edges with work must be the best place to live a life where the sexual needs of the body are not heeded.

At the same time, an American novice master says that the vow of chastity is negative if it 'attempts to flee from the realities of sex and rigidly exclude the physical from thought and conduct'. Sisters must be taught that they are dedicated to God's service as women, rather than as individual angels uneasily enclosed in a body. But that, of course, is exactly what they have been taught.

There is still much written and said about the vow of chastity that must worry a great many people. 'The Spirit abolishes the flesh in us,' opines one theologian. 'It is not celibacy that is the cause of nervous troubles,' snaps an Italian master of novices, 'but a lack of a sense of total dedication.' Yet many of the women I talked to candidly admitted what they feel as real losses. Sister Marie worked during her novitiate in a home for unmarried mothers and their babies — work at which many orders excel. 'You do get times when you just long to have a baby in your arms; you could just sit back and feel distressed about it. And I do regret it, oh yes, I regret not having babies. I would love to have married and brought up children. But there's no use. I'm here for a different reason.'

Nor do religious women these days delude themselves that chastity is any easier for them than for men. 'Both parties,' reckons one superior, 'have their own difficulties. After all, most people say a man cannot resist, but once a woman has a taste of it, she needs it as much as a man. A woman is reluctant to give herself over unless she loves, but once she's had the experience . . .'

There is, even so, still a lot of nonsense talked about chastity. A young woman who is really seriously disturbed about her feelings of sexuality, who wonders whether chastity is sustainable and whether she really has a vocation, is not going to be helped by the advice one sister received to 'go to the chapel and say your prayers'.

All the self-control in the world does not alter the facts: a woman entering a convent is totally renouncing her sexual life. She is giving up the chance of a relationship with a man, and she is giving up her chance of bearing a child. Nuns and sisters are well aware of the love they are forgoing. Sister Morag Michael of the Anglican Community of St Mary the Virgin: 'When I see my sister happily married I think, how gorgeous. But there's something much deeper than human things. It's joy if you're meant to have them, and dust and ashes if you're not. And I'm as sure as I can be that I'm living as God wants me to.'

'You feel,' says an Italian nun, 'that you've had a special call to God, and you mean to give your loving time to Him, and so you can't give it to anyone else. It is a life of self-denial for that very reason: you are giving up the physical side of a profound love. And I can't see what religious life is about if you don't have celibacy.'

The vow of obedience is said to be the very essence of religious life. It is the means whereby the nun's life is framed for her by the canon lawyers.

When she makes this vow a religious binds herself under the authority of the superior of her congregation in whom,

as in God, she must have 'great confidence'. She undertakes
to obey 'all their lawful commands in everything which directly
and indirectly governs the life and work of the congregation'.
Such commands are an expression of God's will which she
must obey promptly, generously and unquestioningly.
'Grumbling or complaining are alien to the vow of obedience,'
says the rule. If a sister is changed from one house to another,
or elected to an office, she may not refuse, though she may
state her case to the superior in cases of special difficulty,
knowing she will 'humbly abide' by her decision. Sister
Marissa of the Poor Servants of the Mother of God devoted
years of her life to teaching subnormal girls in Brighton ('I was
built into the place.') When she was asked to become
superior at another house, she went without question. 'If
you're asked, you accept; you don't say no. That's not God's
will. You'd never be happy again, having refused a work
you were meant to do.'

Obedience can bring special difficulties. It can, says one
nun 'lead to exaltation of the rule, which encourages childish-
ness and mediocrity'. The community used to be thought of
in terms of the hierarchical family, with the head absolutely
and unquestionably obeyed. Out of that idea came several
convent practices, such as bobbing a curtsey whenever the
superior appeared. No wonder the religious psychologists
are pointing out that to attempt to mould young women into
the pattern of their grandmothers is foolish. 'A novice cannot
be trained to passivity, docility and subordination and still
have a mature ideal,' says one.

Of all the religious vows, obedience is today the hardest
for a young, well-educated woman to accept. She is, after all,
used to freedom of thought and speech and her independence.
But it is not practised these days to bring about abdication of
the will as a means of suppressing the individual. Such things
are not long gone, though: it was Teresa of Avila who
ordered a novice to plant a cucumber on its side in the
ground without question, but it is a woman still in her forties
who remembers being told to sweep up garden leaves in a
high wind.

Written into the constitutions these days is a clause stating

that the authority of the superiors 'should not be so exercised
as to govern the most petty details of the lives of their subjects'.
It is no longer permissible for sisters to be 'made to lose all
sense of zeal and initiative over their work, nor be made to
feel that they should be incapable of offering constructive
criticism when it is required'. In today's life, authority is
thought of as a shared thing, as a responsibility. As one
mother superior put it, 'It's just as much the concept of
obedience, but it's thought out'. Margaret Moran, novice
mistress of the Good Shepherd convent in Finchley, London,
feels that 'the whole concept of obedience, authority and
power is dying in women's orders. The great explosion is the
fact that we are a group of adult women who have chosen to
live in community for a certain purpose.'

The time the girl spends in the novitiate is determined by
how she gets on and by the custom of each order. It is usually
not less than one year, nor more than three, and it can be
terminated by either the novice herself or the mother general:
no formal decision on her future in the community has been
taken at this stage.

The novitiate ends with the profession of first vows. Sister
Madeleine of the Augustinian Sisters is adamant that 'if
someone isn't suitable, I won't let her make vows. But they
must come to the decision for themselves, otherwise they'll
feel rejected.' It might take a girl as long as four years to
realize the life is not for her, but Sister Madeleine does not
worry. 'I don't consider being a novice mistress is preparing
future nuns, but helping people find themselves, find their
identity, position and direction, inside or outside the order.
Very often, I'm preparing future wives and mothers, and not
nuns at all.'

Before the first vows are taken, the novice is again considered by the mother general and her council, with the aid of
reports from those with whom she has worked and lived.
Among the Benedictines, not only is the novice examined on
her understanding of the monastic life, the rule, prayer, vows
and liturgy — after which each nun and fellow novice gives her

opinion about the novice's fitness for profession – but the whole community votes on whether she should be admitted; everyone puts a black or white ball secretly into a ballot box. If at least two-thirds are in the novice's favour, the abbess may admit her to temporary vows. The only exception in any order would be a woman who was dangerously ill; she would be allowed to take her vows without a time limit so that she could benefit from their 'spiritual advantages'. If she recovers, she makes them in the usual way at the end of the novitiate.

A woman who is to be accepted then makes a retreat of a few days, although it used to last for three months – the time it took to sew the habit. Until recently, the retreat was preceded by a bishop's questioning. This was a practice known as 'exploration of the free will', a lengthy examination by which the bishop hoped to judge whether the woman really had a genuine vocation. As Eileen Gielty of Notre Dame de Namur remembers: 'The bishop's questions were a laugh, really. They were within their rights to ask you all sorts of things, whether your parents had forced you into the convent, if you were properly fed, and whether you'd walk out if the superior gave you your freedom.'

'*Art thou free and unfettered by any bond of the Church, or of wedlock; of vow or of excommunication?*' asked the bishop of a girl who wished in the fifteenth century to join the nuns of the Bridgettine community. To which she replied, '*I am truly free.*'

'*Does not shame,*' he continued, '*or perchance grief or worldly adversity urge thee to a religious profession, or perhaps the multitude of thy debts compel thee?*' And she answered, '*Neither grief nor shame incites me to this, but a fervent love of Christ; and I have already paid all my debts according to my power.*'

Today the clothing of a novice is rarely carried out in public: where it continues it has become a private 'family' affair. The practice of dressing in bridal white with veils and bouquets has also to a large extent disappeared among major orders. 'The bridal imagery,' according to Sister Maria Boulding, a Benedictine of Stanbrook Abbey in Worcester, 'is right in the Solemn Profession, which is the marriage

ceremony – it belongs there. But this is only the engagement.'
Many of the Benedictine houses dropped the romantic ceremony described at the beginning of this chapter in the mid-
1960s and replaced it with a far simpler service. Although
they had given the habit at the beginning of the novitiate
since the ninth century, they have now reverted to the
original practice of giving it upon profession. Other orders
see the abandoning of this custom not as lack of enthusiasm
for a most touching rite, but as acceptance of the harsh facts.
'More and more sisters,' explains a superior, 'are leaving
before taking final vows. We cannot, therefore, justify putting
so much emotion and meaning into something so early in
their religious life: we'd rather wait for the final profession.'
Mother Gabriel of the Sisters of Mercy was sorry to see the
Clothing go. 'I thought it was lovely, myself. The beautiful
dresses and lace were made into vestments afterwards, there
was orange blossom and singing.' On the day of profession,
those in the novitiate are allowed another half-hour in bed
after the six o'clock bell. Margaret O'Connell, in her book
on convent life, wrote that: 'I lay and thought of the ordeal
awaiting us. There was no greater hour on the earth, I was
sure. How many worldly brides lay as we now lay? They
awaited the hour of their dedication to a man who would die
and pass and leave them only with a memory of passing
pleasure. For us, when the final hour would come, we would
all be gathered together in the land of Judgment.'

Others have more prosaic memories. One twenty-four-
year-old Sacred Heart sister was clothed on a freezing January
day. 'I wore this lovely white satin dress, and underneath a
great big football shirt.'

Each order has slight differences in the ceremonies. The
Carmelites, for instance, have always had a tradition of
wearing roses: it is white roses their novices have for the
Clothing, a symbol of virginity they will wear again at the
hour of their death. The Poor Clares bind their hair with a
crown of thorns. Their novice walks to the superior who
stands with the bishop, and her hair is cut off ceremoniously
and placed in a little rush basket on the table, then the
superior helps her put on her bonnet. In other orders the

bishop performs the haircutting ceremony, then the hair is plaited first and cut off in public, and the superior trims the ends tidily later. Then: 'God forbid that I should glory,' recites the novice, 'save in the Cross of Jesus Christ. By whom the world is created to me and I to the world.'

The haircutting signifies self-effacement but, like so much else about the religious life, there is not one simple reason for it. Cutting off the hair was a sign of mourning in many ancient societies — Egypt, Greece and Rome — which both men and women practised. The cropping of the nuns and tonsuring of monks seems, therefore, to have its roots in the idea that in entering religious life they are dying to the world. Another reason put forward was that a sister who could eradicate her sexuality stood a better chance of becoming holy, and so it became, says an American, 'a point of virtue to make oneself unattractive, for attractiveness was sexual lure'. For this reason mirrors were barred, curves were flattened and heads were shaved — all in the name of virtue. There are orders where the hair is still cut short and the nuns accept it without demur, because 'we haven't time for such feminine vanities as looking after it.' Some women still choose to keep their hair cropped for the sake of comfort beneath the headdress, but no one is now compelled to crop it 'like a convict', as one woman remembers with a shudder. Many used to shave their heads completely: Sister Charlotte Klein of Our Lady of Sion — who now has a head of red-blonde hair which she regularly sets on rollers — used to run a razor over her head every three or four weeks. The majority of women must have found this hard to accept: a young American sister recalls that her hair was tied back with a pink band and the next thing she knew it was all on the floor and her whole head was being shaved. 'The terrible thing about it was the psychological effect, the feeling of how I looked with a bald head.' Others regard it as a meaningful sacrifice. A nun of forty who used to keep her hair cropped, says, 'I can't tell you what immense spiritual joy it gave me, being in that condition. I'd done it for Him, and this gift of one's hair was something very special.'

When the first profession is over, there are parties for the newly professed sisters, though they may be as simple as the breakfast served by the Anglican Deaconess Community of St Andrew for one of their sisters: the days of many-tiered white-iced wedding cakes glowing with candles vanished with the wedding dresses. But some survivals of earlier times are still practised at the first profession. In Italy, the Poor Clare nuns have a skeleton which represents Sister Death. When the girl goes to change, the skeleton is supposed to move forward and embrace her. At least one Poor Clare house in Britain had its own skeleton – until their bishop objected. A young Sacred Heart sister says that every week her laundry would appear on her bed neatly folded: the week after her profession, her brassières were never returned to her.

Dressing in the habit is an elaborate business, with a short prayer to match each garment. This is the wording of the American Immaculate Heart of Mary Community. For the habit itself: 'Clothe my soul, O Lord, with the nuptial robe of chastity, that pure and undefiled I may wear it before Thy judgment seat.' For the cincture and crown: 'O my dear Lord Jesus Christ, Who for my sake became obedient unto death, even unto the death of the cross, grant me the true spirit of religious obedience and prayer.' For the band: 'Place Thyself, O Lord, as a seal upon my forehead, that I may be of the number of those who follow the Lamb.' The coif is put on: 'Create a clean heart in me, O my God, and renew a right spirit within my breast.' The scapular gets: 'O Jesus, meek and humble of heart, teach me to deny myself, to take up my cross daily and follow; Thee O Mary, refuge of sinners, pray for me.' And, finally, the veil: 'Place on my head, O Lord, the helmet of salvation. O Immaculate Heart of Mary, obtain for me purity of body and soul.' The veil is the most emotive part of the habit. Particularly for contemplatives, it sums up the life they will know only from behind it. It signifies the nun's marriage with Christ, and her virginity. 'Receive this veil,' goes the profession of the Deaconess Community of St Andrew, 'the token of purity and modesty . . . that thou mayest at last with the wise Virgins be ready to enter into the joyful marriage of the

Lamb.' The colour of the veil also shows the wearer's religious status: in some communities a white veil is worn until final profession, when it is exchanged for a black one. Other orders, like the Benedictines, give the black veil at temporary or first profession.

Until the beginning of this century a novice would leave the novitiate and immediately make her final profession: there are sisters in most communities who automatically did this. But in 1917 new legislation was brought in, and under the Code of Canon Law a period of temporary vows became part of the preparation for perpetual profession. It was a prudent move, the reason being that a woman needed time to live the life before committing herself to it totally. These vows are renewable each year, and the sister is free to reconsider her decision until she has taken her solemn and final vows, which might be anything from three to nine years later. But the form a temporary commitment takes, and its intention, is exactly the same as that of the permanent vow for which it is an apprenticeship. Through these temporary vows in the presence of the community, she enters the religious state. Some orders make them for three years and renew for two; others renew yearly.

At the Anglican Deaconess Community of St Andrew in London, a young sister is taking her vows for the first time, for a year. The service is at eight in the morning, and before it she stands nervously outside the chapel with the novice mistress. When she enters, there is silence as she kneels before the chaplain. He hears her request to make her profession in the community, then asks: 'Dost thou promise to remain in the holy estate of chastity?'

'God being my helper, I do so promise for a period of twelve months from this date.'

'Dost thou promise to remain in a state of poverty?'

'God being my helper, I do so promise for a period of twelve months from this date.'

She vows obedience in the same words, then her veil is blessed and handed to her, and the cross is settled about her neck; she is given the long cord for her habit, with the three knots marking the three vows.

Not everyone likes the idea of temporary vows. Superiors general and their councils can release a sister from temporary vows, but Rome must be approached before permanent vows can be waived. Some feel that because temporary vows are easier to dispense with than permanent vows, they are less serious. Others regard them as a holding back: one sister found that restriction to annual vows meant: 'I can neither say what I mean nor mean what I say.' Another felt that: 'It's as if I want to get married and promise to be faithful for ever, and I'm being told we can have an affair for a year and then think again.'

Even so, in 1969, following a request made by many superiors, the Holy See issued an instruction, *Renovationis Causam*, which allowed orders to make a different framework for the probationary period before final profession. Under this, a novice does not even have to make temporary vows, but may make a promise to her congregation instead. Theologians define a vow as 'a deliberate and free promise made to God of a possible and better good'. It is made to worship God. But a promise is made to the congregation, to others, and breaking this promise is not regarded as against religion. For one thing, a person 'in promises' is not a religious, as is one who has made temporary vows. There are many religious who see promises as a dangerous compromise, a sort of lower grade for candidates who cannot reach too high, or come to a decision soon enough. 'I do not feel at all drawn to exchanging triennial vows for promises,' was the reaction of at least one superior. 'I think if a would-be nun is not ready after six months' postulancy and two years' novitiate, she will never be ready.' She is one of many women who feel that the whole system of temporary vows *or* promises is psychologically impossible. They argue that making a vow is a commitment, a consecration to God, and that it cannot by its nature be less than permanent. And they see a lack of generosity where they want radical statements and definite commitments.

There is of course an ever-increasing number who argue strongly for the temporary vow and promise system. They point out that the attitude towards entering religious life has changed, that more and more women leave convents at some stage of their training or even when fully professed, that this new system allows them to do so with more dignity, and that both the woman and the Church are made to feel less a failure. At the most extreme, there are even sisters who feel that *promises* are too much, reflecting a trend which seems to be more widespread in the United States than in Europe. The attitude of American sisters is in the main far more relaxed. They accept change more easily; they are accustomed to moving around an enormous country, and they are more open to tackling different work and ways of life. A typical American sister, a girl in her late twenties living in an apartment with a member of another community, says that so far as she is concerned, she does not want to make perpetual profession. 'There's just no way I would ever do that.' She is due to do so under the constitutions of her order in another three years. But her superior has suggested that by that time there might be provision made by the Holy See under which she would be in some way exempted. She is not in any sense refusing to make perpetual profession because she feels she might want to move on to something else. She is a well-educated, highly intelligent, active woman with considerable drive and personality. 'But if I were an ordinary woman, I guess I wouldn't get married either. It's just not the sort of finality I want in any relationship in my life.'

The Anglican/Episcopalian church for a long time objected strenuously to 'irrevocable vows' taken at times of great emotion. In 1885 it was decided that a promise for life should be made to the bishop – and therefore to a man – which would be dispensable. But by 1890 the fine distinction had disappeared, and it was made 'in the presence' of the bishop.

Many young sisters are sure they want to dedicate their lives to God, but less sure they want to remain permanently in the same congregation. Honor Basset, superior of the Society of the Sacred Heart, feels that 'thinking at the moment among the young says that if you make stable commitment in one place, you're tying yourself up against the possibility that God might want you to move on.' It fits in, she thinks, with the modern view of marriage, and 'it's the sort of thing we'd never have tolerated. We'd have said if you're going to give your life to one man, that's all about it.' She points out that if a sister moves on after five or six years in one congregation, 'it's a bit hard on them, since they've put all the money into her training.'

Like the new marriage services, which couples write for themselves, there is now a large section of sisters, particularly in the States, who write their own commitments. This one is a 'Celebration of Promise', a renewal of annual vows, taken by a sister in the Midwest:

> God, Our Father, thank you for giving me your spirit (it's the real thing) and because I deeply feel your actions in my life I am moved today, in the presence of your people, to an ever deeper commitment to the task of search and service as outlined by the Congregation of the Humility of Mary.
>
> Guided by the Spirit and following the example of your Son, I promise to follow a life of simplicity in regard to material possessions, of openness to the Spirit of Truth as manifested by those with whom I live and work, and of celibate community where, together, we can accomplish in your work, what one alone cannot.
>
> Because you have promised that what is asked in faith will be done in truth, I beg for myself and for all here present a deepening awareness of the power of your Spirit and a profound increase in the only real things: peace, joy, hope, love, celebration and sunshine.

From about the fourth century, girls could make their profession as nuns when they were over twelve, and were given a veil of profession to wear. But they could not be solemnly consecrated by the bishop till they were twenty-five.

By the sixth century, no nun was allowed to be permanently bound by a vow till she was forty. Recently, however, final vows have been taken by very young women: several nuns I met took theirs in their early twenties. There is now a determined move to hold this off until at least twenty-five. Then, when it is felt a woman is ready for these perpetual vows, the mother general and her council once more discuss her, reviewing the person she has become and her role in the community. The Benedictines also require the community to vote on whether the junior should be fully admitted. The Solemn Profession at which she makes her vows for life in one of the most ancient ceremonies of the Catholic church comes perhaps five, perhaps nine, years after her first entry.

The night before the ceremony, the Benedictine goes to the chapter house. There, before the community, she has to make her final choice between the cloister and the world. On one table is laid out the ring, the cowl and mitre, the little silver crown of the virgin. On another, neatly folded, are the clothes she wore when she first arrived at the monastery. In this ceremony of tacit profession, she must lay her hand on one table or the other.

If she chooses the cloister, next day she comes once more before the community in the abbey chapel. 'Receive me, Lord, according to your promise and I shall live; and let me not be disappointed in my hope.' The candle she carries is lit – 'And now with all my heart I follow you: I fear you and I seek to see your face.' Then she stands before the prelate who gives her the cowl, the habit of St Benedict, cautioning her to keep her vows, 'so that you may enjoy the company of God and his holy angels and of the saints who have worn this habit before you'. The full black veil of a solemnly professed nun is pinned to her cap and she is given the simple silver ring of the bride of Christ, and the headband that is a token of her virginity: 'With this ring has my Lord Jesus Christ betrothed me; and as his bride he has adorned me with a crown.' She receives her breviary, sign of her right to begin the canonical hours and recite Divine Office. The chart of her vows is read out, she signs, and the abbess lays it upon the altar. Then the new nun goes with the community to choir, where she kneels in the centre while the Collect of Thanksgiving is sung. The abbess takes her hand, and with the mistress of ceremonies leads her to her stall. This stall behind the chapel grille is now hers by canonical right. She is an official representative before God of the Church. 'Behold, that which I longed for already I see; that which I hoped for already I hold; I am united in heaven to him whom on earth I have loved with my whole heart.'

After these ceremonies the nun will keep silence for three days of retreat. Then she returns to community life, sitting in refectory for one meal on the right hand of the abbess, where her place at the high table is decorated with flowers. And when she retires to her cell that night, her bed will be strewn with little bunches of flowers from her sisters.

The most terrible and moving moment of the Final Profession has now been removed by many orders: the moment at which the newly professed nun stretches prostrate on the ground while her sisters put over her the pall, covering of the dead, and place a candle at each corner. There she lies while the *Dies Irae* is sung, as at a funeral, showing all who watched that she is dead to the world. 'It was terrible for the parents,' remembers a Good Shepherd sister, 'and we stopped it because they got so upset.' This order experimented for a time with the sister coming up to the altar with hands outstretched. That, too, has been superseded, and current practice has the sister coming to the altar with her parents, holding amongst them the water, wine and bread as a symbol of their offering.

But the words have changed little and the Final Profession ceremony contains the most evocative religious prose. The blessing said over the finally professed sister of Our Lady of Grace and Compassion begs: 'When you enter the chamber of the Bridegroom, you may carry a shining lamp in your hand and meet Him with joy. May He find in you nothing disgraceful, nothing sordid, nothing dishonourable, but a snow-white soul and a clear and shining body.'

And when the nun is finally professed and consecrated, the entire church turns to her. Now, indeed, she is sweetly dead to the world.

'Thy beauty now is all for the King's delight. He is thy Lord and God.'

4

A CELIBATE LIFE

You can't sublimate it. You can't suppress it. You simply have to damn well sacrifice it.
                    AUGUSTINIAN SISTER OF MEAUX

The most important difference between nuns and other groups of women is that they choose lifelong chastity.

Behind their chastity lies all the weight of ecclesiastical tradition. Yet in our society chastity and celibacy are considered neither desirable nor admirable. Today there is a feeling that the celibate is an aberration, a freak, someone with an emotional if not a physical impediment to normal pleasures, satisfactions and happiness. There are a growing number of nuns who echo this view. One American nun and theologian, for example, who feels that 'the public thinks of celibacy as a negative thing – and the public is right,' argues that 'all this talk about celibacy freeing nuns to serve is just a rationalization. The choice not to marry is a personal one and has nothing to do with efficiency in the service of God.'

Most religious would not agree, however. 'The celibate,' wrote a seventeenth-century Anglican, 'like the fly in the heart of the apple, dwells in a perpetual sweetness, and is confined and dies in singularity.' Virginity has been called a life of angels, the enamel of the soul. 'A virgin,' declared St Ambrose, 'is purity's immolation, the victim of chastity.'

'Virginity,' according to a Benedictine nun, Sister Maria Boulding, 'is something important in the Church, a special grace from God. To those to whom it is given it is pure grace.' It is a virtue extolled by a Church which believes –

as Pope Pius said in 1954 in his Encyclical on Holy Virginity, which continues to be the official document on the subject – that 'our bodily powers and passions darken the mind and weaken the will.' It is considered to be more perfect than the state of marriage. Virginity, it has been said, is of gold, chastity of silver, and marriage of brass. The belief is that a consecrated woman is not important for what she can do in utilitarian terms – the schools where she can teach, the missions where she can work – but because she *is* a consecrated woman, a living sacrifice, her every act is already sacred.

The vow of chastity is a solemn promise by which the nun clears the decks for action and her soul for union with God. It frees her, makes it possible for more than one person to have a claim on her love: it is a means to an end. It is a reminder, too, that before God, man is alone, and that in eternity there will be neither male nor female. She does not consider that through her vow of chastity she is depriving herself of a necessary human experience. 'We're trying,' explains an Episcopalian sister, 'to be more human, not less.' Another said it was like being separated from a marriage partner. 'People wouldn't think you odd if you didn't enter into a relationship with another man while your husband was away, would they?'

But the fact that women in religious orders have given up sexual intercourse does not necessarily mean they lose the desire for it. 'A celibate body,' observes an American sister, 'is still a feminine body.' Such an admission could not have been made ten years ago. In respectable society, let alone in convents, women have never been allowed to acknowledge their sexual drive. Religious orders dealt – and indeed still deal – with the problem by refusing to admit it exists. Anything 'physical' was to be avoided. Even crossing the legs was considered 'unreligious': one elderly nun said she had been very worried, when the young and emancipated sisters in her order started doing so, in case they were breaking their vow of chastity.

The attitude that a nun had to 'put to death one's natural inclinations' (in the words of one) is only slowly disappearing. Women are realizing that it is not possible totally to repress their sexuality – even though some still try. A twenty-seven-year-old Anglican sister describes such nuns as regarding their sex as 'something attached to the side of themselves that they don't use, like a spare tank of petrol on a car'.

Male communities have been very little better than female ones in this respect: one sister remembers talking to a seminarian 'who told me that when he found himself thinking about women, he visualized them just as a mass of blood and bone and muscle, so he wouldn't be led on'. It is a method of suppression about as effective as that of St Benedict hurling himself into a nettlebed, and no more enlightened than the Franciscan monks' belief that 'woman is bitterer than death.'

The suffering brought by total denial has always been regarded as valuable in itself. 'The root and flower of virginity,' as St Chrysostom wrote, 'is a crucified life,' and the pangs of celibacy are called the little crucifixion. One elderly sister volunteers: 'It's not much to give up, when you make that comparison.' Certainly sexual fulfilment is a trifling matter in that context, but surrendering it for ever is none the less a real loss. Failure to acknowledge this has caused much unnecessary unhappiness for women in religious orders. Even today, the fact that chastity brings with it tensions and problems is often ignored: in 1975 Pope Paul VI called the celibacy and virginity of Catholic priests and nuns 'happy and easy sacrifices'.

'I still don't think anyone I've met in religious life,' comments a young English sister, 'admits there's a problem in suppressed sexuality.' Others feel more strongly: 'It's obscene the way we haven't talked about sex in an open fashion.'

'But we weren't given any education with regard to the facts of life,' asserts another. 'Some sisters entered in their teens without knowing them, and they never came to grips with them in a realistic way. And how could a girl with that background truly choose to be celibate?'

The young girl who went from school into the even more restricted and protective convent environment, who met men rarely and formally if at all, and who had no chance to experience any attitudes or life styles other than her own cannot have known what she was sacrificing. She did not choose sexual renunciation at all. It was a piously motivated manipulation. Anne Hyzy, an American Loretto sister in her late twenties, remembers that when she entered not so long ago, 'Things were still very much in the dark. Sex wasn't thought of as a bad thing – it simply wasn't thought of at all. Or if it was, not out loud.' She says that: 'I read books that helped me to understand what was happening inside me. I turned to my friends, and, being women, we have the same experience: they helped me to understand myself in the area of sex. I've had feelings of jealousy, and envy, that I've had to learn to accept. But I know that has helped me to grow.'

Many superiors of the orders, who are in a position to offer help and advice on the subject, are all too often unable to do so because they and their attitudes are those of an earlier generation. The superior general of one major order said firmly: 'I don't think every woman wants to get married or in fact wants sex at all.' She did admit, however, that whenever she had asked her own mother for information she was told she was too young, and she had still been too young when she entered religious life at seventeen. The superior of an Italian order told me that 'discussing sexual matters with young women only makes them morbid,' while another superior, a woman in her sixties, simply could not see there was any problem at all because: 'You never want what you've never had.'

Sister Madeleine of the Augustinian Sisters of Meaux is one of the still rare novice mistresses prepared to discuss sexual matters in public lectures. 'It's perfectly true that religious are alive, vibrating human beings – and the more they are, the better they'll be as nuns or monks: you don't want people impotent in their feelings, with no love to give to God.' At the same time, she does believe that many religious grossly overrate the problem. 'It's simply surprising how, especially if you're not trying to ignore or suppress what goes on in your body, the radiance of your own belief affects even that area. If you feel this fanaticism, if you're touched with fire, then it touches your whole being.' She does however stress that 'someone raving mad with sexual desire to the point where they have to masturbate has not got a vocation.' Nor is she talking theoretically: she herself is in her early thirties and says: 'I've had a spring evening or two. I've had that feeling, like having a toothache, a bit of an ache somewhere. Not to do with any particular person, just nameless and anonymous, and it comes for a little period.

'I can remember – let's see, was it before Rome or after? – lying awake and vibrating, and I thought: What's happening to me, am I losing my vocation? Then I realized the technique. You have to treat it like sleeplessness: if you lie there and worry about it, you'll never get to sleep. I said to a sister, "Isn't it good, I haven't lost my femininity, I'm still normal." And I felt, let it come, let it go. I'm not going to get hung up about it, or masturbate to get relief.'

Current feeling seems to be that the more experience a girl has before she chooses religious life, the better are her chances within it. 'It's no use putting someone who's never faced up to the power of her own emotions into religious life,' is the view of an Anglican novice mistress. And although nuns are celibate, they need not be professional virgins. 'I'm sure,' says a superior, 'that girls who've had sexual experience might well think of becoming sisters and wonder whether this is possible. And of course the answer's yes: it's only a technical thing.'

There are, however, some orders who do insist their entrants should be virgins. The Benedictines, for example, want the girl's assurance on this point before accepting her as a postulant: – 'We don't look her in the eye and say: "Are you a virgin?" We tell her that here we have to be virgins, and then either we hear from her again or we don't. But we don't do it baldly, and if a promising girl comes along who seems to have a vocation but has lost her virginity – and some don't mind at all, they come right out and tell us without batting an eyelid – then we say, well, we do insist on it here, but give her the names and addresses of orders where it isn't so necessary.' At the Solemn Profession the new nun – who is referred to throughout the ceremony as 'the virgin' – takes the three ancient vows of the Benedictines: stability, conversion of life, and obedience. The first binds her to the house, and the second includes the normal vows of poverty

and chastity. Then there is the far older rite of the consecration of a virgin. 'Do you,' asks the prelate, 'promise
perpetual virginity?' and then: 'Come, my chosen one,'
sings the choir 'and I will set my throne in you.' The Benedictines do very occasionally accept a widow, in which case
the Solemn Profession is changed accordingly. In France now
a change has been made which is likely to infiltrate the order
in other countries, by which the insistence on virginity has
been dropped: the entrant is not expected to comment on
the matter in any way, but at the time of profession she can
choose whether she wishes to take the full ceremony, including
the consecration of a virgin, or a simpler version, without
giving any reason for her choice.

The loss of virginity does not prevent a woman making a vow
of chastity in most orders, because religious virginity can be
either retained or recovered. 'It begins,' explains a French
sister 'in the heart, and from there purifies the whole of
one's being.' A nice example of the regaining of virginity is
the story of Aethelthrith, who had an unfortunate aversion
to the married state. A seventh-century Englishwoman from
the fen country, she was married again for political reasons
after the death of her first husband, this time to the heir to
the Northumbrian throne.

The Venerable Bede, the Benedictine monk who has
chronicled her life, says her husband promised a certain
prelate named Wilfrith land and money if he could persuade
Aethelthrith to grant him his conjugal rights. Wilfrith,
however, gave the queen the veil, which involved breaking
all marital ties. She founded a monastery at Ely, which her
first husband had given her. There, she renounced the
splendour of royalty, wore no linen, only wool, rarely used a
warm bath and even, when she suffered from a tumour in her
throat, believed it to be chastisement for her former love of
necklaces. She was renowned for her holiness and was
regarded as the 'virgin mother of very many virgins'. Her
name, with the epithet Virgin, was inscribed in both Anglo-
Saxon and Roman calendars. Her two marriages were not

considered to be any impediment to the title, since Bede tells us she lived with both husbands 'not as a wyfe but as a lady'.

There is certainly no historical precedent for thinking that nuns have never had any sexual experience. Many of the early foundresses were married women who entered on the death of their husbands – and sometimes before. Hedwig, the patron saint of Silesia in southern Germany, was educated in a convent and married at thirteen to the Duke of Poland and Croatia. She founded a nunnery at Trebnitz with part of her dowry, a convent of small houses round a church. She married to follow her parents' wishes rather than her own. 'She hoped,' says the account of her life, 'to secure eternal life by giving birth to children, yet she wished also to please God by chastity, and with her husband's consent practised self-restraint. Whenever she was aware that the duties of motherhood were beginning, she avoided her husband's proximity and firmly denied herself all intercourse until the time of her confinement.' In this way the couple somehow produced three sons and three daughters, whereupon Hedwig 'altogether embraced a life of chastity'. Understandably perhaps, since the first child was born before she was fourteen.

Many married couples have separated in order to enter into religious life. St Bridget was a member of the fourteenth-century royal family of Sweden and she went into the Bridgettine order she had founded once her seven children were grown. Her husband became a monk.

Cornelia Connelly, from Philadelphia, and her husband Pierce, a pastor, had a double vocation: in 1854 he was ordained a priest and she took a vow of perpetual chastity. Leaving their three small children in Pierce's care, Cornelia joined the new Society of the Holy Child Jesus. It led to some acrimony: Pierce gave up the priesthood and, through the Privy Council, claimed restitution of his conjugal rights.

One of the most touching of these double vocations was that of Brother Oswald and Sister Beatrice. In 1931, at the height of his career as a concert pianist, Alfredo Oswald entered the Jesuit order and his wife Beatrice joined the Carmelites. Several times a month he was allowed to visit

the convent and talk to her through the grille, at which times
she had special permission to lift her veil. In recent years,
she was allowed to visit him. In 1963 – still man and wife in
the eyes of the Church – they celebrated their golden wedding.
And in 1972 Sister Beatrice made her last trip to her husband,
to attend his funeral in Washington where he died at 87.

Even so, 'It would be right to say,' according to Sister
Morag Michael, 'that most of those who come to us are
technically virgins, if you'd like to put it that way. Though
it could be that some have had sexual relations with a man
before they've come here.'

Only a few years ago the social climate was such that a single
woman choosing a convent would probably be sexually
inexperienced. Now, the chances are that in the West –
with the possible exception of strongly Catholic countries
such as Italy, Spain and Ireland – a girl entering late in her
twenties will have had some sexual encounters, even if she
has not actually had intercourse. Certainly the majority of
young sisters I talked to had had boy-friends, often regular
ones, or had actually been engaged, and several admitted to
'heavy petting'.

But as yet the difference such experience makes to
these women has not been fully realized by the convents.
When I asked the elderly superior general of one order
whether the more sophisticated and knowledgeable young
women now entering had greater problems with the vow of
celibacy, she replied, 'I don't think we have these problems
if we're frightfully busy and extrovert. And anyway,' she
added after a moment's reflection, 'we wouldn't keep
someone here if they were oversexed: we wouldn't have
eccentrics.'

But: 'Constant and torturing sexual desire in a religious,'
feels one American novice mistress 'is not necessarily an
indication of an "oversexed" person, but of an inability to
relate sex to the finality of love.'

People who enter religious life know what they are undertaking: they accept celibacy – as everything else – freely, not

under compulsion. These are the Church's terms. And the majority of women do genuinely believe that it is more than mere physical continence. 'It is in the soul first,' says a Spanish sister, 'and passes to the body.'

Yet the grey cult of virginity did not begin with Christianity. It is a relic of older, more primitive religions, stemming from a time when men believed in many strange dark gods. An untouched virgin has been held to possess supernatural powers in every culture we can trace. The daughters of peasants dancing with unbound hair through the fields at dead of night to ensure the next year's crop; the virgins of Vesta in Rome, guardians of the sacred fire, who for thirty years vowed themselves to chastity, and who were whipped to death or walled up alive if they fell. In Thebes and Syria, in Babylon and Greece, priestesses had to remain virgins. The Incas of Peru had their Sunbrides, 1500 of them, incarcerated in the convent at Cuzko. From them, the Emperor chose his queen, but if any other broke her vow of chastity, she was killed. The belief behind the insistence on virginity was that sexual intercourse was unclean and defiling, and many regarded the overpowering emotion of sexual desire as inspired by devils.

None of this, of course, would have been consciously in the mind of St Paul when he advocated the single in preference to the married state. He believed that time was short: there was no point in transitory obligations when the Second Coming was at hand. But for more than two centuries after Christ, there was no such thing as an order of virgins. Indeed, anyone taking a vow of celibacy was warned to keep it secret. Tertullian wrote that, rather than boast of her virginity, the celibate maid should 'lie in some sense to men, that God alone should be shown the truth'. The bishop of Carthage, however, urged the local virgins — some of whom were wealthy women — not to wear their jewellery, because they ought not only to be virgins, but to be seen and understood to be so 'by conspicuous plainness of attire'.

None of these virgins were held by any canonically binding vow, nor did they undergo any kind of service. The bishops were specifically told by Hippolytus to perform no ceremonies because 'it is with her heart alone she become a virgin.' It was not until the fourth century that these women were living together in organized groups.

It started in Egypt. In Asia Minor the increasing numbers of orders of virgins began to receive solemn consecration by the bishop. For a long time, though, it was possible for virgins to live individually, quite often in their parents' homes. Others, anchoresses, lived in small houses near the churches, attended by a couple of servants but otherwise alone. They were contemplatives under the solemn promise of obedience, chastity and stability of abode. *Ancrene Riwle* is the early thirteenth-century guide-book for the lives of three of these women living in communicating cells with two maids and a kitchen boy to look after them. They were warned to watch the senses, 'the five guardians of the heart', to have small windows covered with two sets of curtains, through which they must 'not peep out too much or use enticing looks and behaviour'. They had visitors, though, both men and women, who came to them for their advice or teachings. Mother Julian of Norwich was such a woman: 'a simple creature unlettyrde', she called herself, but while she was 'a recluse atte Norwyche', she was famous as a spiritual counsellor, and her *Revelations of Divine Love* shows her to have been a woman both of deep faith and great intellect.

But as the orders became established, these women began to disappear until, eventually, they were no longer recognized in the law of the Church and finally were prohibited. Virgins, 'the choice portion of the flock of Christ', required more protection than their vow of chastity afforded to keep them from 'crafty and insidious violation'. By the end of the thirteenth century the contemplative nun was safely in her cloister, hedged about by laws, under a strict regime, vowed not only to chastity but to total poverty and full obedience.

With the Reformation standards of morality changed. The Protestant reformers – Luther, Bullinger, Becon – opposed the Church of Rome and all the monastic principles. Celibacy, they declared, was odious, and the vow of chastity not only foolish and presumptuous but contradictory to spiritual teaching. They condemned equally the unmarried, the priest, the monk and the nun – and threw in the professed wanton for good measure. A woman, they declared, was to be a wife and mother or she was nothing. Celibacy was a thing of evil. Virginity and continence were equated with impotence and sterility. Clerical celibacy too was rejected, largely because the reformers disapproved of the Roman clergy who, though marriage after ordination was invalid, were not averse to taking concubines instead. Despite that, the Archbishop of Canterbury, head of the Church of England, has at various times been celibate or married according to the feeling of the age. Currently, he is married.

There must be occasions when the nun's celibacy is a genuine inspiration. In 1948 a woman returned to America from Kuching, where she had been held in a Japanese prisoner-of-war camp. Mrs A. N. Keith, in a book called *Three Came Home*, wrote of the experience of being exiled with hundreds of other women without their husbands. Among them was a community of Catholic nuns. 'We secular women, living with our own sex, had already tested ourselves and found ourselves wanting. We could not get on without men, their stimulation, comfort, companionship. But the sisters were different, they were complete. They were wedded to Christ and the Church, and for the first time it became credible to me that they were Holy Brides. We wives had put our minds and hearts on our husbands, which is what a good marriage is; and we were without them, and lost. The sisters had put their minds and hearts on God alone, and they had Him; and only they were whole.'

The nun's freedom from family ties and responsibilities is undeniably valuable. When I met Sister Laetitia Bordes, a member of the Society of Helpers of the Holy Souls, she was about to leave for Vietnam to work with the Vietnamese-American orphans there, in an order where twelve sisters were looking after hundreds of children. 'It's our responsibility to do something: we are all part of that war, we paid taxes that went to maim those children. And I'm free. I see my celibate commitment as freedom. How many people are free to answer this need?'

Another argument put forward by those who advocate

celibacy is that the nun's dedication is a constant reminder of the love of God. But the majority of nuns in the world work among the poor, often in ghetto communities, where the inhabitants may well not be capable of fully understanding the meaning of celibacy. A Loretto sister working in a Chicago slum points out that the people with whom she and her sisters come into contact 'are not very much aware of what nuns are, anyhow – and the concept of celibacy is not something they would have any sympathy with anyway. For them, the family is a great achievement.'

Most nuns – like most women – admit to loving children. A few are fairly dispassionate about them: 'I never wanted children anyway.' Others are more emotional. 'I wouldn't have been satisfied with one set of children,' says a superior whose order runs forty schools. 'I want all the children in the world.' But if they exercise Mary's spiritual motherhood, through which they belong not to one family but to all, the unpossessive love they feel ('the joy and anguish of the celibate,' as one sister calls it) does not protect them from the loneliness which forfeiting the physical expression of sex brings. Sister Mary Agnes, the Poor Clare nun who is also a published poet, confirms that 'Everyone who has dedicated their life to celibacy does suffer from a kind of loneliness. And it is possible to feel lonely in a community where you can't talk to someone – I feel less alone in my cell than when I'm with other people.'

'Last Christmas, I felt so terribly lonely, I thought, *Oh God, I still have to go up to my bed alone.*' This is Sister Marie Keegan of the Belgian Community of the Ladies of Mary. 'It's not just me talking like this,' she adds. 'We all feel the same. I talk about it to my friends.'

Sister Marie says: 'The feeling that I'm going through life alone hits me now and again. And I'm in my thirties, which makes it worse – I've still got a chance, I can still have children, I'm still attractive enough.' She has deliberately chosen community and a shared life, and she wants to do something creative that would not be done otherwise because 'I see the whole world challenging me.' Procreation, as she says, is always going to be looked after by others. 'But there is need for people to experiment with another kind of living, besides the husband and wife relationship.' She says she does not despise marriage. 'I elevate it. If I could live this life and have marriage too, I would. But, in a way, to tie myself to one person would be to cut myself off, and it wouldn't satisfy me. This route does. So I won't give in; I won't give up the chance to be open to all of mankind, in a sense. There are things now that make me happy that I never dreamt of before, an inner core of being in myself that I can get at, and share. But what hits me now and again is the being lonely, the needing someone. Wanting to hold somebody's hand as you go along the street.'

There is one aspect of consecrated virginity that is losing favour among nuns: the idea that they are the brides of Christ. More and more nuns and sisters are no longer accepting what is essentially a masculine conception of their role. As one sister asks, 'If we're the brides of Christ, what does that make male religious – homosexual?'

'We're brides of Christ,' asserts another, 'because the Church will always want to define us in sexual terms, not as people in our own right.' And: 'You have to be an appendage to a male,' snaps a third. 'But I'm an appendage to no man, thanks be to God.'

'I'm not a bride of Christ,' explains Marie Keegan with some acerbity. 'I'm just committed to His work, just as one is committed in marriage. And while it would be terrifically flattering to say I'm married to Christ, it just would not appeal to me anyway, because He's married to so many: I'd choose someone more available.'

But if an increasing number agree with the American sister who urges that 'We must not be hung up on this brides of Christ nonsense: we've got to have a broader vision,' the majority are still happy with this expression. 'A sister *is* a bride of Christ,' confirms a contemplative nun, 'it's very appropriate to put it in a married setting. You go through a courtship, an engagement and then you're married and the love grows deeper as you go on.'

Both religious ritual and literature abound in bridal, marital and sexual imagery. The nuns of the Visitation in Europe in their constitutions were exhorted to 'live, breathe and pant for your celestial Spouse', but this was omitted in the 1948 version on the grounds that 'the Bishop would not like that'. They kept, however, the wording recommended for devout mental ejaculations: 'Let Him kiss me with the kisses of His Divine Mouth.' And in *Ancrene Riwle* there is much use of the Canticle of Canticles, considered in the Middle Ages to be an allegory of Christ's love for the soul. 'Show your face to me, and to no other. If you would have clear sight, look at me with the eyes of your heart. I am not a bold lover, I will embrace my beloved only in a retired place: thus Our Lord speaks to His spouse.' The Benedictines, in their ceremony of Solemn Profession, tell the newly consecrated virgin that 'The King has greatly desired your beauty,' and the prelate prays that Jesus, 'who by the bridal bond binds the hearts of consecrated virgins to himself,' may 'make your mind fruitful through the seed of his divine word.' At the beginning of the ceremony, the chantresses intone: 'Trim your lamps, wise virgins; behold, the Bridegroom comes; go forth to meet him.' When the newly professed nun receives her cowl, she sings of how she has despised all the allurements of the world for the love of Christ, 'whom I have seen, whom I have loved, in whom I have believed, whom I have chosen for my love'. And as the silver ring is placed upon her finger, the prelate tells her it is a sign that she is wedded to Christ. 'Keep perfect fidelity to your Bridegroom, that you may deserve to be admitted to the eternal marriage feast.' And she replies: 'I am espoused to Him whom the angels serve; whose beauty sun and moon behold with wonder.'

One well-known authority believes that 'the idea of the spouse may be rather unhealthy.' Father E. F. O'Doherty, the Irish priest who is Professor of Psychology at University College, Dublin, and Professor of Philosophy of Religion, feels that a nun's relationship with Christ cannot be seen in terms of a relationship between husband and wife. The former is a spiritual experience, the latter concerned with human desire, love and satisfaction. An English Dominican father

comments: 'I suspect if you make your quasi-marital relationship with God, then other people are a very poor second:
they just get a pious spin-off from your primary attention.'

One American priest, Father James Kavanaugh, who has
roundly criticized what he calls the 'outmoded Church', says
firmly that once, if a sister could call herself a bride of Christ
and linger before the altar like a patient spouse waiting for
her man to come home, it was in a childlike simplicity that
has now grown pathetic and outdated. 'Christ,' he insists,
'took no spouse except the Church, nor did He need a bride
to keep Him company.'

Because the idea of a bride of Christ has begun to be
questioned, religious women today are trying hard to change
the image of chastity and project it as a positive, not a negative
thing. 'It is active, not passive,' claims an American sister,
'it is warfare, not peace.'

One of the problems with which women in the church
have to contend is the way in which that Church has always
treated women. Christianity, like so many other religions,
has seen women as associated with evil and sin. At the root of
it all is the fear of menstruation and the devils which controlled
a woman each month. Reproduction was a fearful mystery
which could have only a diabolical explanation, and a woman
was not only impure herself at such times but capable of
transmitting impurity to anything or anyone she touched.
Hindus and Buddhists share this belief and so do Jews, hence
the latter's insistence – which they now rationalize as purely
hygienic – that a woman during her period must sleep in a
separate bed kept for the purpose and attend the ritual baths
when she is 'cured'. A similar procedure is adopted after
childbirth, until which time she does not attend the synagogue.
When Christianity adopted these ideas from Judaism, this
turned into the 'churching' of women. Even today, Christian
women of the Orthodox church will not go to communion
at such a time. (A sixth-century Pope was less unenlightened:
when Augustine of Canterbury wrote to Pope St Gregory: 'May
I baptize a pregnant woman?' he was told there was no contradiction between the gift of fertility and the gift of grace.)

Woman has been seen as Eve, the seductress of men. Canon

law forbids nuns to sing in any place in the church which is in public view because they are regarded as sexual bait, and for the same reason St Ignatius forbade a religious man to look a woman in the eye. Many conventual practices, like the flattened breasts and the shorn heads, could well have been designed specifically to neutralize women. 'And we co-operated,' sighs an English teaching sister in disgust. 'We built heavy walls, covered ourselves in drapery, and made ourselves some kind of middle sex.'

One of the hazards against which convents took – and take – careful precautions are the passions of that middle sex. 'We are,' says a pretty Italian woman, 'obsessed with our personal purity.'

The euphemism used is 'particular friendships', which comes from the French *amitiés particulières*, describing friendships between the same sex and referred to in most convents as 'p.f.'s.' All constitutions contain a phrase like: 'Thou shalt not allow thyself familiarities with others, still less those particular friendships which are a menace to community life.' The superior might be warned to 'be on watch against special friendships, the greatest pest of religious communities, and if she perceive any beginning, she shall hasten to apply a remedy'. If she does not, she is told, such friendships 'always tend to have unhappy effects'.

The interpretations different orders put on p.f.'s vary. 'Special friendships meant exclusivity,' explains an Irish sister, 'which was contrary to the idea of community, because two people could become possessive, which could destroy not only themselves but the community.' Others see it as far more direct. 'When we were novices we knew it meant sensual friendships: we didn't think it meant just having friends sensibly.'

The Carmelite *Manual for Novices on the Cultivation of Chastity* advises: 'Touch no one, and do not allow yourself to be touched by anyone without necessity or evident reason, however innocent. Repress and fly from as a mortal plague, even though spiritual in their origin, particular friendships and familiar conversations arising from an attractive appearance, pleasing manner or an agreeable disposition.'

Most orders stress that nuns 'must not touch each other even in play,' much less 'enter the cell of another sister unless she is ill and they have express permission to enter, and if they are alone in a room with another sister, the door must never be closed.'

'In my youth,' remembers one middle-aged Sacred Heart sister, 'friendship was absolutely off the map. The old nuns said to us novices, "My dear, when you go in twos the devil makes a third".' And another woman in the same order, in her mid-twenties: 'We even had to go out for walks in threes – one postulant and two novices.' The rule that one sister could not sit beside the same person at recreation more than once had the double-edged reason that it encouraged mixing and discouraged intimacy.

'Friendships within the community,' says one novice mistress, Sister Elspeth of an Episcopalian community, 'have come to be regarded with a great deal less apprehension in recent years. Emphasis is laid on the value and necessity of being able to have a natural loving relationship without having to sublimate it into some sort of spiritual competition.'

Even so, she admits the danger of friendships developing into what she calls 'emotional crushes' which have to be worked through. The problem, she believes, is that within religious communities, 'We are often a bit afraid of these things, and feel a certain distaste for anyone wrapped up in such a relationship.'

Some women have bad memories of how the system worked in practice. Anita Caspary of the Immaculate Heart of Mary community in California remembers how, as a young novice sharing a cell with another, 'I once went to late Mass and came home to find all my belongings put into another cell. The superior felt we were "too attached to each other". Only, of course, she didn't explain that she was afraid of homosexual behaviour. She just said my room was changed. So we didn't have a chance to say how ridiculous it was, because we were such casual acquaintances. And I was furious – it just reduced me to a child.'

Certainly there are cases of lesbian affections among religious women, consummated or not. But these are the exceptions: as an American says, 'Almost all the nuns I knew were dedicated individuals, and they hadn't chosen religious life on a whim. Chastity was a rule of the life they had chosen, they believed in its glory – and they lived it.'

Sister Eileen Gielty says, 'I never knew a lesbian relationship in any order with which I have had any contact.' The American sister, Anne Hyzy, feels that 'We live so closely together we could recognize lesbianism right away. When you spend a lot of your life with women, that's one thing you'd be able to spot immediately.' Only one woman, another American, said she had known of a few such relationships between nuns. And added that, though she did not realize it at the time, there was more of a 'problem' with women practising masturbation than was generally supposed.

There is an amazing degree of innocence about the nature of lesbian relationships. 'We have to be very nice with each other,' explained one superior to me. 'Very friendly. But not familiar: we don't touch each other or hold hands, or you'd get lesbianism.'

The danger, of course, in outlawing close friendships is that the emotions are repressed and smothered, resulting in what one priest has called 'an irreproachable vacuum'. As one Anglican father points out: '*Any* real and mature relationship with another person *must* be a "particular friendship".' Rita Hannon claims that, because friendship was very much frowned upon as a potential threat to chastity, 'It's all too easy to meet sisters whose spiritual lives were crippled by such negative attitudes.' To live in chastity, after all, does not mean to live without a heart. 'It is extremely unlikely,' believes one novice mistress, 'that a person will go through religious life without feeling for one or more persons, within or without the community, of one sex or the other, emotions of the strongest and tenderest love. And invariably that person will then feel the ground has gone from under her commitment to God.' And she believes, too, that while a deep human love may lead a woman away from religious life, 'that is far better than to remain stunted or stoical within sexual solitude.'

Attitudes to friendship vary among communities. A middle-aged English sister feels: 'There's much more friendliness in community life now,' but adds carefully, 'I wouldn't say there's actual *friendship* yet.' On the other hand, another Englishwoman from a more enlightened group says, 'We used to call it particular friendship and it was frowned upon. Now we call it personal relationships and it's all right.'

Because the celibate cannot cease being sexual, she tries to diffuse her sexuality in many relationships. And of course many religious have had deep and tender relationships within the bonds of their vows. Diana d'Andolo, who struggled so hard to become a nun, and the second master general of the Dominicans, Blessed Jordan of Saxony, had a total union of hearts, as his letters to her show. And St Francis de Sales wrote to Baroness de Chantal, foundress of the Visitation sisters: 'Know then that I hold myself closely bound to you and seek to know no more, save that this bond is not incompatible with any other, whether of vow or of marriage.'

Convents were always far more worried about the nuns' behaviour with men, which is what custody of the eyes is all about. 'An unchaste eye is partner to an unchaste heart.' In 1279 the Archbishop of Canterbury, after visiting Godstow convent, where he questioned the superior and nuns about the state of affairs there, sent them a list of injunctions rectifying matters. One of these was that: 'Nuns are not to converse with the neighbouring students at Oxford unless they have permission to do so from the abbess, and shall knit no bonds of friendship with them because such affection brings harmful thoughts.' And a sixteenth-century bishop of Ely proposed that the nunnery of St Radegund's should be dissolved because the proximity of the university had 'led to the demoralization of the prioress and nuns'.

Relationships with all men were banned and more particularly if they were religious – yet an American nun eighteen years in religion says that in all that time she knew of no overt relationships between nuns and priests or men in the world. One sister, now in her thirties, went out early in her religious life to work on a mission in Africa. While she was there one of the priests she knew lost his mother. She sat with him one evening, in the dark on the verandah, and he talked about his mother for hours. When the sister got home to England and mentioned this she was severely reprimanded for being in a 'dangerous' situation.

To surround nuns with restrictive legislation and absurd physical barriers, such as grilles in the parlour and padlocked enclosure doors, is considered by many nuns today to be 'an utterly wretched indignity'. (And as St Augustine wrote: 'No one protects the virginal blessing except God who bestowed it and "God is love". Therefore the protector of virginity is love.')

The majority of nuns do consider that when they enter religious life they join a single-sex community. Most do so with fortitude. This is how a young Anglican sister feels about it: 'We do have some priests who come here and have one or two quiet days with us and the other day a young man was here, a student. It's nice to hear a man's voice, a masculine point of view. But it's something you give up willingly, and God somehow gives the strength to channel your love and use it in other ways. You do miss these things. But you can live without them.'

The idea that nuns are not interested in men is one which they themselves consider to be very dangerous. Sister Morag Michael thinks that 'it gives an impression of imperviousness – the ice-maiden touch. And this is a travesty of what one is really meant to be doing.' She stresses that 'we're no less women because we live here. We still have the capacity for homemaking, for receiving and giving love, and the desire to do these things that a woman normally has. But we do believe we are called to fulfil our womanhood in other ways than through marriage: if I can't learn to love in this life, it would be much better if I wasn't in it.'

Just because their company is predominantly feminine, it is by no means without any men. They do not usually meet them in any direct social way, but in some of the houses the sisters do so as part of their work. Other nuns teach in schools where there are many men on the staff, and attend conferences and meetings. 'Sisters have said they miss the stimulation of the male mind in conversation, and this can be so : I think it's important as far as we can to meet and talk to men and women outside. And this does happen far more than it used to.' There are several men on the convent staff doing the heavy work, picking the apples, dealing when the boiler breaks down. 'I think,' says Sister Mórag drily, 'that we can probably mend a fuse.' A year ago they appointed a male steward as community treasurer, a post formerly always held by a sister until the business affairs of the community increased to the point where an accountant was needed.

This community, at Wantage in Berkshire, is still run on highly conventional lines. But many sisters whose lives have now become much freer expect to lead normal social lives. One night recently, for instance, one English nun went with another woman and two men to see a performance of Susanna Anders in London. They had drinks and went to a restaurant for spaghetti Bolognese. By then it was too late for their trains home, 'so I had to take them all back to the convent and find beds for them. Then they wanted to play Mozart and drink coffee till three in the morning.' And this woman now feels that, for the first time in her life, she is actually living out her vow of chastity.

There is no doubt that strict observance of the celibate life protected the nun totally from temptation. At the same time, it was a restraint exercised from outside herself, imposed upon her willy-nilly, and to that extent it was artificial. As Sister Dr Charlotte Klein of Our Lady of Sion says: 'Until a few years ago, there was no alternative to exercising your vow of chastity, because you never saw a man anyway.' She feels that in these last few years she has been very much happier. She enjoys her freedom, and cannot be immediately identified as a nun because normally she does not wear the cross but merely a wedding band. The evening I met her she was getting ready for a dinner-party. 'I lead a very active social life but I would, for instance, not dance.' She has a lot of men friends – 'not boy-friends, people with whom you can exchange ideas' –

all over the world. 'I think this is true and honest friendship. But if there was danger of anything else developing, I hope I'd have the strength of character to nip it in the bud. One would like to talk to people in the community and look to them for support.'

Another woman sees this sort of relationship as a good thing for sisters. 'We're less protected, we're mixing more with the opposite sex, and it's bound to happen to some people at least that they find themselves relating to these men as adults, and they might find the relationship deepening. Maybe they've never had this experience before, but it's not a bad thing that a lot of religious in the last few years have had to go through this delayed adolescence.' She herself, as a missionary sister in an extremely isolated part of Nigeria, was very dependent on the priests for company. 'But I wasn't thinking of forming romantic relationships with them, though I found I was forming *deep* relationships. But they've completely dropped out of sight now because of my community life. It's not a cold thing. I made a choice and I'm still going to continue in that choice: I'm not electing to form a human relationship at that level.'

There are ways in which many women find their relationships with men actually improve. Sister Mary, an Anglican, concedes that: 'It's a question of constantly opening out. I meet quite a few men and, as I see it, relationships are very much more natural now: you have immediate acceptance of the person without any feminine entanglements.'

Sister Madeleine finds that now she is out of the habit many of the old protections have disappeared, and she is aware that all sorts of relationships are open to her now which were closed to a habited nun. In the course of her work she mixes with a great many people: 'It's a fact that a lot of chaps put an arm round me, and I wonder what onlookers think of seeing me being embraced by a crowd of young men. It's possible to have loving relationships with men – loving and tender – and strangely enough, that is when you *don't* have sexual problems. I mean, I'm not leading them down the garden path because there's no garden at the end of it.'

She finds it a strength to know that she can have such

relationships, but admits to difficulties. 'When you enter a relationship, you use a language of words, touches, telling the other what kind of availability you are offering. I know perfectly well what language I am speaking. But there is one older man at college who is hearing something I'm not saying, and when he hugged me, it was quite different. So, very politely, I avoid this situation with him.'

What does become increasingly apparent is that being a nun now does not preclude, for many women, the possibility of love-affairs. 'I didn't,' says one, 'take a vow not to love.' And as another girl in her twenties, the Anglican Sister Christine, points out: 'We make the mistake of polarizing sexuality in our genitals, whereas it permeates the whole of our experience. So people can have a satisfactory relationship without going to bed.'

'Even if you're a nun,' says a French sister, 'there is obviously in all relationships with other people a sexual element.' Liz Thoman, an American Sister of Humility, wears a butterfly ring given her by a boy-friend and says, 'It's very hard. I've had relationships with men, and they love me, and I love them. We've got very affectionate, but we don't jump into bed – we want to, but we don't.' When she entered religious life: 'I was caught up in idealism, and I believe in achieving my independence as a person, as a woman. I've had ten years of thinking my religious commitment through, and eventually choosing it. Now I'm not saying I've had terrific sexual experience but to me, a really fulfilling sexual relationship grows. I know what would be involved in settling down with someone, and I'm not willing to give that kind of time, energy and commitment. So the passion of the moment remains the passion of the moment.'

An American sister in her early thirties, a striking woman with an assured manner, is very conscious of her vow of celibacy – 'I don't call it chastity.' She meets people constantly. 'I have some dear friends. I do find myself making a decision between a commitment and another person. I'm not saying I decide about an engagement ring, but a decision whether you let this develop or carry on with your life. Every time, I have decided to keep it strictly friendship. I love having friends, and I get telephone calls all the time from men I am involved with, and most of them are priests. They make no demands on me, and I make no demands on them. I have to decide for myself whether something will happen or not.'

The relationships this woman has are close and affectionate: 'I've done my share of kissing and hugging, and I won't deny that to myself or the people I'm close to. But as far as starting to live with someone and developing a marriage relationship – I can't do that. I find that unfair to my own work.' This is a young American who, like many others, is reluctant to make her final vows because she feels she would be promising herself to something about which her feelings may eventually change: 'At the moment, living in community is important for me, trying to love and relate to other people, and celibacy is part of it. Though I don't go to bed with men, I have close relationships with men for whom I have a very deep love and strong feelings. But that could change – though it wouldn't necessarily be a formal church marriage if it ever happened.'

So the attitude of many nuns towards the vow of celibacy is changing. It was bound to: the minute the habit and the walls went there is what an American sister calls 'the danger of opportunity'.

On the whole, though, they are very relaxed about the change. Pat Drydyk, a Franciscan sister working in Los Angeles, says that for her, celibacy is 'a day-to-day decision. I very much want to do what I'm doing now, to be where I am now, but there's always that desire for more personal support.' She has been through college and now – partly through her work at the Franciscan communications centre, where religious films are made – enjoys an active social life. 'People take me out to supper every night. I don't call it dating, but getting to know someone better. And it's so natural I just don't think about it. It's part of the evolution.'

Others see the open choice as a strengthening. One English Catholic sister, in her late forties, says: 'I recently had the opportunity to lead another kind of life.' She received a marriage proposal. 'I could have taken it but I didn't and I don't regret it. I dance along the streets when I think I haven't done it. I would have been bored in two weeks, anyway. And I have never wanted children.'

There is, of course, the risk that as the religious life becomes increasingly open, as nuns and sisters work with more and more people, more will transfer their energies to personal relationships in marriage. In fact, numbers have done this already in recent years. 'But that,' says one young woman, 'is the risk of loving.'

'The chastity business is a bore to me really. It's not something I see any virtue in doing.' The nun who said that is highly intelligent, in her early thirties, and a fully professed member of an established order, the Belgian Ladies of Mary. She is no extremist in her views. But there is a growing feeling that celibacy in a religious community is of diminishing importance, and its validity to the life is being strongly questioned.

Many nuns have said they do not want to give up sexual fulfilment ('I don't believe in giving up anything unless you have to'), but are prepared to do so since it is the only way at present in which they can live the religious life. 'But if,' says one, 'there was a way for me to do both, then I would.'

Some of the younger sisters, who have not yet taken final vows, go even further. In America I talked to three – and there must be many more throughout the country – who admitted candidly that they were on the pill. One took it on the advice of her doctor as part of her medical treatment. Another did so because she was a case-worker in a hard-core slum area and was genuinely concerned lest she be raped, as one sister in her community was recently. The third merely said that she 'felt safer'.

The American theologian, Maryellen Muckenhirn, has questioned whether celibacy can even be justified within the traditional convent structure. 'The convent,' she says, 'was too seldom a place of warmth and love. It tended, rather, to be a place of scheduled chapel service, silence, and generalized charity towards all. And celibate love *cannot* always be formal, organized and rule-regulated.' She – like so many of the sisters – finds it doubtful that anyone could grow into serious maturity without living amongst a small, loving group.

Celibate love, she believes, must be 'truly reaching towards the persons in one's life'. Without this, celibacy is meaningless, 'since personal love is the measure of Christian existence'.

There will always be those who defend the celibate state 'for the sake of the Kingdom', and who claim, as one sister says, that 'you are celibate for the love of God and people, so all your resources and energy can be channelled into being available to other people and into prayer. So the religious way of life is centrally bound up with celibacy.' But there is also a feeling that the belief in the superiority of the single over the married state was largely due to lack of understanding of the significance of sexuality. One area where there is already much change is in the celibate priesthood of the Catholic church.

Christianity developed a celibate priesthood out of the Judaic belief in the basic 'impurity' of women: only men who avoided the act of sex with them were thought fit to serve God. There seems little doubt that it is this insistence on the pure priest – and the underlying fear of women behind it – that influences the attitude of the Church and its male hierarchy to women, and the insistence laid on their subservient role. At least one theologian, Charles Davis, believes that the attempt to bind celibacy and the priesthood together have damaged both: he claims that young men who genuinely want to become priests might accept the call to celibacy because it is part of the law, and later in life attempt to compensate for their frustration through power. And all too often, it seems, that power is directed towards keeping women in their place.

There is now increasing realization, particularly in America, that ordination need not be a bar to marriage. While, officially, priests are not free to wed, they are not only doing so but those who do receive permission from the Vatican to marry – as opposed to those who resign their posts – are not being reduced automatically to the status of laymen. And for every priest who marries, a dozen are dating. Father Eugene Kennedy, a Maryknoll psychologist father, advocates optional celibacy not only to preserve the rights of priests to marry, but to preserve the right to celibacy as 'a healthy choice for priests'.

The majority of priests who marry seem to choose former nuns as their partners. Father Philip Berrigan, brother of the poet Daniel, who spent thirty-nine months in prison for burning military draft records, has always held strong views on celibacy which he saw as 'an excuse to flee from the complexities of human love'. In May 1972 he formalized his three-year union with Elizabeth McAlister, who used to be a sister of the Sacred Heart of Mary: they were married in New York by a former Benedictine monk. Father Philip, at fifty, is ostracized from his community of Josephites but is not formally excommunicated. He still considers himself a priest.

It may well be that this will act as the thin end of the wedge to alter the male view of women's role within the hierarchical structure. As one sister puts it, change is possible 'if only we get a healthy way of looking at sex'.

Perhaps the most fascinating development on the question of celibacy is not that there are nuns who leave their orders to marry, but that there are now those who see no reason why married people should not be part of religious communities. The Vatican's Sacred Congregation for Religious has even spoken of the possibility of a religious order in Tuscany where married couples, free from the ties of their families, can enter together to live a fairly traditional religious life while doing pastoral work. The vow of chastity in such a case would mean marital fidelity, though a vow of 'absolute purity' could be taken.

One American women's community has just held a meeting to discuss its future. It does not want to be named here because if it does decide to go ahead with possible plans, 'it'll make us non-canonical as far as the church is concerned. But we see it as a new offshoot into religious communities of the future.' This community already has a group of associate members, about a dozen people who keep their jobs but spend a lot of time with the community. 'There is so little difference between us,' explains a sister, 'except for the vows. And even there, we know they are living the idea of the vows, a simplicity of life, a real search for the will of God in their lives. So obviously the only difference between them and us was celibacy. And all of a sudden, in the light of all these other values and shared experiences, the need for celibacy in a religious community diminished greatly.'

It will be two years before the community decides whether celibacy should be considered essential to full membership. If they do bring in their associate members, then it will be the spirit – not the vows – which unites the community. They believe that if enough groups begin to think and act in this way then 'the official Church in Rome will sooner or later have to deal with the emergence of the non-canonical community and create some new room for them. They just don't have any pre-ordained slots for such an animal.'

The Immaculate Heart of Mary Community in Los Angeles is already a non-canonical community. Members are no longer nuns, and the community defines itself as a group of religious people. Celibacy has been made voluntary. 'We are not,' they say, 'responsible for the personal life-style of our community members.' Married couples have been brought into the group as full members, a step which at first caused 'great anguish'. In many ways it was seen as a threat, the end of religious life. It was the older ,and younger people who worried most – the older because it was such a break from tradition, the younger because they had not confirmed their commitment to celibacy. Among those who have since left to marry are some who protested most strongly against married couples. Finally, the decision was taken that if a couple was willing to give as much as the single woman in service, if they believed as much as the rest, they should be allowed to become full members. The decision was strengthened when one of their single women members, dispensed from her vows as all are, said she was marrying and wanted to remain in the community. She is now on their twelve-woman board of directors.

But the option does not in any way mean that all members of the group are renouncing chastity. One of them, Mary Bowler, has the sleek elegance and narrow waist of a model. She sits on a heap of cushions in the apartment she shares with a sister from another community, wearing a frothy white negligee, and it is quite surprising to hear her say: 'I fully believe there is a place for celibacy and chastity.' She entered at nineteen and, without experience, found the commitment hard to make. She dates, now, but thinks she would not leave the community for anyone. Her worst time was the novitiate: 'I missed the guys, it was hard for me.'

Frances and Nelson Small are both full members of the community. Sitting by the pool at the conference centre in Santa Barbara, a bundle of small children shrieking in the water, they talk about their group commitment. Frances is happily pregnant yet again, and it is hard to believe that she entered the Immaculate Heart Convent at sixteen, and left 'reluctantly' in 1959. After marriage, she found she missed the feeling of community, 'being able to talk about God on a personal level'. So she returned to the convent for a short retreat, and afterwards visited again with her husband. Both found the experience so satisfactory that they decided they would like to become more closely involved with the group. Now the couple and their children spend most of their free time with the IHMs, attending prayer groups and discussions, helping to raise funds and to look after the property. They value the spiritual and emotional gains from the association — and there is no doubt that the IHMs consider themselves enriched by the presence of a large and happy family of children.

Of course this group, because it is non-canonical and not subject to the dictates of Rome, can behave in a way which might be regarded as extreme. There are, however, several orthodox religious communities who are experimenting with mixed sex groups. This is not, surprisingly, a new idea. It is the wheel come full circle. Double monasteries, like that of Abbess Hilda at Whitby, were a feature of medieval monastic life. They existed from the fourth century in France, Spain and Ireland, and appeared in England half a century after the arrival of St Augustine. They grew up largely because of the needs of the communities: the agricultural work could not be done by women alone, and lay brothers were brought in. Gradually, canons joined as well, but it was a mainly feminine community, with a woman invariably at the head.

The sexes were restricted to their separate quarters, and even the churches were firmly divided into two sections. None of these communities belonged to any order recognizable today, except that founded by St Bridget of Sweden in the fourteenth century. Hers was a double order interested in charity, education and the collecting of books. The brothers acted as priests and confessors to the nuns. Their chapels were built with separate stalls and a grille dividing the sexes which though it did not hide them from each other, was kept locked. The nuns lived in the inner precinct, and the men o religion, of whom there were thirteen priests, four deacons and eight laymen, lived round the outer court of the monastery.

Today's double community is very different. Because it is informal and relaxed, because there are no gates and grilles, it is far more difficult to keep cool and separate than when a rigid framework enforced distance.

One woman who has experienced this way of life is Marie Keegan of the Ladies of Mary. A social worker, she spent a year living in an old factory in London's Highgate which served as a welfare base for Irish adolescents away from home. She shared the upstairs living quarters with two other sisters and three Servite brothers. While such an arrangement is usual among lay social workers, for her 'it was the best experience I ever had in community.' She believes that living and working like this brings out the best in both sexes. 'We gave each other a lot because we have a different mentality, a different way of looking at things.'

There were problems. 'I wouldn't like to romanticize about mixed community. It's got terrific dangers. I think we avoided them, but I don't know if we could have continued to do so.' She is conscious that she has no rigid disciplinary codes about herself. 'Although I'm professed, that doesn't protect me from a man. If something is good and beautiful then I go out to it immediately.' She found that living such close community life, 'people's loveliness came out. We had no "particular friendships", because you've got to accept that if you belong to the community, you can't have an exclusive relationship. You must leave or give it up.' At one stage hough, the group did experience emotional difficulties. here was great tension, everyone became depressed. 'But ve recognized the problem, we did face it. We had a meeting nd said, "What's wrong with everybody?" And then people egan to admit and say, "I depend too much on you, I never o a thing unless I think you're going to like it." ' There vere other things. 'People admitted jealousy, and we were ble to talk about being attracted to each other. And talking bout it was our salvation, the problem was worked out. nd that we could sit down and talk about something so very ersonal was hard for the people involved, but it was fantastic rowth. No one was hurt or embittered.'

They all, she feels, achieved greater emotional maturity nd self-knowledge than they could have done in their own ommunities. When she returned to the comfortable de- ched suburban house where she lives with four other sters, 'Everything was beautiful, but I miss this element ost. I realize now that a single-sex community is very much cking in something. It's basically not true.'

Marie Keegan, like the other religious involved in the heme, hopes that what was a year's experiment will become permanent reality. If it should not happen, she would like set up a similar group to do some shared work. While she ould definitely want men to be part of the community, she as learnt some valuable lessons, and would avoid too close hysical proximity between the men and women. 'There ould have to be two separate communities, not in the same uilding. But we'd work and pray together.'

This community was totally experimental, whereas the oyal Foundation of St Katharine, the only permanent mixed- ex religious community in Britain, is based on the com- unity of the same name founded eight centuries ago in 1148.

It lies in the heart of London's East End, down the grubby ommercial Road, past the White Swan public house in able Street. Through a car park there is a little door in the all. Inside is a garden where creamy magnolias flower and arly roses twine round a white-barred gate. The long house ith its Georgian facade is the home of eight men from the ommunity of the Resurrection, known as the Mirfield fathers – the eldest of whom is eighty-five – and six sisters of the Deaconess Community of St Andrew, where the youngest is twenty-seven.

These two Anglican orders came here in 1968 at the invitation of the Queen Mother, who was anxious to re-establish it as the monastic community it had been in the days of Queen Matilda. It used to be a city within the city, with 3900 inhabitants and its own ecclesiastical and civil law, and it has always been patronized by the queens of England. It was written in the constitutions that there should always be a women's community involved, and when the Deaconess community were asked to join the Mirfield fathers, 'we started it very hesitantly,' says Sister Verity, a plump and gentle woman who is one of the three original sisters to live in the house. 'I don't know who was the more nervous: them or us. We didn't know what to expect either from within the community or from our work in the area.'

Sister Verity admits they all, men and women, felt shy at first. 'I'd worked as one of two or three women among many men in the forces. But I'd lived in an all-female home for many years. And we found we took a long time to get used to each other. We really needed time to talk about things that mattered. So every Sunday evening we get together and talk.'

The two orders preserve their own individual 'family life' with quarters in different portions of the house. The sisters have a small and chintzy community room, the fathers chose an imposing apartment in the original Georgian wing where the day's papers are ranged upon a period table in the long window. They breakfast together, but lunch separately because of different community habits: the sisters observe silence, while the fathers regard the meal as recreation time. Sister Christine is the kitchen steward and plans all the meals, though a lay person does the cooking. At night they have dinner together in the refectory, wash up together then lay breakfast and have coffee.

They were determined to keep the two communities reasonably separate because they felt the groups must be strong enough to withstand the change of individuals receiving different assignments and moving on. 'We had,' says Sister

Verity, 'to balance how far our commitment was to this place, how much to our community.' In fact, the sisters did find that every religious person who came to visit them said, 'I suppose you're looking after the fathers?' To which they replied, 'God forbid.' They were glad they had independent jobs, and found they had to stand up for themselves much more than is usual in a women's community. 'We didn't do everything we were asked to do. We had to resist the temptation of being nice and kind and compliant. We had to be quite firm about sharing our responsibilities. A group of sisters came to St Katharine's for one of the regular retreat weekends. Sister Verity reports with amusement how one sister actually curtsied to the fathers. 'When they'd gone, the fathers said, "We couldn't have lived with any of them."'

After five years, the whole community feels that, despite problems, they have learnt a good deal by living together. 'The men,' says a sister, 'are less hidebound by tradition than women. Women are very much more liable to hang on to their traditions for security, and this is where it's so good for us. The changes don't threaten the men so much.' The Mirfield fathers agree. Father Mark, who organizes much of the work of the community – the youth clubs, musical sessions and poetry meetings – says that 'undeniably we gain in richness of life. Men and women are meant to live together. The balance creates the atmosphere.'

Both orders share prayer in the chapel, taking it in turn to read the service, preach, take up the bread and wine. In the early days, there were slight difficulties. The sister who was appointed sacristan was setting up the church and found one of the fathers watching her. 'I bet you're thinking,' she told him, 'that nit of a woman will put out fifty palm crosses for ten people.' There was a stunned silence, because that was just what he had thought. 'We burst out laughing,' says the sister, 'and after that it was fine. We could be rude to each other, we got on together.'

All the sisters feel that since sharing their lives with the fathers, 'we've all become bolder. We have the nerve to do things we wouldn't have done before. We're not shy about things. You have more courage of your own convictions because you don't mind making a fool of yourself.' Another sister particularly values the intellectual stimulus. 'I've found more acceptance between brethren and sisters here than from my sisters elsewhere.' Sister Verity says the nice thing is 'they're not shy of showing affection. The other day I felt ill, and when I went to get my breakfast in the refectory, no one said anything. But then Father Reginald poured my tea, and at lunch-time one of the fathers asked if I was feeling better and another brought my coffee over.'

Father Jack Guinness holds the post of Master of the Court of St Katharine's, and oversees the work of the house, which is mainly conducting retreats and acting as chaplains to groups and individuals. The sisters have more outside work: Sister Denzil is assistant chaplain at Queen Mary's College in the East End of London, helping with problems among the students, and Sister Verity handles local social work, with playgroups and pensioners. She sits now in the warm community room, busily sewing a rag doll for her children, and it is she who best sums up the advantages of this now revitalized form of religious life. 'I have enormously valued being treated like a woman. It's the sort of odd things that women don't do for each other: the little courtesies. It's a subconscious thing, and I suppose I'm flattered by it. I feel valuable as a person.'

These groups, whether extreme like the Immaculate Heart of Mary in California, or orthodox like the Anglicans of St Katharine's Foundation, are giving other religious much food for thought — and perhaps action — about the hitherto rigid concept of the celibate, single-sex community.

None of them would claim that it is an easy thing to give up the satisfactions of the heart. 'There is no substitute for fully sexual love,' says one nun. For her, the absence of a loving relationship with one man in her life is 'a loneliness that no amount of fraternal or apostolic love can overcome'.

'But then, you don't want it to be overcome, if this is your place to be.'

5

PRAYER WITHOUT POWER

Nuns are just ecclesiastical chars.
ENGLISH TEACHING SISTER

The Church is the most exclusive male club in the world.

'What time we get up in the morning, what time we eat and what we wear – all this is still enforced by men.' A brisk woman in her early thirties settles her belt more comfortably round the waist of a grey business suit and adjusts a short black veil. 'Surely', she says, 'nuns themselves are more qualified to handle these matters?'

Her companion, whose delicate face hardly matches the string of degrees that trail after her name, adds: 'It's not that men are *stupid*. But the bishops should *not* be organizing our lives.'

These women – one French, one American – are two who have battered against the stone wall of male prejudice. They at least have made a dent – the freedom to abandon in part the habit, to acquire those degrees – and to sit in a public restaurant discussing them. But the wall still stands, almost as firm today as it was when Teresa of Avila wrote: 'The very thought that I am a woman makes my wings droop.'

She had good cause to feel dispirited. There is a long tradition of anti-feminism in the Church, from that misogynist father, Tertullian, who in the third century told women: 'Do you not know that you are Eve? You are the devil's doorway. It was you who profaned the tree of life. It was you who disfigured the image of God which is man.' A hundred years later St Ambrose endorsed this: 'Adam was led to sin by Eve, not Eve by Adam.' In the twelfth century Bernard of Clairvaux thought: 'Their face is as a burning wind, their voice the hissing of serpents.' 'It is clear,' wrote the seventeenth-century Spanish Jesuit Gracian, 'that woman is under man's dominion and has no authority, nor can she teach, give evidence, make a contract nor be judge.'

Women were actually considered to be deformed men. In the thirteenth century Thomas Aquinas commented that 'in her particular nature woman is something defective and accidental. If a girl child is born it is due to weakness of the generative principle, or imperfection in the pre-existing matter, or to a change produced by external causes, for example by the humid winds from the south, as Aristotle says.'

Even when her biological role became better understood, it was still interpreted as wholly passive. She was the object of male aggressive potency. Therefore, she must also be the receptacle of male thoughts and ideas.

Despite the importance of women who figure in the Gospel, despite the reverence for the Virgin Mary, women were seen by society as the weaker sex. And the Church has always been several steps behind that again. It is a sad comment on the slowness with which it moves that, if Teresa of Avila were writing in the 1970s, she would have little cause to feel more cheerful than she did four centuries ago. It may be accepted by today's churchmen that women have souls – which at one time they hotly disputed – but souls, it seems, are not enough.

This applies particularly to the Catholic church because – from the point of view of nuns – it is the biggest and most hidebound. But to a greater or lesser degree, it is equally true of the Protestant churches.

The power structure of the Church was conceived by men for men. The medieval lawyers who designed canon law believed that women were weak and incapable and needed protection and rigid rules to sustain them in religious life. It is true that male religious were subject to many of the same rules, but it was women who under canon law were classed with children and idiots. 'The Church and women,' says a young nun, 'is a most depressing subject. I hate to think what Freudians would say about a patriarchal church which solemnly refers to itself as "Holy Mother Church".

And I feel intensely hurt for what women have been made to endure in the name of Christ.'

Christianity has done much to keep women in their traditional role of *Kinder*, *Kirche*, *Küche* – kids, kirk, kitchen. Even the cult of the Virgin has been used to teach them an unconscious lesson about their duty to be meek and subordinate. Women religious, particularly, have been subdued by male restrictions, conditioned to please others, not themselves. The Church has used psychological power to subjugate women. It has sought domination in the intellectual, spiritual, religious, sexual and economic spheres. And all by use of canon law, written and enforced by men.

The Church may preach that there are no second-class citizens – yet an economist of international stature was refused the right to address the Vatican II Council of Bishops solely because she was a woman. For the same reason, a journalist was not allowed to receive Communion from the Pope during the council. And it is only under what one nun calls the 'most patronizing circumstances' that a woman is allowed to read in church or distribute communion.

It is a sorry tale of exclusion and suppression. From a human point of view, admits one nun, the ambition of men to monopolize and dominate is understandable, 'but it is not Christian'. It is nuns especially who have suffered. They are given paternal indulgences rather than any rights; rules rather than freedom; dogma rather than room to think.

Many men in the Church, of course, see women as in need of such treatment. An American cleric wrote recently of the temptation for nuns 'at all times to reduce faith to sentiment, devotion to a multiplicity of devotions, the love of God to emotional sweetness and theology to a few narrow, one-sided notions'. Even Cardinal Suenens of Brussels, a man genuinely anxious to open new perspectives for women religious, refers to woman's 'natural subordination which makes her content to lean on a masculine support'.

Not only did woman accept her subjugation, but often she encouraged it. 'Women,' says one Jesuit, 'compete for approval in the hierarchy structure.' A Dominican priest agrees that 'they expect to be exploited. It's part of being a nun. It was a conspiracy between themselves and their founders.' Nuns still show a distressing tendency to accept male superiority. A French superior general, a confirmed feminist, remarked sadly: 'If I tell my religious that I share a certain view, this view carries some weight. But it carries ten times more if I say that it is shared by a *père jésuite.*'

'The Church,' says one extremely articulate and angry young nun, 'has conditioned women to be subordinate to their husbands, and religious women are never allowed to forget they're living in a man's world. There's nothing liberated about that.' Many of the problems, she feels, were brought about by nuns themselves. 'We have surrounded ourselves with petty regulations. In the novitiate we brought up our young sisters to be subservient. We have aped the men in the Church. We are dutiful and follow. But we should be pathfinders; we should be prophetesses.' Others agree. 'The role of the Church,' says an American nun, a Sister of the Helpers of the Holy Souls, 'is to be ahead of society, calling it on.'

Until the mid 1960s nuns were still treated as silent parts of the institutional system of the Church. 'Cheap labour,' as an American sister says scornfully. To a large extent they still are. Despite Vatican II's resounding call for modernization, there is no real route, no official pathway, for nuns to deal with the Holy See or even with individual bishops. The line of command continues through men: from the Pope to cardinals, bishops and priests.

It is not through lack of trying. Each country now has a body formed of the mothers general, provincials and superiors of all the orders, who meet regularly for discussion. In 1965 the American group, the Conference of Major Superiors of Women's Institutes, sent a unanimous petition to Rome asking that it should be represented on commissions dealing with the lives of nuns. This body, after all, would be the logical one for representing sisters before the hierarchy. The request was ignored.

All the conference is allowed to do is to serve as a one-way channel of communication – from the Vatican down to the communities. As one American sister theologian says, 'This s not enough. The superiors are democratically chosen to oster the purpose and common good of their communities. This can be done only if they speak and the hierarchy listens.' She herself believes that part of the failure of the conference to become a heard voice is the average sister's 'ambivalence towards power and politics – the notion that both are tainted'.

Many sisters are particularly incensed that they cannot carry out the smallest change without obtaining permission from their bishop. This has included points as minor as modifying their headdresses. Though, as one exasperated American superior said, 'Any superior who submits habit changes is foolish. She should just phone her tailor and forget about the Sacred Congregation.'

The Sacred Congregation for Religious and Secular Institutes in Rome is the body governing all religious orders. But since Vatican II, more and more communities are questioning the congregation's right to dictate the details of their lives without any reference to their wishes. 'How can some men in Rome say what I as an American woman can or cannot do?' asks red-haired Sister Patricia McKeough. 'They're still labouring under their own culture lag.'

Male domination is not something that can be tackled effectively by individuals, no matter how strong their intellectual arguments. Sister Dr Charlotte Klein tried public debate with churchmen to question their attitudes on deep theological and philosophical grounds. The response? There is indeed a great role for women to play in the Church – as priests' housekeepers. (A view well in accordance with that of Pope Paul who, in a speech about the eagerness of the Church to promote the advancement of women in society, said that women had a role to play in full equal rights with men – but mainly in an area encompassed by the family.)

Another example of discrimination occurred in Louisiana in 1972 when two sisters, Lydia Champagne and Stephanie Bourgeois, were dismissed from their jobs in the office of religious education without the formalities required by the diocese. Bishop Robert Tracy explained his action in a letter to his consultative bodies: 'A considerable number of the clergy feel they would find it easier to deal with a fellow diocesan priest as head of the office rather than with religious sisters.. . .'

The authorities, as one Jesuit points out, 'have refused to understand the aspirations of women in the modern world and have preferred to keep to the old way of doing things, even at the expense of sacrificing these intelligent women.'

The patronizing attitude adopted towards nuns today is even more incomprehensible in the light of their work and achievements. Nuns deal with more of life's harsh realities than most lay people ever see – alcoholics, homicides, drug addicts, deserted wives, delinquent children, prostitutes – the list of a hardened professional case-worker. The Daughters of Charity of St Vincent de Paul, for example, have operated Marillac House in Chicago for more than twenty years. From a settlement house in East Garfield Park they have gone out day after day to serve an area with the highest crime, VD, illegitimacy, illiteracy and poverty rates in the whole of the United States. In another Chicago slum, Woodlawn, a community of Loretto sisters works in a shabby building set among the gaping shells of houses running with rats. Here Sister Therese Rooney, a decisive woman, heads a team deeply involved in putting the mainly black population on their feet both emotionally and financially. The community runs educational courses for those who dropped out of school, teaches office skills to women and has invented a unique training session for people who want to set up their own small businesses. But only within the last couple of years has their work been recognized by their lay colleagues. 'Professionally we were badly treated,' admits Sister Therese, 'as though, in the convent, we didn't know what was happening out there. We got little pats on the head.'

Even nuns who by no stretch of the imagination could be called militant feel that women are ill-used. Anne Hyzy is a tranquil girl, one of the Chicago Loretto sisters. 'I don't feel I'm hemmed in by men; I don't feel I have to be liberated. My way of living isn't in conflict with men, the way women in an office might be: I'm not competing unless I want to be a priest.' But she, like almost every American and European sister I talked to, believes that 'there should certainly be more women in the church holding high-powered administrative jobs. It's pathetic they haven't trusted women that much. After all, there are plenty of women capable of the job who can add a dimension of femininity.'

Such lack of trust is made the more ridiculous by the fact that many mothers general already shoulder immense responsibilities. Some of them govern the lives of perhaps thousands of women. Mother Mary Thomas Aquinas Lee is a perfect example. For many years she has been mother general of the Good Shepherd sisters. She is a woman of wide culture who speaks several languages. She needs to: the congregation has 475 centres in five countries. She has responsibility for 10,000 sisters as well as the thousands of women – delinquent girls, unmarried mothers, state prisoners – in their care.

The problem is that after centuries of subjugation women are wary of power. They have been taught that it is evil, that those who aspire to it are victims of pride. Those who do find themselves in responsible positions fear they will display 'masculine' characteristics, which is how determination and creativity have been regarded. 'That woman,' sighed her bishop of Teresa of Avila, 'should have been a man.'

Perhaps this attitude is more widespread among the older generation of sisters, such as Mother Gabriel, mother general of the vast Sisters of Mercy order: 'Those Women's Lib nuns say the authorities don't understand us – but of course they do. I think they're marvellous men, I do really. They're not affected by sentiment and temperament and jealousy and everything else.' Believing that 'canon law is very just,' she finds it perfectly acceptable that the bishop must be consulted if the sisters wish to sell property. 'After all, we might be fools, we wouldn't know anything about it, we might be had.' When, recently, she was sent a questionnaire in which she had to say whether she thought women were capable of understanding finance, she answered 'No'. But even Mother Gabriel does not think 'they should boss us too much. There's not much logic in thinking anyone in charge of a big order could be a fool.'

Many women feel that the role of the nun, by its very nature, precludes too much self-determination, like the enclosed contemplative who believes: 'We can't engage in Women's Lib, we are not fighting for our own rights.' But it was an enclosed Carmelite nun who became one of the first to speak out publicly in Britain against the male rule of the Church – and found little favour for doing so in the eyes of her community. Sister Margaret Rowe is an articulate Australian who worked in a Canberra science laboratory before becoming a nun twenty years ago when she joined the Carmelites at Bridell in Wales. In 1968 she wrote an article for the *New Christian* magazine in which she accused bishops and male superiors of 'interference and arbitrary suppression,' and pleaded that as it was Human Rights Year, a few words should be said for the 'oppressed minority' of religious women. 'There is still little recognition,' she wrote, 'that institutions are for persons, not persons for institutions, and it is not fitting that one man, or one woman, should suffer in order that the prestige of authority or the structure of any other thing be maintained.'

What chiefly worried her was that those who enter religious life forfeit no human rights, but 'when are religious women going to be treated as mature, responsible adults, capable of managing their own lives?' She cites as an example the 300-year-old order founded to take poverty-stricken young people off the streets to educate them. This order felt it was merely duplicating the work already done by the social services, and wanted to move into a different field. To do so, it needed permission from men in Rome 'who might not understand the conditions that exist in the East End of London'.

Sister Margaret drew a reprimand from the prioress: 'She has done us a disservice. Quite frankly, I am aghast that this should come from a nun of our order. The church protects us and helps us to lead a life of solitude and prayer. We are not aiming to seek equal rights for women.'

But an American sister says: 'Until sisters get involved in their own liberation, they're not much use to anyone else.'

The speaker is Sister Ethne Kennedy. She is sitting behind a table full of what is – in religious terms – revolutionary literature. From her office on the corner of Superior and North Rush Street in Chicago she runs NAWR – the National

Assembly of Women Religious. She is the chairman of the group, which started in 1967 with one aim: to find out what effect sisters have on society 'and if they have none, why not?' She wants to release women from the 'patronizing attitude' of the Church which so oppresses them that 'we are not even aware of our potential.' Women, as she points out, 'are the largest minority in the Church and society, but we've been locked in this modified, monastical society in which men do the decision-making. We're taught that psychologically, theologically and every other way, men are superior.'

She herself is a member of the Helpers of the Holy Souls. She chose this order mainly because of its liberalism. But she found that in practice it was not so liberal that Vatican II did not mean profound changes. And the members of other orders suffered more. 'Sisters were in little piddling groups – you were a Sister of Mary or a Sister of Charity. I felt they wouldn't get any further till I did something about it.'

At that time the major superiors of various orders would meet at conferences where perhaps 170 women took decisions that involved 176,000 more. NAWR encouraged Sister Councils at which the sisters in each diocese, whatever their order, could meet for discussion. Sister Ethne organized one meeting where 400 sisters talked to major superiors with the apostolic delegate present. The result? 'Flack from the bishops.' Bishops, she claims, do not on the whole like the idea of their sisters banding together and finding a unanimous voice. Their reasons range from believing that sisters have enough to do already to the conviction that keeping them divided is the best way to ensure their own continued rule. At present, forty-five American dioceses are not allowed to have a Sister Council.

Nor do all sisters approve the idea. A woman who wanted to join was told by her superior she could not because 'one sister per convent is enough.' Another problem is finance. Ethne Kennedy found that NAWR simply could not survive on a yearly subscription of $3 so raised it to $5 – and they lost 2000 members. 'Nuns just don't have the money.'

Even so, almost 2,000 sisters from all over America attended the last conference to talk about work, renewal – and equality. 'That's the question most raised,' says Sister Ethne. 'It's a question of how you see yourself. Basically, society is having a terrible struggle for power between men and women. As our role changes, so does theirs. And it changes at the most profound level, the level of personality.' She does believe, though, that the traumatic period – certainly for American religious – is over. 'I think we've had a real breakthrough with mass communications. I think sensitive men realize that men and women are complementary, creating a new society. And I think a lot of things are going to drop by the wayside.'

But the battle is not won yet, and she thinks, too, that the place to seek the greatest upset is in the basic structures of the hierarchical church. 'Because the structures are perpetually oppressive, and the power system of the church is pretty obsolete.'

Be that as it may, the power of the bishops is still very real. Almost all the European nuns to whom I talked were in close contact with one or more bishops. To enter the Carmelite monastery in Llandovery I had to seek formal permission from the bishop of the diocese and the abbot of Caldey. Possibly this was due to the fact that normally no outsider may enter an enclosed community – but the invitation had been extended by the mother prioress herself.

There are communities which seem to like operating in this way. The Anglican Deaconess Community of St Andrew, for instance, is visited weekly by the Bishop of Kensington, and the Bishop of London comes to the convent for professions and life vows. 'We can't make major decisions without consulting them,' says Mother Joanna. Even though neither bishop would query any minor decision made in chapter, they are still informed by letter of what has to be done. The sisters admit they 'would be very bereft if we didn't have this interest'. None the less I find it hard to accept what one French woman superior general claims is true: that 'women religious need a man and, deprived of the continued interest of a priest, their natural tendencies to sadism and masochism wreak havoc in the community.' Yet she was a practising psychiatrist before becoming a nun.

At one time there was a reason for the bishop's visits,

which had to be made at least once a year: to ensure that no nun was detained against her will or maltreated. Today such visits are unnecessary – 'After all, we aren't holding parties till five in the morning with men.' Some sisters find them an irritating hangover from the past. Even though the visits are now made on a purely friendly basis and conducted with the utmost goodwill, they hate what they see as interference. The hierarchy of England and Wales,' snapped one sister, 'try one's patience to the utmost.'

The trouble is that the Church has no constitutional safeguard against tyrants, benevolent or otherwise. In Rome there is absolute monarchy, and power is almost exclusively male. There are some hopeful signs. Late in the 1960s four nuns were named to the Roman Curia, the central government of the Church, hitherto made up largely of men in their seventies. It was hoped that the four women – American, English, Spanish and French – would influence the Curia to liberalize rules. But so far their influence would seem to be slight. Canon lawyers are only now revising canon law on the principle that women can no longer be treated as minors.

The rights of women in the Vatican have not improved much, despite Vatican II. It is, of course, true that the people closest to the Pope are women: his own community of attendant nuns. But they are housekeepers, and get into the news only upon the occasion of the Pontiff's birthday when they bake him a cake. Although there are now a number of nuns and laywomen holding jobs in various departments, including the Congregation of the Faithful and two pontifical commissions, the tradition still stands that even ranking diplomatic representatives accredited to the Holy See must be men. When in 1970 the West German government nominated a woman as Second Secretary there, she was turned down.

But 'Equality,' points out Letitia Brennan, an Ursuline from New Rochelle taking her doctorate in psychology, 'is not about to be offered to women. To be recognized, they must take the initiative themselves.' Others agree. 'They must insist on assuming their own responsibilities,' says another. 'They must insist on being treated as adult member of the Church.'

In the early days of religious life, women in religion wielded enormous influence both in their monasteries and beyond. Indeed, it was accepted that few communities could vie in intellectual and social significance with the foremost communities of women. The eleventh-century princess Sophie abbess of the German settlement of Gandersheim, mastered common law so that she could enter disputes with learned men and successfully oppose them.

In the seventh century Abbess Hilda of Whitby was one of the most influential women in Britain. 'Mother of All' they called her, and her biographer Bede says that 'her prudence was so great that not only did ordinary persons, but even sometimes kings and princes, seek and receive counsel of her in their necessities.' She was visited constantly by church dignitaries 'on account of her innate widsom', and during her thirty years as abbess first in Hartlepool, then Whitby, no less than five of the men who studied under her became bishops. Her successor, Aelflaed, was equally impressive. Given into religious life by her father as a tiny baby, she was only twenty-five when she became abbess and shortly afterwards was the chief speaker at the Synod of Nidd: yet after the Council of Trent it was 1971 before a woman – the internationally renowned economist Barbara Ward – was again allowed to address the World Synod of Bishops.

The power of the abbess was at one time absolute: she is spoken of as 'Sovereign' and 'Majesty'. She ruled her own lands, held her own courts, decreed punishment and penance, and sent her own knights into battle for her king. Many religious settlements were founded by royal or imperial families, whose daughters then became abbesses as of right often while they were still only children. In the tenth and eleventh centuries abbesses of the chief houses in German lands had numerous privileges: those of Quedlinburg and Gandersheim were even able, under Otto I, to strike their own coins bearing their portraits. Abbesses were in close

ouch with the royal courts and affairs of state, partly because
of their family connections, and partly because monasteries
were used as hotels by well-to-do travellers, including
members of the ruling families. So worldly were these abbesses
that Abbess Mathilda, of the Saxon settlement of Quedlinburg,
virtually ruled the country as guardian of the baby Otto II
when his father was killed in Italy in 983, and was praised for
the determined measures by which she fought off invaders.

The abbesses of these two royal houses, Quedlinburg and
Gandersheim, had both the privileges and duties of a baron:
when war was declared they issued summonses for their
contingents of armed knights. They were summoned to the
imperial Diet and went in person until the sixteenth century.
These women held, as did heads of women's orders in other
European countries and some abbots, the power of a bishop
within their own territories. They carried with them emblems
of their episcopal power, the pallium and the crozier. They
wore the mitre and cope, and even the episcopal ring. They
conducted all their own church services except the Eucharist,
for which they were not ordained. And on one occasion the
Abbess of Hradschin in Prague – who was also an arch-
duchess – even performed the crowning of the new Queen of
Bohemia in a magnificent ceremony in Vienna's Chapel of St
Wenceslas.

Not only were these abbesses laws unto themselves; but
they often had separate nunneries under their jurisdiction. In
France and Spain, for instance, the Cistercian abbesses were
enormously powerful. The abbess of Las Huelgas near Burgos
was appointed head of twelve other nunneries. They held their
own General Chapter in Burgos, and the bishops assembled
together with six abbots and seven abbesses, each of whom
was entitled to bring with her six servants and five horses.
From then on, the power of the abbess of Las Huelgas increased, until a thirteenth-century abbess actually refused to
see the visiting abbot of Cîteaux, the Cistercian head office –
for which she was excommunicated.

In England, abbesses were among those to whom the king
looked when he needed help in defending the country. In
the reign of Henry I the abbess of Shaftesbury found seven

knights for the king's service and regularly received writs
asking that she send her quota of soldiers into the field. In
March 1282 when an insurrection started in Wales against
King Edward I, the bishops, nineteen abbots, four abbesses and
the prior of Coventry all received such writs. Heads of major
religious houses, bishops and the archbishops of York and
Canterbury were all summoned when Parliament sat – and
this extended to abbesses: in 1306, for instance, fifteen abbots
and four abbesses were called to Westminster.

The power of these women was well-founded in goods and
land. The oldest were the richest, and the Benedictines were
richest of all: it was said that if the abbot of Glastonbury were
to marry the abbess of Shaftesbury, their heir would have
more land than the King of England. Nor was their spiritual
power confined to the women beneath them. In the double
monasteries of medieval times, when men and women in-
habited the same religious houses, it was always under the
rule of an abbess. There were priests who ministered to the
nuns spiritually, and lay brothers who did the hard manual
work. When the Benedictine revival abolished the organized
male community, the nuns still retained their chaplain and
male servants. The Swedish Bridgettines appeared in England
at the great foundation of Syon in the fifteenth century.
This, too, was a double monastery under an abbess who ran
the house, arranged the lives of all, appointed chaplains and
canons, and controlled lands and revenues. Clearly there was
no objection to women holding power.

Gradually their influence waned. As a result of social
change, the possession of property shifted from the hands of
women. They ceased to found nunneries, and where men –
abbots and local landowners – did so, they curtailed the
power of the women. Only the abbesses of the older orders
retained their influence.

But it was the Council of Trent in 1545 which really took
away much of their power, and it did so in two ways. Bishops,
who formerly had no right to enter the houses of abbesses with
episcopal jurisdiction, were now able to do so as delegates of
the Holy See. Even more damaging, however, was the cur-
tailing of their movements: nuns were forbidden to leave their

enclosures. It was this that removed the privilege of attending the Imperial Diet from the aristocrats who ruled the German foundations. It was this that kept abbesses of the oldest and richest religious houses in England from answering the summons to Parliament. And it was this, finally, that began to stem the power of those haughty Spanish abbesses of Las Huelgas, for no longer could they hold their General Chapter in Burgos. Even so, despite the loss of privilege, it was 1874 before the episcopal role of the abbess was finally ended, and it was again due to a combination of factors. In France, the lands and houses confiscated from the Church during the French Revolution were not returned, and later Napoleon made heads of all religious houses subject to his appointed bishops. In Spain the abbesses of Las Huelgas continued to be powerful for another fifty years, until the old idea of the nobility's right to rule disappeared as democracy took over, and women had no voice or vote.

The rule of enclosure is still rigid. Any enclosed nun leaving her house without permission risks exclaustration, which means she is no longer in any way a member of her order. Or, if she is under solemn vows and there is some scandal attached to her going, the penalty may be excommunication from the Church. Though in earlier days the walls were used to keep the world out, they gradually became part of religion itself, so that a religious became by definition an enclosed person taking solemn vows. And the protective measures that developed were sometimes almost unbelievable: in Assisi, at St Damian's, it is still possible to see the ordinary door of the convent high up in the wall where it can be reached only by a ladder drawn up at night.

When, in 1609, Mary Ward founded the Institute of the Blessed Virgin Mary in England, she and her sisters were known as the Galloping Girls because of their refusal to have enclosure. 'Show yourself as you are,' she told them, 'and be as you show yourself.' Although the Pope supported her, churchmen were horrified: she was imprisoned and a decree of suppression issued on her sisters. A century later, when St Vincent de Paul was scheming to keep his order uncloistered and active in France, he warned them that they must always tell the local bishop that they were not in religion. 'Should some muddle-headed person appear among you and say, "We ought to be religious, it would be much nicer," then, my dear sisters, the company is ripe for Extreme Unction, for who says "religious" says "enclosed".'

Enclosure was carried to extremes. When one English branch of the Carmelites founded a house in another town in the nineteenth century, they travelled in a coach with all the windows painted black. This order had arrived originally from France, to be met at Victoria station by friends who insisted they see a little of London, much against their wishes. A young sister asked one what she had seen, receiving the indignant answer: 'We saw nothing, of course. We are enclosed nuns.'

Churchmen wielding power frequently use it to enforce what seem to be undue restrictions. As late as the 1960s, the eminent prelate of a large American diocese ordered that no sister venture outside the convent after six in the evening and several other bishops followed his lead. But now, thanks largely to Vatican II, a sister from that same diocese says that 'even appearances on late-night television are considered part of the apostolate.' In the late 1960s Cardinal Antoniutti wrote to the School Sisters of St Francis in America that he felt their new freedom was leading to practices that were not only dangerous but a source of scandal, such as 'late hours, indiscriminate visiting . . . and worse'.

The attitude towards contemplatives has always been even more strict. At about the same time Cardinal John Carberry wrote to the 4000 contemplative nuns in America saying that he understood that contemplatives had been seen at religious meetings and workshops. 'This,' he wrote, 'may have serious effects on their contemplative vocation,' and he 'respectfully requested' that they abstain from attending such gatherings while the question of their renewal was under study.

One nun publicly and furiously contested Cardinal Carberry's moral right to tell 4000 women what to do – moral because there was no question but that he had the right canonically. In 1969 this woman, Sister Margaret Ellen Traxler, formed the liberal National Coalition of American Nuns to prevent the oppression of women in religion. One of her first acts was to tell men to keep their hands off the running of religious orders of women – though it was couched in more formal terms. 'We protest any domination of our institutes by priests, no matter what their hierarchical status. We uphold as inviolable rights of self-determination for religious women.'

The impact this had was reflected in a headline in the Chicago *Daily News*: MILITANT NUN'S FIGHT FOR SEXUAL EQUALITY ROCKING THE CHURCH. Today Sister Margaret runs an influential organization from an office in South Wabash Avenue in the heart of Chicago. One in fifty of all American nuns are NCAN members, and those who join are active and vocal; together they are capable of making a considerable impact on the system. NCAN sets out to be a conscience for the Catholic Church in America. They have campaigned for good teachers for the negro colleges in the Southern states, and their organization CHOICE sent the first whites to these campuses. They have supported civil rights marchers and picketing farmworkers; Jews in Russia and American Indian dropouts. They are fighting to get the Equal Rights Amendment to the American Constitution ratified in all states, since they believe there is little point in fighting for equality within the Church so long as women outside do not have it.

Probably the most militant feminist to remain in the ranks of any religious order, Sister Margaret would never dream of leaving the Church: 'I really see my life as a commitment to God and I'm not going to go back on that.' She is a member of the School Sisters of Notre Dame, but far from representing their views, she is totally opposed by many of her fellow nuns. (At a conference at the mother house in Rome a group of Austrian sisters asked recently that she be denied a vote at the meeting because of her stand on priestly interference.)

Some of NCAN's criticisms are undeniably justified. There are no women at all in decision-making positions in the Church – yet women represent well over half the membership. In the autumn of 1972 the American synod of bishops met to talk about justice and not a single woman representative was present. 'Imagine!' exclaims Margaret Traxler. 'They're talking about justice and half their membership is denied a presence, much less a vote.'

But if Margaret Traxler refuses to see herself as a daughter of a male bureaucracy, if she advises that it is better to ignore canon law than try to fight it, if she sees the hierarchy as an anachronism, she sees also the reality. The Sacred Congregation for Religious can dissolve any order at any time, and acquire their houses and property. 'And women have to understand this before they can link arms and fight against it.'

There is another area where the Church is tied to centuries of tradition: women are also excluded from the priesthood. A woman is one of the two classes of persons absolutely barred from ordination, the other being those who are not baptized. Yet an exclusively male priesthood is of human, not divine devising. There is no theological justification for excluding women, only an emotional one. (One bishop has said with a shudder: 'Priestesses would be a shift to pagan creeds.') A lecturer in psychiatry at the University of London suggests that woman is seen as imperfect, 'just as a man who is a eunuch or has severe corporeal deformity is held incapable of receiving Holy Orders'. He points out that the passionate reactions against the idea – *disgusting, repugnant, shameful* – show there are 'powerful unadmitted or unconscious motives at work'.

There are currently moves towards ordination for women in many churches, mainly in the form of qualified and consecrated deaconesses, of whom there are seventy in the Church of England. By 1971 the United Presbyterian Church in America had ordained eighty women, and the American Baptists appointed a woman president, while in Sweden the first ordination of women took place as early as 1960 (although it is true this was considered so shocking an innovation that many men ordinands immediately resigned).

In 1973 the body of Catholic bishops in America set in motion a study ostensibly to decide whether women should be ordained – a step which militant nuns regarded as no more than an empty gesture. Meanwhile, eleven women were ordained to the priesthood in the Episcopal Church in Philadelphia, only to be told their ordination was invalid because the bishops who performed the ceremony were not authorized.

Curiously, nuns are not much interested one way or another. There are of course those, like Sister Honor Basset of the Society of the Sacred Heart, who feel that 'women who are religious-minded would love to have been priests.' She considers that since being a nun is the only opening for a girl, 'it's got muddled in people's thinking.'

But almost all the ones I talked to seemed unconcerned beyond the point that they would like to see the possibility open, and felt sure that eventually it would come. When they do discuss it, even aggressively modern women tend to do so on the most superficial level. Typical is the English sister who liked the idea of women as priests, but said that personally she only regretted it now and again, as when 'at Easter we couldn't pass the chalice from one to the other: it was passed over to us by the priest from the bishop.'

It seems a short-sighted attitude. The question of ordination for women is one which could vitally affect all nuns and sisters. The hierarchy of the Catholic Church is particularly complex and deeply-rooted. The nuns' chances of changing this system to acquire greater self-determination are minute. But it is not the principle of the hierarchy to which nuns object. Obviously there will always be a power pyramid, as there must be in any organization as massive as the Catholic Church. It is the fact that it is a wholly *male* hierarchy which is the problem. Women do not object to being answerable to a bishop as such, they simply resent the fact that it is a man who arbitrates so much of their lives.

It is surprising that nuns do not put more thought and effort into trying to break the emotional barrier and get women priests accepted. For tomorrow's woman priest might be the next year's female bishop – and by 1999 a woman cardinal!

The question of women priests does raise one issue which concerns nuns, and that is the teaching of theology. In the past nuns tended to receive what teaching there was second-hand and at the most rudimentary level; after all, they were not expected to be interested in such a complex subject. But as the education of nuns improved, so did the need for better theological training. 'You can't,' exclaimed a highly qualified French sister, 'expect intelligent young women with trained minds to sit and listen to the little vision of Sister So-and-So.'

The importance of training in theology and philosophy becomes even greater as nuns and sisters move further out into the world. As the American Sister Bertrande Meyers says: 'When a nun is asked for advice, she can't just say, "We'll make a novena to St Jude for this," or, "Just keep up your prayers and everything will be all right."' Certainly no one wants to confuse being a nun with being a theologian, but one woman who has a good working knowledge of all the different orders says that the ideal situation would be if 'at *least* two or three nuns in every convent had theological training'.

Regina Mundi, founded in the mid 1960s, is the only European theological college provided solely for women. The course in theology, however, is simply a massively abbreviated and simplified version of that given to men at nearby universities. It is no wonder that nuns who have taken the course describe it as 'hopeless'. At least one is now re-reading theology at King's College, London.

In 1965 Cardinal Heenan founded the Corpus Christi theological college in Bayswater, intending that it should become a centre for renewing religious education after the Vatican Council. Out of every 1000 students, 750 were nuns. Then, early in 1972, the entire and distinguished academic staff resigned over disputes with Cardinal Heenan, chairman of the governing body. There were several points of contention, one of the most revealing being Cardinal Heenan's objection to the policy of giving the same course in speculative theology to priests with years of study behind them 'and to untrained nuns and laymen'.

While 'untrained nuns and laymen' are still lumped together in the minds of the men of the Church, it is useless to suppose that women can achieve any kind of voice. Even promises of equal status turn out to be empty.

In 1966 the Holy See published the decree of the Council,

Perfectae Caritatis, which said that the institutes themselves were responsible for renewal and adaptation by means of general chapters. This was a revolutionary move since, for the first time, instead of the Roman Curia rigidly controlling all discipline, the Holy See had recognized that each order could formulate its own constitutions. But when orders tried to put this into practice, it became apparent that the bishops had no intention of relinquishing the reins of power.

There was in America one attempt at renewal and self-expression by the Immaculate Heart of Mary Sisters in Los Angeles. The resulting clash with the hierarchy rocked the Catholic Church in America, as the sisters defied California's Cardinal McIntyre by refusing to retract any of the reforms on which they had embarked in response to Vatican II. 'All we were trying to do,' they claim, 'was to search for new ways. We sincerely serve the church – but we objected to being dehumanized.' The outcome was unprecedented: they are now, under canon law, 'defectors'.

The story of how what one religious sociologist has called 'the battered remnants' of the sisters of the Immaculate Heart left the religious life and became a lay community is extraordinary. It is also peculiarly American in that no European community has experienced a similar upheaval at this point even though renewal and adaptation have brought difficulties to many of them. But even in America, the Immaculate Heart sisters were not the first to give up their religious status. (The Glenmary Sisters were the first; they now serve as secular members of their 'communities of service' because the restrictions laid upon them by religious life interfered too much, they felt, with their work.) Nor will they be the last. They will, however, undoubtedly remain the most famous.

The Sisters of the Most Holy and Immaculate Heart of the Virgin Mary was founded in Spain in 1848 as a semi-cloistered community, and twenty years later ten were sent to California as missionaries. Scarcely pausing to learn English, the community opened two schools and became the first teaching order in southern California. In 1924, by now with a fair number of

American sisters, it broke with the Spanish foundation. This made little difference, for even when in previous years the sisters from America had returned to Spain, the rules were so strictly observed they were not allowed to join the Spanish community behind the grille.

As early as the 1940s the community was becoming more progressive to the point where it was criticized by churchmen for giving courses philosophically ahead of Catholic teaching. The members did not consider themselves at all radical: 'We just answered the needs of people more immediately than most orders.' The sisters ran the college and high school built by the community, nursed in their modern hospital, or worked in their conference centre. Then, in 1962, the community received a canonical visitation – a rare event – from His Eminence James Francis Cardinal McIntyre, of California, a man of conformist views. 'If you're going to be a nun with your mother house in his diocese,' commented a sister about him, 'he's going to see you do it his way.' The visit was not a friendly one. At this time, women throughout the world were beginning to leave religious life, and every order was suffering. His Eminence, however, chose to attribute the number of dispensations being requested by IHM sisters to the inadequate training they received. He questioned the community's theological training, pointing out that it was not the thinking of recognized contemporary theologians it should be following, but his own. Unless the sisters conformed, he told them, they would 'pay for' their views. Later that year he returned to tell them that experimentation was 'dangerous', and that the changes the community had adopted – which allowed more freedom in the observance of silence and manner of prayer – were contrary to orthodox religious life. He gave the sisters sixty days to conform to traditional religious practices.

But these changes had been legislated by the order's general chapter in 1963. The IHM community is a pontifical institute, able to make changes in the internal life of the community unless Rome disapproves. It is the work of the diocese and public worship which come under the head of the diocese, and his approval is not necessary for general chapter decisions.

The mother superior, Mother Mary Humiliata, was so worried by the implications of Cardinal McIntyre's ultimatum that she went to the ultimate authority in Rome, the Sacred Congregation for Religious and Secular Institutes, and as a result Cardinal McIntyre modified his criticisms: the matter seemed closed.

It was reopened when the IHM general chapter, in accordance with the directions of Vatican II, met to discuss renewal of religious life. The changes the community wanted this time included allowing the sisters to resume their own names and handle a small personal allowance. The sisters also wanted to be allowed to choose work other than teaching and nursing, and to experiment with suitable lay clothing. They wanted, in short, to be allowed to dress and regulate their lives like normal women. The sisters anticipated the objections of Cardinal McIntyre and consulted eminent theologians and canon lawyers on the soundness of the proposals: it made no difference. The cardinal took the new decrees as a statement of defiance. He refused to accept the arguments of the IHM sisters that the traditional habits, fixed hours and firm government he considered indispensable to 'religious' life were a hindrance to women working in modern schools and hospitals, and insisted that if the decrees were not dropped the sisters must withdraw from the schools in the archdiocese.

The response of other religious to this was widespread. Superiors of major orders defended the IHMs and there was a nationwide petition of support. Some theologians considered the decrees were a splendid response to the call for renewal, while others rebuked the sisters for disobedience and labelled them 'Hollywood types'. Nuns and sisters accused them of trying to kill off the religious life. In the midst of all this, Mother Humiliata — or Anita Caspary as she had become — went again to Rome for advice. Her answer came when Cardinal Antoniutti spoke to the major superiors of women's orders in Italy in January 1968. He said Vatican II did not authorize experiments which would obscure the meaning of religious life, create confusion or provoke scandal. Changes affecting the nature of the institute were forbidden, and as to clothing: 'In the army no one is allowed to choose his own uniform.' Thus with a heavy Curial foot did he help stamp out the IHM attempt at renewal.

The Sacred Congregation, 'conscious of conflict,' as Anita Caspary drily puts it, now took a hand, and presented the IHMs with directives with which they must comply. One was the retention of the habit. The second was a set prayer schedule with all sisters meeting at least once a day for prayer. The third concerned the importance of spiritual works over apostolic ones, and the fourth was that they must co-operate with the local bishop. When Anita Caspary protested at these directives, a pontifical commission was set up to study the case and four American bishops arrived to question the sisters. The advice they gave the community was 'pay lip service — have a habit, keep it in your closet and wear it once a year on feast days.' 'But,' says Anita Caspary, 'we didn't want that kind of hypocrisy.'

So the community split. A group of fifty of the older sisters accepted the four points and continued as they always had under a new superior. Some left religious life altogether. And 400 sisters remained with Anita Caspary when it became evident they would have to sign their dispensations. 'When you make a decision in common sense,' says Anita Caspary, 'and are told to reverse it for obedience, your whole being is torn apart.'

The first sister to hand in her dispensation was Sister Anna, who made her first vows in 1905. At ninety-nine she signed the mimeographed document with a firm hand and announced: 'I am now going to the chapel to make my vows to Jesus.' Until her death at 101 she continued to wear the full habit of the order. Anita Caspary herself found it hard to leave religious life: 'I'd have made a terrible divorcee. To find that church people seemed to disregard completely a lifetime of service and dedication, to find the Church didn't give a hoot what happened to your whole life.' She did not even have the satisfaction of knowing why the IHM sisters were singled out. As the Catholic press pointed out, what was being done in Los Angeles by the IHMs was being done throughout the United States by all kinds of orders. Indeed, much of their support came from religious who were putting simila programmes into action. The affair ended officially in 1970, but it is very far from finished in the eyes of the religious world: Anita Caspary still spends a good part of her time travelling and taking part in television programmes about her community all over the world. The BBC and CBS have both made documentaries. In Germany, no sister of any order would consent to appear on a television discussion programme with her.

It is worth looking at what has happened to the women who have stayed in Anita Caspary's group. In what direction have they moved, now they are no longer under the direction of the cardinal or the Vatican? Have they become as radical as Cardinal McIntyre feared they would?

In many ways they are extreme. The members no longer live as a closed group – but then neither do many other members of religious orders. On the other hand, they still retain the *feel* of a religious community. They call themselves 'a community of religious persons' because if they became a secular institute they would be right back under the jurisdiction of the Sacred Congregation for Religious and Secular Institutes. The members now live where they choose in 'a community without walls.'

Just off the Hollywood Boulevard, between the hills and the smog, there is a large white-painted apartment house, No. 1832. Behind the wrought-iron gate a Madonna smiles, and inside, balconied rooms rise round a courtyard set with café tables and chairs. A fountain plays, and the blue of a swimming pool glimmers in the distance. This is the hub of the IHM community, and in an upstairs apartment lives Ms Anita Caspary IHM. She is an elegant woman with upswept hair and an expensive dress, sitting in a cool antique-furnished room, a bowl of glass grapes at her side, pink flowers in tubs nearby. It is hard to realize she was once Mother Mary Humiliata in long purple robes, her hair hidden away. Now she is President of the Immaculate Heart Community, whose 247 members include a cellist with the Los Angeles Philharmonic orchestra, the china and glass manager of Buffum's Department Store, two psychologists, an electronics assembler for the Vidar Corporation and three men. Some of them live here, perhaps with dependent relatives – Anita Caspary has her mother with her. Others have apartments, shared possibly with a member of a different community. One sister lives alone in a flat above a garage. The idea is that communal life is created by the members by participation in the life of the whole community. 'We're talking about a network of people with the same ideas living different life-styles.'

The pattern of life is relaxed – no bells, no fixed hours for rising or sleeping, no formal recreation. But it is in their membership that they have made the biggest break with tradition. In 1970 the community admitted married couples to full membership, which members feel adds a dimension of which they could not previously have dreamed.

Anita Caspary is justified when she claims that: 'Anything that is happening in religious life with regard to vigour and vitality is happening through women.' Whatever happens to the IHM community now, however successfully they resolve their problems, the Church will not profit by their example. The only way to change the structure is to stay and reform it from within, and the IHMs had little choice but to leave. Anita Caspary believes that in the Church at this moment 'the situation couldn't get much worse – and something drastic has to happen soon.'

But the men of the Church must change their way of thinking about women. From the parish priest to the bishops and cardinals pacing in purple through their celibate days, there must be an acceptance of the ability of women to govern their own lives, to accept responsibility, to make valuable contributions.

'If the Church is going to be saved,' says Anita Caspary, 'it's got to make use of its woman power.'

6

THE SLOWLY CHANGING CLOISTER

A lot of things need changing in the religious life. Unless they are thought out and not swept under the carpet, the religious life is done for – and justifiably so.

A YOUNG ANGLICAN SISTER

Until ten years ago the pattern of life in religious communities of women had not changed noticeably in fifteen centuries. The nun was not so much preserved in amber as pickled in formaldehyde.

Change is coming now. For a few it is a radical re-thinking. For others it takes the form of cautious reappraisal. And for some orders it is still remote.

Yet without change, many orders will not survive this century. They will be dismissed as out-of-date and irrelevant, and their novitiates will go on dwindling.

Peter Hebblethwaite, who left the English Jesuits and editorship of the prestigious Catholic review *The Month*, comments: 'We are not keepers in an ecclesiastical museum but guardians of the human future and mankind.' But it is purely as ecclesiastical museums that many orders totter on. Their behaviour, way of life, and attitude to authority; their clothes, ideas and rules have changed little since the time of their foundation, perhaps hundreds of years ago.

For nuns, life has been too detached, physically and emotionally, from the world. Within their walls they became isolated, and their perspectives distorted. They were the last strongholds of the studied manners of the middle-class woman of the nineteenth century. They became, says Cardinal Suenens of Malines-Brussels, 'like a fortress whose drawbridge is only furtively and fearfully lowered.'

Segregation from the world has left nuns and laity facing each other across a gulf of incomprehension. The trouble has been intensified over the last few years because convent life has taken little note of the emancipation of women outside its walls. Often, the rules and regulations for nuns are still those laid down for young women totally dependent on their parents until marriage, when they would become dependent on their husbands. They were not expected to earn their own living outside the home: they were not even expected to go out unaccompanied. For such women, religious life could not have come as much of a surprise. But for today's women, to be suddenly wrapped in the rigid corset of conventual behaviour must be constricting.

Convents are governed by regulations, as all organizations must be. But they are so numerous and so ancient that, in observing them, religious communities are forced into curiously dated behaviour patterns and quite literally withdrawn from modern life. This was never intended by the founders, who would surely be horrified to learn that regulations made for practical reasons should have become, with the passage of time, sacrosanct in themselves. Some of these regulations are found in the rule, which concentrates on the charism or spirit of the order. It is meant to be a statement of the direction and task of the community. Too often, brought into line with canon law, the rule has become merely a legalistic document dictating duties and obligations, a petty god directing each detail of life: novices in some orders still learn it verbatim and recite it on their knees before the novice mistress. Even in a relatively young congregation, the rule may still be centuries old. Many orders, for instance, adopt that of St Benedict and use it as the pattern for their lives. Yet St Benedict wrote it in AD 540 for his monastery of Monte Cassino.

Then there are the constitutions and customs which vary from order to order. These set out information on the government of the community: details of each stage of the life; strictures regarding votes for officials; even minute directions regarding such niceties as skirt lengths.

The regulations may have been written to suit the situation in one part of the world. Teresa of Avila, for instance, writing in Spain, laid down instructions about buildings which were suitable for that climate. Yet when the Carmelites first came to England and put up their great stone house in Notting Hill Gate, the architect was horrified that it was to include no heating at all. It took the insistence of a cardinal to persuade them to put in heating – and then he had to declare that it would not constitute diminution of the Primitive Observance, since Teresa herself would have supported him wholeheartedly if she had ever experienced the English climate. He used to write them notes every autumn pointing out that it was no luxury but plain common sense to light the boiler now they had it.

Every detail of convent life was dictated with equal firmness. Being dressed in a particular way, walking always in icy cloisters, eating at scrubbed tables: all these things came to constitute the very identity of nuns themselves. Although a foundress might have been a woman of quite staggering courage and independence in her time, her modes of thought and behaviour were bound to lose their pioneering flavour with the passing of centuries. But her community continued to cling to the old observances. So the original spirit of her order – the fearless innovation and the brave initiative – was lost, drowned in a welter of archaic absurdities: the refectory regulations patterned on the eating habits of eighteenth-century French peasants; the stilted recreational practices on those of a Victorian household; the clothes on the garments of sixteenth-century Belgian widows.

At present regulations vary not only from country to country but from convent to convent. There are orders like the contemplative Cistercians where there has been no discernible change since they were founded in the eleventh century: they live in total silence, without any common recreation, sleeping fully dressed on pallets of straw in a shared dormitory. Others, like the Society of the Sacred Heart, have recently come out of strict enclosure and are now allowed such freedoms as speech at meals. Although they were teaching sisters, adult women had to be accompanied if they were forced to step outside the convent door. One sister remembers how she once found waiting for her a seven-year-old boy who announced: 'Me mam's ill but I'm here to look after you instead.' She recounts it now in a London restaurant as an amusing anecdote: unbelievably, she is talking of a time five years ago. And there are orders where the change from an over-regulated life has been carried to extremes. This is most obvious in convents in America's Midwest: the Sisters of Loretto at the Foot of the Cross, for instance, were one of the first orders out of the habit and their sisters are free to work where and as they wish, and are as unconfined and liberated as any Western career woman.

The communities having the hardest time with the problems of change appear to be those which realize the need for adaptation but are uncertain in which direction to go. The more involved a community or an individual becomes with modern life and the problems of its people, the more absurd become the rules and regulations designed to protect the nun from contamination by the world. If a woman has spent her day coping with aggressive adolescents in a slum school, it is clearly ridiculous that she should have to miss a meeting with their parents because the convent rule insists she be inside by six p.m. And the reason for this was, quite simply, that 'timing used to be geared to before the invention of electric light,' as an American sister explains. Less than ten years ago her order rescinded the rule that had every member of the convent inside by eight p.m. in summer, six p.m. in winter and in bed by ten o'clock. Other orders' ill-considered 'modernization' allowed the sisters to stay up late for reasons of work – but insisted they rise at five-fifteen next morning: 'We tried to live modern nights and medieval mornings.'

The result of hanging on to obsolescent regulations was that nuns and sisters often simply defied them. 'A parent would come to see me at night,' recalls a young American, 'and I'd learn later they'd been turned away because it was my time for prayer. I wasn't supposed to talk to people on the street, yet that was my best place to get to know them. I felt my belief in the gospel message was very simple and beyond a rule – so I ignored or broke the rules.'

Nuns were also trying to do modern jobs under a medieval system. It was part of their obedience that they were never consulted about the tasks allotted to them, but simply expected to carry them out to the best of their ability. In active communities sisters would be sent where they were most needed, regardless of their inclinations or talents. At one time, this was a perfectly acceptable part of religious life, but the system began to break down when nuns moved into more specialized work for which lengthy training was required. The woman who laboured for her degree in English and then spent a decade teaching Latin felt understandably unhappy. So did the American sister who 'entered for the poor – and then I was dismayed when they sent me to Rome for theology'. One sister taught mathematics in an American parish. It was a subject she hated, and for more than four years she grew increasingly depressed. Her superiors knew that she had entered to work with the sick, and she had been assured that after her training she would do so. But when the time came, she was told to deposit her personal judgement in the hands of her superior. God, she was repeatedly told, wanted her for another work. After several requests were ignored, she left the order. Another sister spent six years doing secretarial work and accounts 'which horrified me. I can't type, and I can't add two and two. It couldn't have been more repugnant.' She did, even so, find unexpected advantages. 'I learnt that the way you did the job transformed it.'

Sisters used to be put through university by their orders quite often as an obedience whether they wanted to go or not. Sister Honor Basset was sent to Oxford, much against her wishes. 'It didn't seem to be in tune with my vocation: I'd entered for the religious life, not higher education. The order wanted me to get a degree but I didn't want to become a bluestocking. But it was an obedience. So I went.' She found 'a lot of the life excessively hard, and I went through a very bad time'. Part of the problem was psychological: the sisters had been taught that interest in the world was wrong, yet they were expected to get the best out of the life. They had to obtain special permissions to attend lectures, and had to be chaperoned everywhere by another sister. 'I remember waiting around for two hours in the cold for my chaperone's lecture to finish so we could go home.' At the end of her three years, Sister Honor did in fact fail. 'I talked it over with the mistress of studies and Reverend Mother. And they said, "You know, we want you to get a degree." So I started again.'

A nun in the same order's house at Leamington Spa entered at the turn of the century and studied for her degree from inside the convent. Under university rules she had to turn up at the university for the final examination. The problem was discussed, and the order felt she should not go dressed as a nun. At that time, like all religious, hair was cropped. So she was given stage clothes and a wig. Because the exams were from seven to nine at night, and Greater Silence would be in force when she returned, she promised that if she felt she had done well she would leave the wig on top of a box.

After university it was common practice for a sister to return to the convent with her degree, only to be given some job such as working in the kitchen, which in no way used her new-found knowledge. 'The greatest sin,' according to a woman who experienced this, 'would be intellectual pride.'

While the sister was at university her schedule was supposed to follow as closely as possible that of her order. The 'pattern of day' was rigid and was exactly that – a day divided neatly by bells into half-hourly intervals. For a contemplative, this worked perfectly. For a busy university student or a teaching sister, it imposed an extra strain to which the brevity of the recreation time allowed merely added. The average sister in teaching order started her day at five with chapel, then meditation for twenty minutes, the office of Our Lady for fifteen, then Mass which took an hour. This would be followed by breakfast and a full day of school, with fifteen minutes of prayer at midday, half an hour during the afternoon in chapel for Adoration, then another twenty-five minutes of office in the evening.

'And you had to get in your rosary for a quarter of an hour

and then night prayers. When the children's dormitories were closed we used to go to bed at nine o'clock; it was marvellous.' In all that time recreation was half an hour of spiritual reading in the community room or listening to a book while doing needlework.

For a great number of congregations of women, these practices – or similar ones – are still current. So a twentieth-century girl who decides to enter a convent may well find herself experiencing what amounts to culture shock.

Sister Madeleine of the Augustinian Sisters of Meaux says: 'In the convent you're suddenly brought into a cultural situation that is not really Victorian but positively feudal. And this causes tremendous conflict inside yourself.' The entrant must, it is laid down, allow herself to be moulded by the rule into the pattern of the order. She must give up her opinions and her tastes, 'reveal her repugnance to her superior', and obey. She must respond with deference towards those in authority, move on the instant when a bell rings. 'And when,' says Sister Madeleine, 'you go to the chapel or lunch, you may be told very sternly to bow down low somewhere and whisper your apologies to the superior before carrying on.'

In the past those entering accepted such authoritarianism stoically. 'You took it just as you had at home,' explains an American, 'where you conformed to your parents' wishes.' The discipline was applied as rigidly to a woman responsible for teaching college as it was to the youngest novice. 'I once returned home feeling terrible,' remembers an American history teacher. 'I said to the superior, "I think I have a temperature. May I go to bed?" She said, "Yes, but go to the chapel first and say all your prayers privately". So, after a full day at school, feeling really ill, I stood for an hour in the chapel.' And it extended to all aspects of life. In one enclosed order the nuns wore heavy cloaks in choir. It was a custom retained from the time of the eighteenth-century founder when the stone-floored choir in winter would have been freezing. A nun remembers asking her superior why they continued to wear the cloaks despite the over-efficient central heating. 'All these things,' she was told, 'are part of the life of penance and mortification which we embraced when we made our vows.'

A nun in her eighties, now living in a far more relaxed atmosphere in her updated convent than when she entered sixty years ago, comments on the system: 'All I can say in its defence, it certainly made a dead set at self-will.' It did even more than that. By such minute ordering of detail, the convent implied that its nuns were incapable of decision.

But there was a reason. Community. 'The important thing was always the community,' says a sister who believes she would have left if her order had not begun to change at the first possible moment. 'The individual sisters were only important in so far as they made up the whole.'

Uniformity of life and habit did indeed attempt to obliterate all personal differences between nuns. Eileen Gielty, an immensely talkative Irishwoman, says that when she replaced the portress during the school holidays, and took over the door and telephone duties, 'People would ring and say, "What's your name?" And I would say, "I'm one of the sisters." It wasn't false humility, it just didn't seem relevant to say what your name was, because you weren't expected to come across as a person.'

Such diminution of personality, combined with the strict rule, had the effect of making many nuns feel remote from each other. 'We felt deprived of relationships,' confesses one elderly woman, 'lonely for sheer companionship.' And if the nuns were isolated within the same community, different orders were as little known to them as foreign countries. 'Nuns in convents down the road didn't have anything to do with each other. It's only in the last five years that I've met members of any community other than my own.'

When Mother Turnbull, the great musician of the Sacred Hearts, went to teach Gregorian chant to a community of Carmelites, she was not allowed to enter the enclosure, but had to do as best she could through the parlour grille. When nuns went to another house in the same order before the changes of Vatican II, equally strict segregation was observed. 'They had rooms separate from the rest of us,' remembers one sister. 'And they didn't even eat with us but in a little parlour.

Now there's much wider hospitality among nuns — they can even come and share our meals.'

Until recently, there were no holidays. Everyone lived — as the enclosed still do today — the same pattern day in, day out, year after year. Then communities would follow the contemplative practice of observing 'Lot', or cell days, when rules were relaxed, and they might talk more than usual, stay in their cells and read, or go into the garden. The name 'Lot' derives from the custom in medieval monasteries of letting blood three times a year, after which the nuns spent four days getting their strength back.

Only five years ago, even active orders did not allow their sisters to go home for emergencies. Now, even the majority of contemplatives would permit this. Many of the sisters to whom I talked still feel bitterness over the deprivation their parents suffered as a result of this restriction. 'After I entered,' says one, 'I never saw my parents except in the convent parlour. My father died alone during the war: that wasn't Holy God.'

Another nun, whose brother and sister were also members of religious orders, says, 'I knew I couldn't go home, and my mother knew it. When she died, my sister and I were not allowed to attend the funeral. And looking back, I feel how lonely my mother was.'

Some orders were lucky enough to own or share 'holiday' houses, convents by the sea, perhaps, where sisters could go for a week. 'Then you could get up at half past six because you were on holiday. You still had your duties to prayer, and the morning prayer had to be made before nine o'clock, and there were certain strictures with regard to time. But on the whole, you were free to go for walks or generally lie around.' Even there, a certain code had to be observed. 'You couldn't lie out flat on the grass, it wouldn't be religious.'

Gradually sisters were allowed away from their convents. 'We considered it a holiday to go into retreat, or perhaps your superior would send you on a course.' Then, in 1950, an international Congress of Religious was held in Rome. This august assembly decided that the real purpose of recreation was to restore soul and body. Sitting round the superior in conversation was not to be recommended for this. Useful and agreeable pastimes, such as light manual work or the playing of games, were preferred. Nor did it like the idea of religious being allowed breaks. 'One should beware of vacations and furloughs, lest in giving recreation to the body, harm be done to the soul.' Even less did they like the idea of religious going home. 'The constant and prolonged contact with worldly persons – it makes little difference that they are relatives, friends or acquaintances – puts the soul in the frequent occasion of failing in its duty and of assimilating, little by little, the spirit of the world.'

It was 1960 before Cardinal Suenens urged that the sisters should be allowed home, 'for contact with the realities of life will give them more understanding of others'. He deplored that many religious were lucky if they got one day's holiday a year. Many sisters expected to go home for seven days once every nine years. Then this was revised – to seven days every six years. 'You felt,' remarked a sister in such an order 'very much out of things when you went home for the first time.' Once home, the sister was expected to 'endeavour to give edification by her deportment' – scarcely an incitement to relaxation.

Often the sisters themselves do not want such freedom. Mother Gabriel of the Sisters of Mercy considers: 'If you become a real nun, you should be committed fully to the life. Some aren't, you know.' At a time when her order allowed a visit home every three years, her mother became ill. She had never returned home. 'In the old days, you wouldn't need to go home, because your family weren't derelict. When my mother was dying, my family asked if I would go. I said, if she asks for me, I'll go. And if she doesn't, I won't. And she didn't.'

Only within the last few years has the rule of enclosure been relaxed sufficiently to allow nuns who need medical treatment to enter hospital. Previously, they had to be treated within the convent. Members of some orders, such as the Sacred Heart, did not even leave for operations: the surgeon came to the house. But doctors will not operate under those conditions now, and it would be hard to find a dentist prepared to bring a foot drill. (Though at least one contemplative community has an old-fashioned drill kept on the premises, and their dentist comes in to give them treatment. The elderly nun who showed it to me commented with some acerbity when asked if they would prefer the new painless water drill: 'We would not go out of our way to avoid discomfort.')

When long-established European communities started new branches in the United States, problems arose. In America, where in many places a car is the only practical form of transport, even sisters in car-dominated Los Angeles used to rely on kindly-disposed lay people to drive them around, since driving was considered 'unmonastic'. In Europe, this particular barrier has taken a lot longer to break down.

It was the same stern approach that kept many religious communities from modernizing their domestic arrangements. 'Monastic simplicity', in the minds of many religious, means nuns on their knees polishing floors to a fine finish by hand rather than using floor polishers. They were often told they would only get to heaven on their knees – be it praying or scrubbing. That many still believe this is evidenced by the rows of white-habited novices I saw crouched in the hallway of a large Sussex convent, rubbing away in sweating silence.

Much of the more primitive labour has now vanished. Most convents now have, for example, washing machines instead of tubs. There are photographs of St Thérèse, the consumptive 'little flower' of the Carmelites, working away with her sisters at the washing, kneeling round a large pool kneading linen by hand. This usually took place every six weeks or so. It was the reason why each sister had to have a trousseau of several complete changes when she entered. It was not unknown for novices to have their hands badly skinned and bleeding after a full day's washing, from the pure ammonia poured into the water.

The Anglican Community of St Mary the Virgin has in its huge washing room at Wantage, Berkshire, great copper vats, the real Victoriana, in which the wash is boiled. Until recently the ironing was done with heavy old-fashioned steam irons: convents must be the only places in the world still using such beautiful and antiquated machinery. Sensibly – but sadly – this community has just changed to conventional electric irons.

Not all convents have abandoned the old ways. For some, it is a matter of asceticism. Spanish nuns, for instance, make it perfectly clear that they think American sisters lax and soft for their use of electric machinery. Others simply cannot afford modern conveniences. In one old Benedictine monastery in Britain, for example, there are just three bathrooms. One in the infirmary, one in the novice quarters, and one reserved for the abbess. All the rest of the nuns wash in bowls on the floor of their cells in true monastic fashion, standing upon bathmats of sacking.

It is the emphasis in the rule on decorum, on modesty and purity, that above everything else has dictated the behaviour of communities of nuns. 'We were always living many years behind the manners of the country, and ladylike behaviour was demanded of us.' This caused, thinks Sister Madeleine, 'a terrible strain between your inner beliefs and aspirations and the things you do spontaneously as a person of twenty – rushing downstairs, putting your feet over the arm of a chair, relating to men in the way of our time.'

The Rules of Modesty ordain how the nun must behave. In many orders they are still followed to the letter, while in others they have given way to behaviour more natural to women of today. These rules insist that hands must be joined in a special position, clasped together at waist level. It is a breach of discipline to hurry, much less run: their walk must be measured except in case of pressing necessity, and even then they must 'as far as possible have regard to religious propriety'. Then there is 'custody of the eyes,' which have for the most part to be cast down, while care has to be taken lest they wander from side to side. 'Men,' states the rule of one order, 'should not be looked at indiscreetly.'

Nor should anything else. Curiosity is to be avoided at all costs, and it is stressed that if the sister looks at the person to whom she is talking, she is creating a dangerous situation fraught with temptation. Some prohibitions are obvious, if a trifle pathetic. Looking in shop windows, for instance, is worldly and could be a distraction. And if a sister is talking to someone in an office, she must on no account allow her eyes to stray to the papers on the other's desk for fear of curiosity. It is, indeed, a minor breach of rule to raise the eyes unnecessarily, even for a moment, in choir or refectory. This is to avoid distracting the thoughts, which should be applied to God. 'Vain, perverse and wandering thoughts' are to be guarded against. So carefully were they guarded against, indeed, that a lively girl in her late twenties says that in the novitiate, 'after two and a half years we'd never been allowed to look at the pictures in the corridors.'

The rule also insists that the head should not be turned to the side unless there is need. It is to be held straight, inclined forward, without leaning to either side.

And the sisters are exhorted at all times to 'show joyousness in their countenances rather than sadness or other less regulated feelings'. The lowered voice is also an essential part of seemly behaviour: nuns are expected to maintain 'calm composure' and avoid 'vehemence'. Equally important is treating everyone with perfect consideration. The rule expects that in conversation nuns will wait 'with perfect patience' until the speaker has finished. One nun new to the convent infirmary was told to cut the bread and butter especially thin for one patient, 'because Sister is blind'.

Behaviour in the refectory is also rigorously controlled. Meals are not to be thought about in advance because such gross and sensual thoughts would be unmonastic. The convent is no place for gluttony. 'You feed your body just enough to get a certain amount of work out of it.' The sister should never retire from the table without having mortified herself in some slight way – not having a glass of water, perhaps, when she wanted one. Though she must not scruple to eat and drink what is provided, 'accepting from the hand of God indifferently what one liked or did not like'. It is possible to be reprimanded, as one nun was, for 'eating her soup in a worldly way', while saying something was nice would bring the retort that it was a worldly attitude to be a gourmet.

Many of the more curious mealtime customs began when

orders from one country started houses in another and, in th
name of simplicity, retained the rule with regard to meals
The Sisters of Notre Dame, a French order, had one plat
which had to be wiped free of grease with a piece of bread
There would be no cups, just a handle-less bowl for water
They had both knives and forks – but everything had to be cu
at the start of the meal, then eaten with the fork. 'We wer
absolutely never allowed to use the knife during the meal
but it had nothing to do with religious life – it was part of th
French and Belgian customs, when a poor family shared th
only knife.' At the end of the meal a scrap plate went up an
down the rows of sisters, collecting everything that coul
not possibly be eaten. An extra penance would be taking an
eating something from this dish – a remnant of a custom
practised now only among austere contemplatives, when th
nuns go from table to table in the refectory asking that the
be fed 'for God and Our Lady's sake', as they beg a mea
which they eat squatting on the floor.

Throughout the meal, silence is observed. 'If you dro
something you get down and kiss the floor for offending agains
the silence of the house.' There are gestures to be learned t
express different wants: the index finger and thumb close
for bread in some orders, in others put flat upon the table
For salt, a circle is drawn with a knife, for butter the knife i
pointed; while water is requested by rapping the goblet or
the table. And since eating is so gross an occupation, th
mind is occupied with listening attentively to reading. I
America, communities have started to tape these reading
for convenience.

The rule of silence in the house is observed so that nuns ca
listen better for the voice of God. The shadows of silence, th
spaces of recollection, have always been considered indispen
sable to the religious life. As one eighty-year-old says: 'There'
a lot of talk about abolishing silence, but that's rubbish: yo
can't have peace if you don't have silence.' And it does, says
superior of the Deaconess Community of St Andrew, 'hel
you focus on God rather than on one's busyness'. There ar
other advantages in silence. 'When you didn't have to talk,
says a sister, 'you could get away with murder – you didn'

have to express an opinion.' If there were times when silence, as the Poor Clare poet Sister Mary Agnes has written, seemed to be 'pressing steel plates about my ears', there were times too when it was a protection from irritation, and gave some measure of privacy. In some orders, if speech was absolutely essential, permission to speak would be asked with a bow and two fingers to the lips. The nun so approached would answer, '*Benedicite*', to which the answer was '*Dominus*', before anything was said. Or another order might use '*Ave Maria*' with the response '*Gratia plena*'. But like so much else the rule of silence became a fetish, so that even the accidental slamming of a door was an infringement. Lapses had to be reported to the superior. 'You had to kneel and she would give you a penance and you'd kiss the ground.'

There are official times for admitting faults. Among the Benedictines, for example, when the Chapter of Faults takes place, the abbess calls on six nuns to make full and clean confession to any fault, any wrong done. On their knees they confess to every unkind thought or careless action, the idea being that the community takes each other's shortcomings and sinfulness and shares it. Some communities called this process the 'culp', a corruption of '*Mea culpa*'. Marie Keegan of the Belgian Ladies of Mary recalls: 'It was usually in the dining-room. Six or seven of us lined up at a time, back to back, then you lay down on the carpet, face down with your arms at your side and said, "I confess to you, dear Mother, and to you, dear Sisters" – and then you read it off a bit of paper. A typical culp would be, "I thought uncharitable thoughts, I spilt milk and didn't say anything about it." A great one if I was really stuck for something was, "I broke the night silence." Then you got a penance.' In addition, there were all sorts of extra penances. Any sister who wished could prostrate in the refectory for five minutes to show she was a sinner and that everyone might trample on her. Another penance, carried out weekly in many houses, was the kissing by the novices of the feet of the entire community in a gesture of humility.

One of the areas where women's communities have always been stricter than men's is in passing on information. 'The

idea of passing news of any sort in a convent was anathema
ten years ago,' says a French sister. 'If you even missed
something someone said in conversation, you couldn't ask
what it was.' One nun remembers that when she entered only
one daily paper came into the house, and the community was
allowed to read only the one middle page of news. When the
Duke of Windsor abdicated, the news was considered so
unsuitable that the paper was stopped for a week. 'I only
heard the scandalous story years later.' A woman who
entered just before the invasion of Belgium in 1914 never
saw or heard a single news item about it throughout World
War I. Occasionally a nun would hear from the superior about
a relative killed or wounded. Then after four years the bells
were rung and the superior announced the war was over.

For many communities, even reproductions of sacred art
were considered unfit for contemplation, and the pages of
illustrated books were glued firmly together. Statues were
clothed neatly in white flannel petticoats. At the other extreme,
a Sussex convent in 1963, in all innocence, commissioned
frescoes by a curious and talented painter known as Frantz
Salieri: they caused a scandal in the Church of Rome. A few
years later he emerged as the director and designer who
helped make the ambiguous world of transvestism into an
art form.

Even information that seemed useful to the nun in her work
might be withheld. A nun who became infirmarian after World
War II knew nothing of medicine. Her family sent her a
modern *Encyclopaedia of Nursing* which was immediately
confiscated, containing as it did so much which it was quite
unnecessary for her to know. Although such censorship may
appear extreme, it can be justified in monastic terms; super-
fluous knowledge clouds the mind which should be filled
with thoughts of God.

The reason so many of these medieval practices survived lies
in the history of the religious orders themselves. For long
periods of time they virtually disappeared in various countries,
and when they returned they looked to the past for inspiration.

In Britain during the reign of Henry VIII, for instance, and in France at the time of the Revolution, religious life all but died out, while in America it had not begun. When it was once more acceptable, it merely started up again where it had left off. When the Anglican sisterhoods were developing in nineteenth-century England, they were very much a restoration rather than a renewal: Gothic architecture and romantic novels were fashionable, and this was mirrored in a burst of nostalgia for medieval Christianity. Equally old-fashioned in many ways were the native American communities which, in the nineteenth century, appeared in the wake of the established European missionary orders already there.

Yet rigorous as the regulations were and are, it would be wrong to assume that all nuns suffered under them. As Sister Margaret Moran of the Good Shepherd points out: 'I have the theory that in fact the more people conformed to such a set of regulations, the more individual some of them became. They came through as fantastic characters, lovely to meet.' But a docile character may well be broken – many nuns have had nervous breakdowns. 'Mind you, they weren't always recognized, and one in my order never really got over it.' Most nuns would agree with the English member of a teaching order who feels that 'because we had this very basic idea of committing your life to Christ, you would put up with a lot of things. When you went into the convent you knew a certain kind of behaviour was expected of you and you just conformed to that. But there were other things in your life which were meaningful and which compensated.'

Even so, admits a mother superior, 'only now are we learning how many older sisters suffered an almost constant frustration which they accepted willingly – but not always cheerfully – as part of the cross they bargained to carry in following Our Lord.' Sister Russell, a superior in the Society of the Sacred Heart, remembers: 'I went in very uncritically and accepted anything they said must be done: I think even in that state I loved it. But I can see now that we stopped questioning and thinking. People thought it was possible to be a good religious without thinking.'

The regulations encouraged the nuns to be passive and childlike. Recently a Mirfield father visited an Anglican women's community where he asked for a glass of water. 'I'll just ask Mother,' was the response. Even today, 'firm yet motherly' is the phrase used by a congregation formed in the 1960s to describe the qualities needed by a superior. This, too, is a harping back. Most communities started as small families, with rules and regulations which suited such a structure, and the omnipotent figure at its head. No training was considered necessary for the post. A superior received the grace of her office, and her inadequacies and shortcomings were divinely overcome. It did not always work. One enclosed nun I talked to was elected superior, though she felt from the first she could not undertake the office. Within weeks she had a nervous breakdown and actually ran away from her convent without telling anyone – for which the penalty, waived in her case, is exclaustration. She was of course penniless, but took the money from a collection box, promising herself to return it. She ended up sitting in Westminster Abbey without a clue what to do next.

Although many women are capable of filling the role superbly, a problem is that the very structure of convents encourages autocrats. 'Harassed superiors,' observed one priest 'have been known to treat their subordinates as if they were unwilling conscripts.' 'A convent,' snapped one American sister, 'should not be run like an asylum – or an army.' Sister Audrey Kopp, an American nun and a professor of theology, observes: 'Although canon law states that any decision that affects the whole must be made by the whole, it doesn't always work out quite so democratically.' She points out that the superior can if she so wishes manipulate the ideas of the sisters. She is the person who controls radio and television, and censors newspapers and letters.

Enlightened superiors have always worried about the question of obedience, well aware that an over-rigid 'mother' may use the rules unjustly to make her own life easy but that of her nuns intolerable. Teresa of Avila, who had a particular devotion to this virtue, retails with horror what happened when 'to another prioress came a nun and showed her a very large worm saying, "Look how beautiful it is." The prioress in jest replied, "Then go and eat it." She went and fried it. The cook asked her why she fried a worm and she answered, "To eat it," and would have done so. Thus through the great carelessness of the prioress that nun might have done herself much harm.'

This does show how little justification superiors need give for their commands. It is, for instance, quite possible for a superior to forbid a young sister 'imprudent behaviour' – cinema visits, or accepting invitations to people's homes – without having to define what 'prudent' behaviour actually is.

There are many women – some still inside, some outside – religious orders who have talked to me about what, to an outsider, sound like cruel and unnecessary restrictions. The Brazilian nun who was told never on any account to touch the small children in her care, even to hold a hand; the contemplative forbidden to write poetry in her cell since it was 'self-indulgent'. But some stories have more dangerous overtones. There are women who have known themselves to be in need of help for psychological problems which elderly superiors were quite unable to comprehend. One sister, unable to sleep in a tiny room because she was beginning to suffer from claustrophobia, was asked if she expected hotel accommodation and advised that this was her cross and she must bear it. Another woman, who at a time of considerable stress had walked in her sleep on to the roof of the convent, was accused of 'attention seeking', and had to 'speak her fault' before the entire community.

It must be stressed that all too often it seems not to have been lack of sympathy but of understanding which led to such situations. This fact, however, can have given little comfort to the American sister who went to her superior for spiritual help – only to be handed the keys of the community car and told to go to a drive-in movie and have a hamburger.

The major safeguard against abuse of the role of superior has always been the process of election. A religious cannot usually be considered for the post of superior until she is over forty. Elections are held every three years in most orders and re-election is usually possible only once. It was not until the eleventh century that heads of many religious houses were actually elected. Before that, the rule generally passed from mother to daughter: a woman of royal blood would often found a religious settlement with her marriage portion and retire there on the death of her husband. This system meant that many heads of religious houses were little more than children themselves.

The ceremony of electing the head of a monastic community is full of dignified ritual. Today, among the Benedictines, the abbot president, head of the congregation, arrives at the monastery on the appointed day with two monks who are the scrutators. The voting is held in the locked choir, and under oath. A list of all those eligible is handed to each nun, who cuts out the name she chooses. This process is repeated until one name achieves the necessary number of votes. It is a serious business. 'Conspiring to be abbess' is forbidden by the order.

When the choice is made, the abbot president confirms the new abbess in the name of the Holy See, hands her the pectoral cross, the ring, seal and keys of the monastery. Then the choir is unlocked, the whole community enters, and the abbess is taken to the abbatial chair where, one by one, all her nuns kneel before her and put their hands between hers in the age-old gesture of homage and obedience. And to each she gives the Pax, the kiss of peace.

Up till now the religious community has been very much a two-tier society: while uniformity was considered desirable, the social patterns of monastic life were positively class-ridden. Not for nothing was the head called 'superior' – and not until Vatican II was the word 'inferior' for her subjects outlawed. Any woman who entered took with her the status she had in the world outside. Although in the religious life they were discouraged – to the point of being forbidden – to discuss their backgrounds in order to avoid jealousies and comparisons, their role in the convent was decided by who they were and what they brought with them.

The choir nuns were educated women who brought with them an often handsome dowry. They could speak Latin, follow the prayers, and read and make music — hence the term 'choir'. A large number of early convents, indeed, accepted only those who were nobly born. So much so that in the fourteenth century the Pope had to intervene before the Order of Franciscan Minoresses would take members of the new landed gentry. Apart from daughters of dukes and barons and the Lord Mayor of London, there were later included daughters of a skinner, a draper and an ironmonger, and two whose fathers were fishmongers. Presumably their financial status was acceptable.

Other women, entering without benefit of education or dowries, were the lay sisters — sometimes known as claustral or coadjutrix sisters. Working women who wanted to dedicate their lives to God, they lived largely separate from the choir nuns. Their prayers were different, being simpler — they did not say Divine Office — and they often had their own chapel. Their clothes were less elaborate; they took their recreation separately, and sat in the refectory at special tables; they even had their own mother assistant. On them, the smooth running of the monastery depended. They scrubbed and polished, washed the floors, and cooked, thus freeing the choir nuns for study and writing, the fine art of music, and illuminating religious manuscripts. Then, too, medieval nuns had both male and female servants — not only to work the vast tracts of land, to farm, or keep their herds of cattle and sheep, but often to serve indoors. In a document written about 400 AD the nunnery at Barking records that the clerk to the abbess was paid thirteen shillings and fourpence, her yeoman cook twenty-six shillings and eighteen pence, while her groom cook and pudding wife get a gown a year worth two shillings. And the abbess and cellaress both had double portions of food, presumably to feed these servants.

While the lay sisters were exhorted to 'look in a spirit of true humility upon all members of the community as above them', the choir sisters were told to look upon their lowly and obscure duties 'with a secret appreciation and a certain kind of envy'. Gradually the attitude towards them changed. It became common for choir nuns in most communities to do their share of heavy work, usually under the supervision of the lay sisters. 'When I was young,' remembers a Sister of Mercy superior, 'we washed the convent walls ourselves. I get a man in now. I wouldn't let my girls do it.'

In enclosed communities the lay sisters are of course still essential: they are the inmates' hands and feet to the world outside. And no one is more staunchly defensive of the old caste-system than the lay sisters themselves. At the Carmel in London's Notting Hill, where the lay sister is still outside the enclosure, she is fiercely proud of her role, and dislikes intensely the new freedom beginning to creep into enclosed orders. 'My vocation is looking after cloistered nuns. I can't do with them running out all over the place.'

This class system is among the factors making change both slow and painful. Another is the very nature of a religious community: it is not a commercial, industrial or professional organization based on self-interest, but a state of perfection, founded because each member seeks her own sanctity — and that of others.

For most communities, it is not the young sisters who find the idea of change difficult, nor the older ones, who accept it philosophically. It is the sisters in their middle years, their forties and fifties, who find change a painful ordeal. It is hard for them to accept practices to which they are accustomed as suddenly militating against the good of the community. And it is in this age group that the superiors and mothers general of the various orders are to be found. 'The mothers general are scared,' commented one American sister. 'They don't understand how deep the changes will be.' It is certainly true: talking to me about renewal, one superior sighed heavily and said, 'They want dinner when they feel like it, that sort of thing.'

It is ironic that while the male Establishment of the Church neither eagerly seeks nor really welcomes change ('Like a mighty tortoise moves the Church of God; Brethren, we are treading where we've always trod,'), by 1948 even Pius XII was telling religious superiors to adapt or perish. Yet when, in the mid 1960s, Cardinal Suenens published his revolutionary

The Nun in the World, advocating change for orders of women, it was a mother general who, it is said, asked the Pope for his head on a plate. She was not altogether joking.

She was too late: the tide had already turned against the old ways. The rigorous apartness of convent life, the icy firmness of the rule, tilted and began to break up in the rough seas of World War II. Adaptation had to come, and the old ways never quite recovered. By 1956 the Holy See had established the Conference of Major Superiors, of mothers general and provincial who met to discuss all sorts of problems, including education. The Holy See had wanted a priest as president, but the women refused and elected instead the mother general of the Adrian Dominicans. The Sister Formation Conference devised a curriculum of study for religious to encourage communities to train their women to professional standards.

Religious women were beginning to speak out. 'The totally regulated life,' declared Sister Charles Borromeo Muckenhirn, the best-known woman theologian in America, 'is not human, especially under the pressures built into modern life.' 'I want to live a religious life,' insisted a French nun, 'but not in a medieval way.' By now, even some of the men of the Church – though not the more hidebound – were beginning to come down on the side of change. A French bishop declared that his nuns were tied by their rule and hampered by the habit. 'Religious life seems like a cage – they cannot go out and fight the enemy where he is, outside.' An Italian bishop accused his sisters of 'proceeding at the same old sedate trot', with no idea of the rapidly changing conditions outside. 'They are sleeping through the time for action.'

In 1962 when the Second Vatican Council opened in Rome 2600 cardinals and patriarchs, archbishops and bishops assembled under Pope John. 'We are going,' he said, 'to shake off the dust that has collected on the throne of St Peter since the time of Constantine and let in some fresh air.' Pope John did not last out the Council, but under the Curia, the cardinals who govern beneath the pope, the council continued as Pope Paul was elected.

Then, in accordance with their instructions to return to

their sources, religious orders looked to the pioneering spirit of their founders. Behind the convent walls there was much prayer and heart-searching about the future. Hundreds of different orders considered how they might remodel their way of life to fit more usefully into the world. They saw Vatican II as a green light, and responded eagerly. There were renewal workshops and community discussions. Professors of canon law and moral theology were invited to give lectures. The rule and the books of customs were rewritten.

One of the first orders to start modernization was the American Sisters of Loretto at the Foot of the Cross. Their mother general was Sister Luke Tobin, the only American nun to attend Vatican II. The order gave up the habit, and moved into work it considered more relevant than the original teaching, nursing, and orphanage jobs. Nuns began to work with drug addicts and the Job Corps; they made themselves part of the community in a new way.

For others, change was harder. Not every community made the jump to modern life so successfully: one Anglican community now expresses some regrets over their decision to close down their embroidery school and send the sisters out as chiropodists.

The Italian and Spanish orders in particular face a two-fold problem. First, the women of these countries are, as one Spanish sister carefully puts it, 'not advanced'. They feel, in the words of an Italian nun, that 'here, there are always the regulations. We would not be the first in Italy, we would not lead the way: we have to be so quiet all around the Pope.' In these countries today the nuns are still heavily veiled, the grilles still firmly in place.

Some orders are quite simply reluctant to change. 'Religious life,' remarked a French nun sadly, 'used to be a sort of pinnacle.' A middle-aged sister regretfully agrees with her. 'It was a very rigid life, but clear as daylight what you should and should not do. Now it isn't so clear, there's continual flux and adjustment. You have to learn to interpret independence in the right way, freedom in the right way, liberty in the right proportion.'

That women have always found it hard to interpret the

rules is confirmed by Father Gilbert Volery, who is secretary
to the Conference of Major Religious Superiors in Britain.
'Women religious know the laws better than men, often
enough. But they cannot reason with them – they take them
en bloc.' He ascribes this to their lack of training in philosophy
and theology.

This difficulty is exacerbated by the fact that in many
convents the decision-making machinery is beginning to
change. The role of superior is being looked at and found
wanting. Many communities have decided to replace her with
an elected president, or an executive officer. In American
convents there are even chairnuns. The superior's position
is no longer one of unquestioned power: she is expected not
to be a policy-maker but an implementer, carrying out
decisions taken by the councils and co-operating with other
people. 'I've never made an individual decision,' says Sister
Barbara, who heads the huge American Maryknoll order.
And superiors are getting younger: Sister Barbara herself is
forty-seven, while the average age in her community is
fifty-one.

In some places the superior has gone both in name and role.
Indeed, her image has become so tarnished that many orders
have dropped the term 'mother house' altogether, and now
refer to their 'house of formation' or 'head office'. Orders
which had no particular plans for abolishing the role of
superior found they did so perforce, like the Sisters of Charity
of Nazareth, founded in Kentucky. They decided to renew
by forming several small communities and discovered that
no one would accept such responsibility for a group lest she
be misinterpreted as assuming the role of superior. Other
orders deliberately decided to have a team in place of the
superior. This happened to the mother general of the English
Congregation of Our Lady of Sion, and she was absolutely
delighted. It proved, she said, that she had been doing the
work of four people.

In really small groups, the need for a superior disappeared
automatically. 'We're missing it,' says a nun living in a
house of five. 'It was nice in a way that the superior spoke
for everybody. You have to pay for liberty.'

Even where the mother superior does exist in a more or less unchanged situation, attitudes towards her have undergone a transformation. 'Mother — ' said a pretty Anglican, 'she's the peg on which we can hang things.'

Another problem which hinders change is the generation conflict. 'We're more open to ideas now,' says a forty-year-old sister in an Episcopalian community, 'but we've got a long way to go in certain pockets of resistance. At a recent chapter I was very conscious that the young group weren't looking to the mother to suggest ideas. They wanted independence of thought and action. And they were genuinely suffering because they were being denied it. And the older group, I could tell, were thinking, "Why should they have it all their own way?" '

There is no doubt that the older sisters are afraid of stepping out of line. They have a certain conception of obedience which does not question accepted customs. Of such women, Cardinal Suenens gently observed, 'Seen in this light, any innovation seems doomed in advance.'

In such congregations, the young occasionally attempt blockbuster tactics. A thirty-year-old American Sister of Charity says: 'There were enough of us in the order to say, "Look, we have to go where we want to go, because the Church and the order are not relating to social needs." Twenty-four of us formed a Committee on Renewal and Experimentation, and we hashed out a policy to present to the general chapter meeting, demanding progress and change. The majority were still conservative, but they weren't organized into a power group.'

Along with the total authority of superiors, the absolute obedience they once demanded has vanished too. The pattern of day has become more relaxed, the rule amended to fit with differing timetables. Sisters are encouraged to go out to clubs or lectures or extra-mural classes. They are able to catch up on sleep they miss, and make their private prayers when they choose, so long as they fulfil a certain amount in a week. 'The accent now is on personal responsibility,' explains

sister two years away from her final profession. 'Each person
works out what she needs in time of prayer.'

For many convents formal recreation has also been relaxed:
have been at recreation in one Catholic community where a
whole roomful of elderly sisters sat upright on hard chairs
happily watching a children's puppet programme on colour
television. Not all have softened, though. Some orders still
make it obligatory to take recreation as a community exercise,
and in numerous houses a book is read aloud to sewing sisters.

One change that met with mixed feelings is the relaxation
of silence. Several houses I visited, having found that living in
community is far more difficult where free speech is permitted
('Now we have to cope with a lot of people's problems and
difficulties'), plan to reintroduce at least a partial return to
the rule of silence.

Other changes are so slight as to seem to outsiders scarcely
worth mentioning. It is hard, for instance, to realize the
difference a telephone makes to an isolated community.
Other freedoms struck many sisters themselves as outrageous
when they were first introduced – the possibility of going to a
cinema, for instance, or smoking a cigarette.

Some changes are undoubtedly for the better; others have
probably been made too hastily. Too many communities have
needlessly flung away centuries of tradition in a desperate
attempt to adapt rapidly, and it has recently become apparent
to many orders that the more they strive to modernize, the
fewer entrants they get. Figures published in Britain show
quite clearly that the moment habits were adapted and
nuns made themselves hideous by cutting off the bottoms of
their habits, vocations dropped. Oddly enough, the reaction
to such modernization for at least some women in America
is just as traditional as it is in Europe. 'I would have joined the
Maryknollers,' said a cheerful American girl to me, her face
framed in a monastic wimple, 'only I wanted to wear a habit.'

The habit remains the most potent symbol of religious life.
'The bridge that takes you over into convent life,' says one
Belgian sister, talking of her time as a novice, 'is a sort of

romanticism. Particularly about the habit.' The nun's clothe
are important. If she wears a habit she has chosen to be 'a sig
of God in the world'. She is announcing exactly what she is.

It is, however, an announcement that increasingly larg
numbers of sisters are flatly refusing to make. 'I don't believe,
says Marie Keegan of the Belgian Ladies of Mary, 'that when
walk down the street in a black habit, people will say, "Ther
goes a visible witness of God." Hell, no.'

A young American sister, Liz Thoman, with long hai
flicked up at the ends, blue eyeshadow, pink lipstick an
handfuls of rings, sees no reason not to wear sexy, allurin
clothes. 'I will not hide behind a false front in order to b
"not available". The biggest thing is your own response, an
your availability from your response. In California, no matte
what you wear, people are going to stare at you. I can't kee
from being who I am.'

This attitude is a dramatic break with tradition, fo
distinctive clothing has always been part of the religious life
In the old monastic orders men and women wore virtually th
same clothes: robe, scapular and sandals, with the additio
of a veil for women and a hood for men. These garment
have a beauty of their own, a quality of timelessness an
simplicity. They are also highly suitable for the life for whic
they were designed: nothing could be more practical tha
full-length serge in cold cloisters and stone-floored cells i
November. These clothes came to be seen, by nuns as wel
as lay people, as religious in themselves. So identified wer
they with the essence of a vowed life that 'taking the vei
became another term for entering. The original function c
the veil – protecting the wearer against the evil eye an
devils – has long been lost, and early in Christianity it becam
a sign of constancy. At the time of Tertullian a bride wore
betrothal veil from the moment she was first spoken for unti
the wedding day, to symbolize fidelity.

Even in the early communities, the rules of dress were no
always strictly observed. In 1397 the nuns of Nun-Monkto
in Yorkshire were visited by the archbishop of Richmond
who accused the prioress, Margaret Fairfax, of allowin
various kinds of fur – especially grey – to be worn in her house

He objected to the wearing of silk garments, silk veils, finger rings and embroidered or ornamental jupes. And as late as the sixteenth century, several convents found it necessary to specify in the rule what must *not* be worn. At Syon, the Bridgettine house on the Thames, a document from 1500 says that the mistress of the wardrobe shall make clothes 'which shall not be over curious but plain and homely, without wearing of any strange colours of silk, gold or silver, having all things of honesty and profit and nothing of vanity after the rule, their knives unpointed and purses being double of linen cloth, and not silk'. At the same time, though, she was charged with providing 'mantel furres', fox skins in particular being mentioned. In the nearby convent of Godstow at about the same time, the nuns were warned that 'linings of dyed woollen shall not be worn; nor red dresses, nor other unseemly clothes wide at the side.'

Many nuns and sisters today are finding clothes an increasing problem as attitudes change within the orders. When, for instance, Mother Mary Joseph founded her English Vocation Sisters, she put her sisters in calf-length skirts, much to the chagrin of the orders with whom she was working. 'They said we lowered the dignity of religion by the length of our skirts. Now some of them are shorter than ours.' But even if Mother Mary Joseph is prepared to shorten skirts, she is determined to stick by her dark green habit. 'The Vatican Council said the nun must be a sign in the world. How can she be, if the world doesn't see she's a nun?' She also sees the habit in purely practical terms. 'We have made a vow of chastity, and I do think when a religious sits down, you shouldn't be able to see up her skirt.'

There are other positive advantages to the habit. 'You say to yourself, well, thank God I don't have to worry what I'll put on tomorrow. It's the same tomorrow as it'll be in another hundred years' time.' Another nun finds the habit a safeguard against herself. 'Scratch the surface and I'm just as open as any woman to the distraction of wanting this kind of hairdo, this colour dress.' It is a small sacrifice, they consider, in exchange for so much: one nun remembers that four months before she entered, she bought a scarlet suit. 'I love scarlet.

It costs you to give that up for black and white. And it should cost – that was being a woman.'

The habit is also seen as a badge of authority, which would otherwise be lost: 'Would you take so much notice of a plainclothes policeman?' A sister working with disturbed adolescents felt: 'The boys needed someone to look up to, and the habit proved I was genuine. They could understand me doing this work for God. What they hated was the idea of someone doing it for them. So they accepted me more readily than the social workers.' The same feeling was expressed by the young lay social worker working with girls who had been through the police courts on drug offences and were sent to her on probation. 'Those girls were impossible – I couldn't get a word out of them. Then I started taking them, two at a time, down to the sisters. The results were fantastic: the girls knew the nuns weren't being paid to be interested, that they really cared.' By the same token, the habit can provide protection: one of the Little Sisters of the Poor, the feminine branch of the order founded by Charles de Foucauld, says: 'We couldn't go to some of the places we do if we didn't wear it. If you're living in a slum among Moslems in Algeria, working in local jobs, they'd think it very odd if they couldn't see what you are. And although it's true sometimes people are hostile to religion, we want to go in as religious – and break down those barriers.'

There is a protective aspect to the habit, though this would seem to be failing a little at present: several American nuns wearing it have been mugged and had their handbags snatched. It remains, to a degree, an extra safeguard for the nuns themselves. 'I saw those sisters,' said one superior of a highly conventional order, 'laughing out loud, uncontrolled. Now you couldn't do that, in a habit. You know all the time who you are.'

One nun advanced a practical reason for travelling in a habit: the fact that in the United States nuns can fly clergy rates if they wait for standby seats. 'And if you're not in a habit, it's hard to be identified.' The same applies in parts of South America, where religious are allowed a ten per cent reduction in fares, though there, claims a sister, 'it's to get you on the plane so it doesn't go down.'

Older sisters in particular cling to the habit. They have neither the means of dressing themselves properly nor the figures to get any sort of pleasure out of current fashion. 'At seventy-five I don't have enough hair to go without a veil.' An Anglican superior finds the habit the most comfortable garment she has ever worn. 'It's made to fit and it's not too tight. Having been in the forces with a hard hat and a collar and a belt tied to give you as much waist as you could manage, I'm much happier in this.' The majority of her age group do not even want to shorten their ankle-length hemlines: 'At the moment we can get away without stockings.' And they are very conscious that the habit is a great disguiser of age. One ex-convent schoolgirl says she was amazed when she made a return visit not long after leaving to find a lot of ageing women in baggy skirts instead of the gracious nuns she remembered.

There are increasing advantages in the habit now that nuns are more and more invited to social occasions. The head of one training college, whose order was half into secular clothes, was invited to attend a civic dinner on behalf of the college: 'I felt it ridiculous to buy an evening dress for one occasion. I was far better off in the habit.' Then, too, it gives quite a lot of immediate information about the sister who wears it. From her habit it is possible to tell a woman's order, the type of work she probably does, and often even her nationality. Some of them are quite explicit about the allegiance of the order they represent. The Bridgettine nuns, in their muted grey habits, wear a white linen wimple, veiled in black, with the crown of white linen bearing a cross with five red drops of blood.

Some feel the advantages the habit gives them are unfair: 'When you're wearing it, you've got instant, easy respect. It would take me *years* to earn the respect I get just by having a veil on my head.' This is confirmed by the superior whose argument for preserving the habit is: 'You lost prestige at once in a poor house if you put on secular clothes. I can ring the bell in any poor home and I'm let in at once: you're one of the sisters, you're accepted.'

Yet often, the work a sister is doing might be hampered by

religious clothing. One Anglican sister who accompanied a group of chaplains to the Munich Olympics with the British teams, says that at first the habit really erected a barrier. 'If I hadn't worn it, an awful lot of time would have been saved.'

'It's kind of spooky,' claims an American, 'to be dressed as a nun when people don't care what nuns are.' This is something missionary sisters often find. In Nigeria, for instance, even native sisters now wear short dresses and bright headscarves because the people, often Moslem, would immediately reject them in the habit. 'Children and dogs,' says an Anglican sister, 'are put off by black.' That the majority of nuns and sisters still have black habits is another relic of former beliefs. For although black was the colour of mourning, again symbolizing the death of the religious to the world, it was equally worn because of the ancient belief that, cloaked and veiled in black, human beings were invisible to the spirits and therefore free from evil molestation.

Clothes are important to women as a way of expressing individual personality and taste, as well as background – and a woman in uniform is denied all three possibilities. They also give a psychological fillip at times, which is why one of the worst things about the old conventual habit was not being able to change it. A nun might start her day at six in the morning, do a hard day's work, and then go to a meeting in the evening: all she could do would be wash her face and put on a fresh linen band. 'It felt very nice to have secular dress,' says one American Loretto sister. 'You feel much more feminine and clean.' Then, too, the more open and varied a sister's life became, the more she needed change. 'To have just one dress for classroom, sports, Eucharist, cooking, shopping, travel, formal dinner, and public concert, may seal off for many women a good exhaust valve,' feels another American.

On the whole, the more sophisticated the work of the sister, the more eager she is for change. Nuns attending secular universities, for instance, had a hard time. 'It was a bitter experience, getting used to the students in my habit. You were supposed to conform, you felt caged in. I wanted to say, "Oh, for God's sake, I'm a real person."' Another sister was the only nun in the mathematics faculty. 'I was the centre of attention, and they were extremely nice. But all the same, you are different.' Sometimes they even came across active objections. 'Why,' asked a lecturer in philosophy of an American sister, 'must you shout at me that you're a sacred person?'

The voluminous clothes do have an unfortunate effect on the beholder. 'They suggest,' claims a nun who is also a psychiatrist, 'smugness and self-righteousness. They enclose the nun from the touch of others.' Another sister feels that 'the habit cuts me off from society. I hate the fact that people make assumptions about us – such as that we're not allowed to talk to men.' But the clothes of a woman in religion were never intended to have this effect.

Ancrene Riwle, the thirteenth-century directive for anchoresses, was quite explicit about the role of the habit and quoted St Paul: 'Keeping oneself unspotted from this world . . . in this lies religion: not in a wide hood or a black cape, not in a white rochet or a grey cowl.'

The founders and foundresses – of whatever period – followed this teaching, and when they began their orders they merely wore the clothes of their day, choosing for their convents what was available and commonly worn: this was true until the nineteenth century and the Gothic revival. They never anticipated that such clothes would come to be accepted as part of the rule itself, so that any change, any modification, was unthinkable. With the result that today there are still nuns walking around dressed exactly like widows in the 1840s, bonnet, cape and all. 'It's very dignified and beautiful,' comments a young sister now in secular dress, 'but it looks like a theatrical costume.' 'Stylized costume dolls,' snaps an American sister scornfully.

The Notre Dame sisters, an early-nineteenth-century order, until very recently wore virtually unchanged the peasant dress of their French foundress. In their Lancashire house, says one, it looked 'incongruous'. It had a cross-over bodice and a gathered skirt in black serge. The bodice was pinned with the nineteenth-century equivalent of a safety-pin, a long steel pin which not only became increasingly difficult to purchase but was also dangerous to use. 'You had to learn how to put them in without jabbing yourself.' Press studs would have been easier, cheaper, and more comfortable – but the foundress did not mention press studs . . . Equally bizarre were the buttons of the Society of the Sacred Heart. The order was founded in France just after the Revolution, and the habit was finished with many tiny engraved buttons, the exact design and size of which was laid down by the foundress. In England, these became increasingly difficult to obtain, and eventually they had to be ordered specially from France at enormous cost. 'Hardly,' comments a superior, 'in line with religious poverty.'

Some of the odder dress styles had been curious even when they were first worn, and quite often represented the ideas of suitable fashion held by the male advisers to the various orders. The Sisters of the Most Holy Cross and Passion, for example, founded to help working girls in the industrial areas of Manchester and Bolton, were enlightened enough to wear secular dress when going to teach in the schools. But they wore, in the mid-nineteenth-century, a long black mantle, a large black straw bonnet and voluminous black crêpe veiling. It caused so much attention, even then, that they had to abandon it.

With clothes, as with convent rules, eccentricities began to creep in as religious orders spread from the country of their foundation. Uniformity of habit was seen as a means of binding together different houses. Every house, no matter where, wore the same habit, kept the same hours, lived in all respects an identical life. Climate was allowed to make no difference. The Immaculate Heart Sisters, arriving in San Francisco from Spain, dressed as if the Californian climate did not exist: the violet blue habit and scapular covered with the heavy mantle for chapel and feast days; the stiffened coifs ('They would be just soaked with perspiration'), the square band, soft transparent veil, and the heavy black one over it.

When the Sacred Heart nuns founded houses in South Africa and the Congo early in the twentieth century, they went out in the same hot black robes they needed for European winters. 'Finally it was recognized to be a limitation, not an advantage,' says Honor Basset. 'We were allowing local

eeds to be dictated from Rome.' And the American Mary-
noll sisters remember all too well how it felt working in
ome of the world's hottest climates in the full habit. 'The
eil fitting tightly against your head, then all those layers down
our back, the scapular and the cape.' Just one concession
vas made to the heat – the habit was in white.

By far the most elaborate parts of the habit were the
ollars and headdresses. 'We had to have twelve enormous
ichus, feet and feet long, of a beautiful lawn. These had to be
emmed by hand, because you were never allowed to do
nachine work.' Then there were the caps. 'Ours had a
hing on the top to give fullness, called a caterpillar, and held
ogether with incredibly little stitches. Then there was the
rill. It was the length of a room, of fine gauze that was
irtually impossible to sew. It had to have a centimetre hem
nd be whipped on a very flat needle with a cord. As you went
hrough it, you pulled every fifth frill until this huge length
f material was the length of your face. Then this had to be
ewn on to the cap, and if each side wasn't exactly even it
vould be bulgy and couldn't be properly goffered on the
offering machine.'

These massive confections were totally impractical. 'You
ould never go out in the rain, the pie-crust just lay down
nd died.' And they had to be specially cared for by a woman
vho was employed by the convent to do nothing else. Each
ne took an hour and a half to starch, and she did sixty every
ortnight. 'We knew it was totally unrealistic. But we didn't
et nylon frills until 1966.'

The headdresses of many orders were bonnets with long
idepieces which were actually designed to act as blinkers,
o that the nun could only look straight ahead towards God.
These continued to be worn even when the nuns started to
earn to drive cars. One Sacred Heart sister, deputed to be
lriver, took the test endlessly until she discovered the
nstructor had no intention of passing her while she continued
o wear her headdress, since he was convinced she could not
ee a thing. And the American Immaculate Hearts were
fficially asked by the authorities to adopt a driving veil.

Headdresses came in so many layers – eight was normal –

that nuns developed a system of securing each layer to the next and simply lifted the whole thing off at night and kept it on a hatstand or a broom handle in their cell. They would then don a bonnet or a soft night coif: Sister Charlotte Klein remembers going at the end of the 1960s to an international conference held in an expensive Wiesbaden hotel. She got back to her room after a convivial dinner to find her bed turned back, with her nightdress and bonnet carefully laid out by the maid.

By this time, cropped and shaven heads were recognized as being culturally odd. The elaborate headdresses with which they were covered, like the complicated habits, were making nonsense of one of the major reasons advanced for keeping the habit: that it was simpler and cheaper than normal women's clothing. This may once have been true, but not in today's world of non-iron fabrics and simple hairstyles.

When nuns did start changing to secular clothes, their hair presented a problem. After years and years under confining headdresses, what hair they had left was in a poor state. 'Thin and ratty,' is how one woman described hers, 'and odd lengths where I'd cut it short.' Others had deep indentations above the eyebrows where for years the tight headband had rested continuously. Even going to the hairdresser was an embarrassing experience. 'I didn't know what they'd think of me or what I should ask for. I'd entered at eighteen, and I don't think I'd ever had a proper hairdo. I said to my superior, "I haven't got the courage to go in there, I feel such a fool." In the end, she had to take me in, and explain it was an experiment, and ask them to make me look presentable.'

The vanguard of those orders who have modernized started around 1967. The first extravagance to go was the pie frill round the face. Then simple dresses were adopted, still with a scapular and belt. The first nuns publicly to abandon the habit were the Sisters of Loretto at the Foot of the Cross, who were in suits by the spring of 1966. Soon afterwards the Sisters of Humility of Ottumwa, Iowa, received amazed press coverage when Sister Jean Reidy, taking her degree in philosophy at Notre Dame university, appeared in nothing more radical than black and white store-bought clothes. It was, she says, only then that people invited her to their homes. By 1970, an American sister returning after a missionary stint of ten years found a profound change: 'I went to a leadership conference of major superiors and out of 650 women, seventy-five per cent were in lay clothes: modern, professional-looking people.'

By this time the majority of orders which wanted to had at least one sister with permission to experiment with different types of suitable clothing. Currently, many of the European orders have several different sets of clothes being worn by different members of the community. One order I visited had four variations. The superior wore the full-length black habit, veil and all, the only compromise being that it was of synthetic fibre and the collar and veiling were of nylon. A teaching sister had a black, long-sleeved, mid-calf-length dress, with a back-of-the-head veil. A university chaplain was in a dark grey suit with a white blouse and no veil. And a fourth sister, setting off on holiday, wore slacks and a sweater.

But in September 1972 the Sacred Congregation for Religious and Secular Institutes issued a warning. The traditional habit might be modified to accord with practical requirements or hygiene, but might not be abolished altogether or left to the judgement of individual sisters. Although the nun must be recognizable as a religious, she is allowed to wear purely secular clothes if the nature of her work demands it, though 'even in this case the dress of religious women should always be in some way different from the forms that are clearly secular.' This letter was sent to papal diplomats around the world with a request that they ensure that the dress rules were kept in their areas. The directive was sent by Cardinal Antoniutti, showing once again that men are more determined to retain the habit than women. Abandoning the habit was one of the four points over which American Immaculate Heart of Mary sisters broke with the Church establishment. They had been given permission for one sister per house to experiment, if this was done with 'a terminal end in view'. Which meant, they discovered, 'if we promised to stop'. And in North Carolina recently Bishop Waters insisted that nuns had to wear veils, and sent an announcement to all major superiors that unless their sisters conformed, they would no longer be welcome in the schools there. The result was that out of only 110 sisters in the diocese, ten left to work elsewhere.

The churchmen who want their daughters in religion to be veiled and robed insist they do so to protect them, to preserve their modesty and chastity as much as to make them a sign of God in the world. But it is surely significant that in other societies where women are so treated, covered up and hidden from sight, it is not done out of any kind of respect but because they are scarcely seen as people in their own right. They are the property of men, and in a masculine society they are second-class citizens. No wonder the overwhelming reaction of nuns who have abandoned the habit has been that for the first time they feel they have achieved liberty.

There are, however, some arguments advanced against change which are persuasive. It is becoming increasingly obvious that attempts to 'modernize' a habit dating perhaps from the sixteenth century frequently result in women who look as if they were dressed exclusively at jumble sales. Such habits, with their billows and belts, full sleeves and fichus, simply do not lend themselves to shortening or narrowing. The worst possible advertisements for religious life are the sisters who hack three inches off their hemlines, shorten their veils into headscarves and wear thick cotton stockings and plastic shoes. They look underpaid and underprivileged – depressed drudges in dusty black. That they are aesthetically displeasing is not, perhaps, important except in so far as, like it or not, our society is a material one, and people are judged for better or worse on appearance. But what such unsuccessful updating does show is a terrible timidity. They are making a token gesture which is failing, and such compromise simply points up their inability to adapt to current needs. They would do better to scrap what so clearly is not working and start again.

It is this possibility, of course, which really frightens churchmen. It is true that, fashion being what it is, almost any contemporary fashion chosen by an order today will in ten years' time look scarcely less archaic than the original arrangement. But it is men, not women, who shudder at 'the thought of a mother superior with the latest copy of *Vogue* under her arm'. It is men, not women, who growl that, 'if you're not careful the sisters will all end up looking like nurses or air hostesses.' And it was a man, not a woman, who commented after talking to 'liberated' sisters in Paris, as they sat in their lay clothes smoking and drinking apéritifs: 'It was as if I had encountered for the first time a maiden aunt in hot pants.'

It is not difficult to find styles that will look neither flashy nor forlorn, that will not date quickly, and that will suit most wearers: like the Little Sisters of Charles de Foucauld in their blue denim dresses with matching veils, who perfectly accord with the council decree for religious on clothes that habits should be 'simple and modest, at once poor and becoming. They should meet the requirements of health and be suitable to the circumstances of time and place as well as to the service required by those who wear them.'

But there does seem to be a strong case for suggesting that religious should either stick to their original clothes where circumstance permits, or abandon them totally. There is no obvious reason why enclosed contemplatives should, as American Carmelites have done, adopt a skirt and jersey. On the other hand, it is clearly ridiculous for nursing sisters to dress, as the Poor Servants of the Mother of God did until only three years ago, in heavy black serge with a blue scapular and huge buttoned-on oversleeves. Underneath went heavy petticoats, on top a black veil and blinkered headdress, and the whole thing was finished off with heavy black shoes.

Some women, having modernized to a degree, would not dream of going a step further. Hilda Mason, a Sacred Heart nun, 'couldn't go out of black and white. So much has happened to me, walking round with the veil on. People come up and ask for prayers. Sometimes I have coins pressed into my hand for the poor box. I'm asked to put mentally deficient people off the bus at a certain street. And in Lancashire, the conductors pay your fare.'

Others are not interested in modernizing at all: they just want to get out of the habit. An English nun who abandoned it five years ago did so after thirteen years in the convent. One morning she was walking in a park when she saw a young couple embracing on a bench. As she approached they tore themselves apart and sat with their eyes cast down in guilt. 'I realized that what my clothes were saying to them was that I was a representative of God, of Christianity, and therefore had a hatred of things like this. I felt so terrible, I wanted the crocuses to go back into the ground. I – or at least my clothing – was saying that life, vitality, sexuality, were dangerous and possibly dirty. That's what my *clothes* were saying, despite my personal beliefs.' Her community was already discussing change, and she returned to the convent and said: ' "I won't wear the habit for a minute longer." I had a very understanding superior, who gave me an open cheque. I couldn't go to the shops in my habit, so I put on some very odd old clothes which I found, and went out looking extremely queer.' She took herself straight to Oxford Street, to the first shop she saw, which happened to be the department store, Bourne and Hollingsworth. 'I bought a pinafore dress, an ill-fitting coat, and even worse shoes. I wanted to look inconspicuous, and ended up looking strange.'

Abandoning the habit is an emotional experience. 'Can you imagine what I felt like,' asks one sister, 'when I took off all those voluminous garments? I felt so vulnerable, like some little creature that had been skinned.' Others found it a relief. 'It was a great revelation when I changed into ordinary clothes and people met *me* instead of a cardboard image.' And: 'I can walk into an airport terminal,' claims an American, 'and not have everyone within five hundred yards know I'm a nun.' Others still find it hard to remove the habit totally – like the German sister who opened the door to me wearing dungarees, a sweatshirt, and a veil.

Most women have encountered considerable difficulties over buying clothes, not least because of the cost: 'When I saw how prices of dresses had gone up since I entered, I wouldn't touch them with a bargepole.' The dilemma between the vow of poverty and the cost of maintaining a semi-respectable wardrobe is solved in many cases by home dressmaking and buying at sales. The smartest sister I met, an American Maryknoller in a navy and white dress with matching two-tone shoes, said the dress came from her sister, the handbag from her mother as a birthday present, and the shoes were the only new item.

Individual taste provided unexpected hazards. 'We're discovering now,' said one superior drily, 'that some people have no taste at all.' The majority appreciate that certain clothes are unsuitable. 'I could never wear a low neckline because I'm a consecrated woman,' says Eileen Gielty of Notre Dame, 'and what would people say if they saw a sister in red? It's a sexy colour, it does have this image. And we're not trying to attract people.' Another woman, who admitted red was her favourite colour, says she compromises by always having a maroon jumper.

And, of course, even when modern clothes are accepted, that is still not the end of it. In Western society the woman who does not make use of such basic 'cosmetics' as deodorants is regarded as an eccentric oddity. 'If we're going to appear as ordinary women,' insists Eileen Gielty, 'we should at least look decent.' Communities are moving towards the attitude defined by the young English Sacred Heart nun who says: 'We can use discreet make-up as long as it's not to please other people but to look like everyone else.' They are still very much aware of the reactions this provokes. 'People throw up their hands in horror,' comments a pretty young sister 'at the very idea of nuns wearing make-up. But I don't think we should live as if we were behind bars.' So far, Americans are the only nuns I have met who wear more than a soft lipstick and a lick of mascara. And they will use eyeshadow, nail varnish and perfume. They also wear jewellery and fairly dressy clothes, but with restraint. Earrings, for instance, would be worn as a 'luxury' at a public event or other formal occasion.

The superior of one European order which has just decided to go into secular clothes ('I'm glad to get out of that veil, it caused so many migraines in the past'), says that at first they thought a habit would be suitable for formal occasions, like jubilees or funerals. 'But then we decided that really we couldn't find anything that constituted so formal an occasion that a suit couldn't be worn.' Other orders have dropped a formal habit because, like the Little Sisters, they felt it an unwarranted expense to have a white habit worn perhaps twice a year.

The real revolution is that young women entering religious life now simply do not regard the habit as essential, and refuse to hide behind it. 'They want to be entirely genuine,' remarks a novice mistress, 'and to them, any sort of habit is dressing-up.' An American in dungarees and a patchwork poncho confirms this: 'You're no longer yourself. You just become "a nun", an artificial thing.'

Many conventionally-habited nuns see the new easiness of dress as unfair: 'They have the best of both worlds' is the view of one woman in her fifties. 'The freedom of the world, and the security of the convent to return to.' Others consider abandoning the habit to be nothing less than the thin end of the wedge: 'When you put on secular clothes, that's one foot out straight off.'

While most of the changes in religious life are greeted with relief — 'We were too much of a hothouse before, too artificial' — there are women for whom they are too much, and in the wrong direction. These women see freedom to eat in public and to wear pretty clothes, and the lack of rules as petty. They interpret irregular hours as instability. Father Edward Heston, Secretary General of the Sacred Congregation for Religious, the Roman overbody for all orders, says: 'You should see the stacks of mail we have from very good religious who are complaining about the excesses of renewal programmes.'

In the United States a group called Consortium Perfectae Caritatis (Perfect Charity) dedicates itself to trying to defend religious life against the 'false ideas' of freedom which have developed. These nuns, who number about a hundred, believe the Second Vatican Council has been wrongly interpreted, and they seek to follow the directives 'more accurately'. They believe that nuns should continue to wear the habit and respect the authority of the male, and consider that too many have replaced a life of prayer with a life of action.

If the Second Vatican Council went too far for them, for

others it did not go far enough. Many do not believe that Vatican II has succeeded nearly as well as it might have done. Father Andrew Greeley, an outspoken Chicago sociologist, speaks of the 'tragic mistakes' that have been made in the American Church since the Vatican Council. This, he says, released tremendous social and intellectual forces. If these forces had been properly understood and properly channelled, then there could have been tremendous creative growth.'

For some orders, the new way of life has arrived with a vengeance, like the American house where at breakfast – a meal provided by a catering company – the superior arrives in curlers to say grace. 'Good food; good meat; good God; let's eat.' Yet others are still suffering from uncertainty about which way they are going. One community, the Ladies of Mary, which started advocating renewal as early as 1956 from their mother house in Brussels, feels: 'As a congregation, we're going through the doldrums. The ground has been taken from under us. There's something to replace it, but as yet it's not crystallized under people's feet.'

'There is so much discouragement, so much frustration, so much despair in the American Church at the present time,' believes Father Andrew Greeley. Yet he believes too that somehow there will be a renewed religious life. 'An institution which has served human needs for fifteen hundred years is not likely to vanish completely: but a heavy price will have to be paid, in terms of both wasted energy and personal suffering.'

Many nuns are not sure even of that, and use harsh words of themselves: 'of *paralysing* mediocrity' was the way one young sister described women's communities today. Intelligent women feel hampered by restrictions a masculine Church still imposes upon them. 'They don't understand,' explodes Sister Charles Borromeo Muckenhirn, 'that we have to get out of ourselves. We can't sit forever and listen to our arteries harden: we have to get out of our little nunny world.' Such women feel passionately that nuns should be providing a blueprint, discovering new paths, attempting to live out the kind of life other people are not free to risk. Religious orders all too often see virtue in doing what they did well in the past. There is inertia and static rule-treading where circumstances demand change and social concern

There are still a lot of discontented women in religious life. And change comes from discontent. Thinking sisters believe their future is in hazard. 'What is happening to nuns now is what has happened to women in the last hundred years,' says Sister Honor Basset. 'The world is developing an attitude to women, and this is part of that development. Either we are going to be of use today or we are not, and if you have really got a call to serve God in today's world, you have to consider this very carefully.

'I think the feeling is that nuns must move forward or they will die out.'

7

THE NUN IN THE WORLD

I don't know what we're going toward – but it's something new.

SISTER PEARL MCGIVNEY

Most nuns are in active orders living, to a greater or lesser degree, in the world. Many are working at jobs which may be directly bound up with their community, such as teaching in convent schools or nursing in their hospitals. Others, however, are undertaking tasks which are far from the conventional work of nuns – the rehabilitation of drug addicts or the care of women in prison. And there is yet another group who are more radical still: nuns and sisters who are increasingly becoming involved in areas and activities which five years ago would have been considered unthinkable for a woman in vows.

Sister Pearl McGivney is an example of those sisters who believe, in the broader sense, that the nun's place is among those who need her. While the enclosed nuns of Carmel pray for the world's salvation, a continent away Sister Pearl is fighting for human rights.

The Coachella valley is five and a half hours' hard drive from Los Angeles, between the luxurious pools of Palm Springs and the Mexican border. It is not yet four in the morning, and already the temperature is soaring into the nineties. In the darkness, the Mexican farmworkers are out in the fields, picking the sweet grapes. earning an annual income of less than half the national poverty level of $3000.

The picket lines are out too, and Sister Pearl in her brief red skirt is with them, tramping the dirt roads round the fields, crunching underfoot the dry shells of dead locusts, and carrying the banners with the black Huelga thunderbird,

the ancient Aztec eagle with square-edged wings that Cesar
Chavez has taken as his symbol in his fight for the equality of
the Mexican workers.

All summer, the Coachella has been the scene of America's
most prolonged and bloody inter-union battle between
Chavez's tiny United Farmworkers Union and the huge, rich
and ruthless International Brotherhood of Teamsters. The
Chavez pickets want the farmworkers to strike with them
for realistic wages and decent conditions. 'Strike,' they shout
into the dark fields. 'Huelga. Vengánce, señores! Para su respecto
y dignidad! Huelga, compañeros, huelga.' Sister Pearl starts
singing 'We shall overcome', and the Teamsters retaliate by
turning up their loudspeakers to drown their voices, playing
'Bye Bye, Blackbird' full blast.

Sister Pearl, with her heavy coils of dark hair, her gentle
face and anxious eyes, looks like the last person to be involved
in this struggle. Yet two years ago she went from her New
York convent of the Sisters of St Joseph of Brentwood down to
California for three weeks to see what Cesar Chavez was
doing for the Mexican farmworkers. She never returned to
her community.

It is a strange life for a nun. The violence in the valley is
terrifying. The Teamsters want to finish off the UFW and
Chavez – they call him El Perro, the dog – and keep the farm
workers subservient and poorly paid, as they have always
been. The threats on Chavez's life come daily now, and he has a
squat bodyguard and two Alsatians for protection. The day
before I arrived in the Coachella, six Teamsters were arrested
for throwing rocks from a track at the car in which he was
travelling. While I was there a Mexican was dragged from his
car and stabbed six times with an icepick before the Teamsters
realized he was not the man they wanted. And the following
day one of Chavez's aides, a Catholic priest, was sitting in
the Trukadero restaurant when a Teamster standing 6 ft 4 in
tall came over to the table, broke the priest's nose with one
blow, and walked off. A month after this incident, a picket
at another town was shot dead from a passing car.

Sister Pearl has seen much of the violence. Everyone knows
she is a nun – she wears her habit often on the picket line.

deliberately to show the Church is on the side of the farm-workers, and the Teamsters resent her. 'I've never,' she says, 'been called a broad until now. They shout, "Sexy – you ought to be ashamed."' And not long ago there were a thousand people picketing in ten lines of a hundred each, and I was with a nurse. We got split up and found ourselves caught between two Teamsters' cars with marchers behind us. One car came alongside and a man asked, "When's the last time you worked in a field, Sister? How do you know what it's like?" Then he grabbed the flag on the car and scraped the wooden stake up my arm.'

Sister Pearl, who is now thirty-one, became interested in the movement when she was studying theology. 'Some migrants came in to talk about their situation and ask for our support. And I knew I had to do something.'

Before Sister Pearl had even heard of Chavez, she went down to Long Island, New York, where the potatoes are picked by Puerto Ricans and blacks from Florida and Georgia, and lived in the camps there with two Dominican nursing sisters. 'The thing that struck me was that they were broken men, and we were treating them like children. We were putting bandages on the wounds and giving them aspirin, but not changing anything at all. It was work of social concern, but it didn't change the system.'

Migrant farmworkers are vital to the American farm system. They move round the country, from state to state, harvesting crop after crop as fruit and vegetables ripen. The majority, like Chavez, are Mexican-Americans. Some, the Chicanos, are American-born, while others are Mexicans allowed over the border. They are open to exploitation by the growers who run the vast foodbowl that is California, in a situation that has not changed essentially since John Steinbeck wrote *The Grapes of Wrath*. In those days, it was poor whites who did the work, but now the Mexicans suffer more than they did. A minority only now becoming articulate, their presence in poverty has no place in the American dream. Often illiterate, their children receive minimal education because of the constant travelling, so they cannot better themselves. They have neither social security nor old-age pensions. They live in primitive shacks provided by the growers and pay inflated prices in food shops owned by them. And the work itself is back-breaking: stooping and bending in that blinding heat – it is impossible to continue beyond midday – usually without even the most primitive sanitary arrangements.

It is the passion which Chavez brings to this cause that made Pearl McGivney join him. 'When I first met him, I thought, he's a good man and he does his job. It's when you talk to him that you realize what a great man he is. And religion is at the heart of everything he does. I wanted work with something that was hitting at the worst problems, and the migrant workers were in the most horrible situation. I guess that's why I chose the union, because it helps people control their own lives, it gives them dignity as human beings.'

Pearl told Chavez she wanted to work for him. He said, 'What are you going to do for the people? They need medical care.' There are many accidents in the fields, not least from the dangerous pesticides the Mexicans have to use, for which protective clothing is almost never provided. But no doctor will treat a Mexican without prior payment. Over 500 accidents each year are to the children who work illegally in the fields. California law allows twelve-year-olds to do so in the holidays, but an estimated 800,000 – a quarter of the labour force – are under that age: seven-year-old girls picking strawberries, nine-year-olds spending ten hours a day in the lettuce fields.

With Chavez, Pearl developed a medical insurance plan and her job is to open clinics to serve the workers. These have to be organized and staffed, and she is also in charge of the necessary recruitment, much of which is done through personal contacts. 'We're trying to find professionals with social consciousness. And we've got great people: I never met such people in my life.' There are four permanent clinics in California with full staffs providing total care. These are in the busiest areas, and Pearl is now developing the clinic system so that mobile units can follow the farm workers as they move. She spends weeks at a time travelling from clinic to clinic. 'And I've learned how to fix a flat tyre.' When she arrived: 'I didn't know one person. Now I go an place in the state and find farmworkers, people on the staff, sisters. I always have a home. That's the exciting part about a religious living fluidly: there's always somebody there.'

But 'home' really means La Paz, the mountain headquarters of the United Farmworkers, where 250 people live, both families and single volunteers, as well as the five other nuns who are now permanent members with Pearl. There are other sisters working with Chavez – the Maryknolls from New York help the women learn child care and basic hygiene, and many nuns and priests march regularly on the picket lines and frequently get arrested for doing so. But none of the others actually live as part of the Chavez group.

The six, from various communities, have made two rooms in an abandoned hospital – La Paz used to be a sanatorium – into a living-room and a bedroom with three mattresses on the floor and white-painted walls. They clubbed together to buy a freezer for $15 out of the $5 a week each gets as a volunteer. Pearl was so delighted with this bargain she never thought to ask if it worked. Luckily it did.

When Sister Pearl decided to join Chavez, she knew two things. 'I knew that I would do it, and I knew that I wouldn't leave community.' At that time she was the only sister involved, but now apart from those with her, there are letters and phone calls constantly from sisters who want to join them. 'It's *the* form of living the religious life right now.' At La Paz there are also two brothers, one of them a Xavieran. 'Every day we all try to have prayers, and we talk. We even sing. It's very informal. And it's very real.'

Sister Pearl's own community is supporting her both morally and emotionally. 'We're all open to the possibility of a new Community of the Sisters of St Joseph out here. But the great possibility is that something completely new will emerge from this.' What she would really like is to develop a new community, of both brothers and sisters, all from different orders. 'I don't think individual communities, as one distinct from the other, is a very balanced concept today. The idea of sisters in free movement is completely new: it's something I dreamed about and hoped for from the beginning.' Although her community can ill spare her, she knows they will continue to back her: 'When we discussed it, the community said, "If this is of the Spirit, it won't fail. If it is of man, it'll fail by itself."'

One of the other sisters in Coachella is Mary Jean Friel, who joined Chavez six months after Pearl herself. A devastating girl with long brown legs under her blue denim dress, she wears tiny silver peace dove earrings half hidden by her streaky blonde hair. She does Chavez's secretarial work, but more than that she helps him co-ordinate his programme. She is with him almost always, taking notes at the meetings, answering phones, helping him meet people, fending off those he does not want to see.

Chavez is a man who seems to inspire maternal feelings in his helpers: small and quiet, for La Causa he has sacrificed his energy (and some say his health) for the last twelve years. He has given up much of his family life – his wife had all but two of their eight children in his absence.

Mary Jean decided to join him after considerable experience of the problems of migrant workers. She is a Sister of Loretto at the Foot of the Cross, a community founded in Kentucky in 1812 by a French priest. She became a sister because 'I realized I had some kind of responsibility for being so happy all my life.' Her community was asked to work with migrants in Colorado, and her job was in a labour camp looking after the welfare of the families. In 1969 she became involved in a strike with the carnation nurseries there. 'A Mexican family taught us what it meant to be non-violent, what it meant to be a striker. I didn't know really what it was all about: it just meant people I liked suffered an awful lot.' The evening before that strike ended, Mary Jean told the twenty-two sisters in her convent that there was a bad day ahead. 'Not all the sisters were for me, and some were very much against the workers. But I learned a beautiful thing. People support you even if they don't approve of what you do. I had to get up at 5.30 that morning, and when I came downstairs, a sister who had argued with me the day before had hot oatmeal waiting. She insisted that I eat it, and she told me she'd pray for me the whole day.'

Mary Jean and Pearl share an office in Coachella, on the

corner of Highway 86 and 6th Street, where a huddle of empty shops faces a petrol station and, beyond, the massive range of mountains that encloses the valley in a heat reaching 120°. The office is a large whitewashed room full of odd desks and chairs, every surface cluttered with posters and papers, banners and badges. Twelve people are sweating away despite the air-conditioning, typing, telephoning, talking. There is a knock on the door, and a short man holding his hat mutters nervously in Spanish. Sister Pearl goes out with him and unlocks the room next door: piled inside are sacks of provisions, boxes, parcels. She fills his arms, and he beams and backs out. He is a striker, and the food supplements the wage the union is paying him.

Sister Pearl's first thought when she joined Chavez was to become a transient teacher, moving with the children from place to place, getting them above the fourth grade which is the highest the average migrant child achieves. Experiments are planned with both children and adult education centres among the workers at Delano, but for the moment, 'It's more urgent to change radically the whole migrant situation. Cesar wants to end migrancy. Not today or tomorrow. But in the end.'

Chavez himself sees the sisters as a moral asset to his people. And he believes they are safer than anyone else. 'No one is going to run over a nun, you know. You'll run over a priest maybe, but not a nun.' He mimes a fierce nun: 'I dare you. Run over me.' Pearl and Mary Jean are marginally less confident of their imperviousness. Both have sat in the back of open trucks while Teamsters threw rocks at them. And they were asked by Chavez to lead 800 people in a march round one of the nearby shanty towns for fieldworkers, where many were known to be against him. 'We walked round with our banners shouting, "*Huelga*, boycott, *Viva* Chavez." It's terrifying not knowing what's going to happen – Mary Jean grabbed me by the hand.'

Both sisters are appalled by the squalid conditions under which the large families live. They enjoy talking to the women, and Pearl went to Puerto Rico specially to learn Spanish before joining the UFW, for which the Brooklyn diocese gave her a scholarship. But if they are shocked by the way the Mexicans have to live, they are prepared to share it. 'Some places we live adequately. In others it's at subsistence level. We moved into a migrant house infested with roaches and rats, and from April to May we slept on the floors. There was a toilet but it didn't have a door. Very few houses have water, and we try hard to enforce sanitary regulations.'

Their Coachella apartment is three small rooms currently shared by eight women – five sisters and three temporary volunteers who are not all members of the permanent La Paz group – in a block a short walk from the headquarters. By late afternoon the heat of the day has subsided a little, and the temperature is down to 110°. The apartment has one fan, which Pearl hastily switches on. Her community has contributed the only decoration, a green and white felt poster which says, I SHALL BE WITH YOU BECAUSE I LOVE YOU.

Most evenings, the sisters eat late, perhaps at nine-thirty, taking turns in cooking while the others bathe. Mary Jean, eating her bananas and yoghurt, observes: 'It takes mature people to be able to live like this.' She gets the milk out of the freezer and giggles. 'Even though we're all beautiful, we do have a few thorns here and there. You have to know your own limitations and work within those.'

They are strict – not rigid – about their formal religious life. There is a resident chaplain at La Paz, and two priests in Coachella. But it is hard to regulate times for prayer when you are getting up at two-thirty to join the picket lines every morning. For Pearl, 'Faith in God is my reason for living.' Yet, despite that, 'The price of religious life is loneliness. You have yourself and God. I'm convinced it's not possible unless you have a real prayer life, so you're strengthened and refreshed: it makes me more alive.' Her apparently haphazard life seems to her closer to the original concept of religious life than the current, conventional convent system. 'The founders had the mobility to follow the Spirit where it led.' And in this last year, she says that she has become much more aware of her vocation. 'I guess it's because I have to review every day who I am, and what I am. And I keep saying yes '

Sister Pearl is quite convinced that she could neither live

as she does, nor do the job she wants to do if she were not a nun. She jumps to her feet, ties a vast apron round her waist, and attacks the washing-up. 'It frees me for responding with love.'

Women like Sister Pearl and Sister Mary Jean are rare, even in the United States. But they are not unknown. Nuns are becoming concerned with politics in a way that would have been impossible before the Second Vatican Council. Until then, the Church hierarchy said categorically that politics was not the concern of any religious. A great many people still feel that way, but more and more religious in the States are beginning to feel that they cannot stand on one side and watch injustice continue.

This does not seem to be so true in Europe, where the only active political participation I came across was one lone sister who donned her habit to protest outside the Houses of Parliament at Westminster against the hedging that was going on over the bill concerning discrimination against women. In countries like Holland, where religious are in many ways liberated — I saw not a single habit there — the idea of a nun involved in political activity was greeted with blank stares.

It remains very much an American phenomenon. The militant nuns of America are into everything, from spending a month in jail to study the penal system and write a report, to issuing a statement on the unnecessary brutality of Black Panther Bobby Seale's sentence for contempt. When James Meredith was murdered in Mississippi in 1965 the negroes were forbidden to go to Montgomery in protest, and state troopers moved in with guns, tear gas, and dogs. Fifty-two nuns in full habit stood between the state troopers and the marchers: 'The troopers were afraid to club us.'

In 1971 nuns made a concerted effort to get justice for the natives of Alaska, who were being forced to sell their land to the government for oil speculation at absurdly low prices. As a result, the Justice for Alaska Natives Bill was pushed through Congress. The following year five Sisters of Charity were charged in a Louisville court with 'disorderly conduct' after demolishing a derelict house there. It was a desperate attempt to get the city to realize the dangers of 'rat-infested fire traps' in an already deprived urban area. Although the house was condemned and abandoned, the city had no plans to remove it, or similar houses surrounding it. The Sisters of Charity ended up with $10 fines – and the support of the president of the Senate of Religious in the diocese, who called it 'a courageous moral act'.

And in 1973 it was a nun who went to Wounded Knee as part of a task force following the uprising to study every aspect of the Indian situation there – from the problems of children forced to attend distant boarding-schools to the appalling housing conditions in the area.

One order deeply involved in politics is the Sisters of the Humility of Mary, a group founded in France in the mid-nineteenth century to work with the poor. They came to America as missionaries, teaching and nursing, and their range has widened to take in experimental scientists and public relations consultants: one sister is a law student in Washington who plans to educate the poor to make the law work *for* instead of against them. Two sisters have served as delegates in county conventions in Devenport, another was one of the key people working to get a candidate into the Iowa legislature, doing full-time recruiting and research. They feel such involvement is totally justified, since it concerns social issues. 'We get reforms to state and national power through the county conventions.'

It was one of their sisters, Eleanor Anstey, who became the first nun to run for the Iowa Senate. She was asked in 1972 by the citizens of Muscatine to put her name into the Democratic primary for state senator; she accepted and took the nomination unanimously. She then spent the next three months learning about the Iowa Senate, the major issues, the needs of the district, and the whole process of campaigns and elections. A colleague from her order researched her campaign, there were press releases, stickers, an advertising campaign – all on a $1000 budget. She found the experience extraordinary: 'It was a strange feeling to be driving down the highway and hear your own radio spots.' Although in the end she lost by only 4000 votes to the Republican candidate, she intends to continue in state politics. 'So many decisions, affecting the lives of thousands of people, are made in the Legislature.' She sees a real need for more women, particularly sisters who are free from political pressure and have no vested interests, to be there when decisions are made about criminal justice, the care of the elderly, prison reform, the environment, revenue sharing. 'I saw so much apathy in government. I think we've got to have more people who care.'

Another sister who agrees with her is a forty-seven-year-old member of the Dominicans in Memphis, Tennessee. Sister Mary Anne Guthrie ran for Congress in August 1974 as the first nun ever to do so. A Democrat, she faced four men in the primary. She wants to bring women to the forefront of government because 'I do not think woman, herself, has recognized her own potential. I would like to see more women in leadership positions.' She sees no conflict between her religious profession and being a member of Congress.

If more and more sisters are concerned with social reform through participating in the established political and legal systems, there are also increasing numbers who see no mileage in such peaceful methods. Of all political issues, American religious have reacted most strongly to those where war is involved. It was in protest against the war in Vietnam that twelve Anglican nuns in New York received communion in St Patrick's Cathedral and then lay down in the aisles wearing white sheets bearing the words: ANOTHER PERSON DEAD IN INDOCHINA. It was in protest against American troops being sent into Guatemala in 1966 and 1967 that Marjorie Melville, the half-Spanish Maryknoll nun, and others doused draft cards with home-made napalm and ignited them. Thus, along with the Berrigan brothers, America's rebel priests, she became one of the Catonville Nine.

In the Baltimore courtroom she spoke of American terrors; the dropping of napalm; planes missing their targets; the bombing of peasant villages. 'I know these people,' she said. 'They are not statistics to me. They are just looking for a piece of land to support their children. They are not trying to overthrow the United States. That is the last thing in their minds. I wanted to make as effective a protest as possible to US military intervention across the world, not only in Vietnam, but in Guatemala where I had seen it.'

Marjorie Melville was imprisoned in March 1970 for two years.

If such behaviour appears unlikely for a woman who has vowed her life to God, who is concerned more with things of the spirit than the body, more with the next life than with this, it is worth remembering that historically nuns have a radical tradition.

Nuns were the first 'professional' women. From the earliest times until almost the present day, a Catholic woman had only two honourable choices open to her: 'a husband or a wall'. She could either marry, produce children and run a home for her family, subject to her husband. Or she could choose the convent walls.

In the first days of Christianity religious houses for women were centres of learning and provided the only education available to girls. In the sixth century the Bishop of Arles, Caesarius, persuaded his sister Caesaria to leave her Marseilles convent and rule over one he was founding: the nuns, he said, should learn to read and write, to spin and weave their own clothes, to nurse the sick.

The religious houses of northern France were famous for education. They were the finishing schools of the aristocracy, and young women were sent there from England as well as from France. Towards the end of the sixth century Tours was known as the predominant religious and cultural centre of the country. And in Poitiers a settlement of 200 women was established by Radegund, a woman who was born a Thuringian – a German race – captured as booty by a Frankish king and made the fifth of his seven wives. She was extremely literate: the poet Fortunatus said in his life of her that 'she refused to take meat unless her mind be satisfied. All pious teaching is food to her.'

Nor was it only French convents which cultivated such

women. One English nun, Lioba, who was educated at Wimborne in Dorset and left England around 748 to settle in Germany, did so at the request of Boniface, who wrote that 'her reputation for holiness and virtuous teaching has penetrated across wide lands and filled the hearts of many with praise of her.' We know from the biography written of her by the monk Rudolf of Fulda that: 'She never laid aside her books except to pray and strengthen her slight frame with food and sleep – Old and New Testaments, grammar, liberal arts, writings of holy fathers, canonical decrees, laws of the Church. She was aware that inclination is necessary for prayer and for study, and she was therefore moderate in holding vigils. She always took a rest after dinner, and so did the sisters under her, especially in summer time; and she would not suffer others to stay up too long, for she maintained that the mind is keener for study after sleep.' Her learning brought her a busy social life. 'Princes loved her, noblemen received her and bishops gladly entertained her and conversed with her on the scriptures and the institutions of religion, for she was familiar with many writings and careful in giving advice.'

The convents of the German lands of Saxony also achieved enormous intellectual and social importance as the ruling families realized there were advantages in a union between religion and state and vied to found religious settlements. They sent their daughters there to be educated, and those who did not marry were thus assured of powerful positions, while those who left to wed often returned in later life. Herford in Westphalia was renowned for its learning: Gandersheim, Quedlinburg and Essen were all important until the Reformation. They were not only centres of artistic industry where girls learned spinning, weaving and embroidery, but they operated almost as endowed colleges for women interested in learning: religious and classical writers were studied, as well as law.

It is quite obvious why girls were so eager to enter: the boredom of life in a damp medieval castle must have been excruciating. When their fathers and brothers were away fighting, attending court, or running their estates, there would have been little for the women to do. There was almost no communication with the outside world. Books were rare and precious, and not found in private houses. It must have been a relief to be sent away to a convent, usually from the age of seven until perhaps fourteen, then considered a marriageable age. It was not until the fourteenth century that convents began to lose their importance as educational centres. They no longer kept up the standard of earlier years, though they were still providing the only education and training outside her home a woman could get, since universities ignored women. But morality was changing, the nuns were kept in stricter seclusion, and there were few women of the intellectual capacity of Lioba or Radegund.

At no time did the nuns go out to teach. Not until 1535 did Angela Merici found the Ursulines in Italy – St Ursula was the traditional patroness of girls – to teach girls and the common people; no one else had considered such work necessary. She received papal approval, but twenty years later the Holy See ordered the suppression of all female congregations not in enclosure and subject to common vows. To survive, the Ursulines acquiesced and donned the habit for the first time.

It was soon afterwards, in 1597, that two men tried again to avoid enclosure and establish free schools, this time for day pupils and boarders with the Canonesses of St Augustine. St Peter Fourier and the Blessed Alix Leclerc both wished the needs of the school to override the rules of enclosure: 'I have always thought that it was necessary to say that they were first and foremost schoolmistresses, for fear they should be thought to be religious first and foremost.'

Canon lawyers impeded them, and Pope Urban VIII rejected the idea of teaching nuns on account of a passage in St Paul: 'Suffer women not to teach.' The order continued, the work of teaching was approved, but they had, like all the others, to operate inside the ordained framework.

It was nuns, too, who became the first professional nurses. Until the twelfth century, the attitude towards disease was anything but Christian. Although people had no idea of contagion, a much later concept, they had a healthy sense of self-preservation, and anyone visibly disfigured was shunned by their family and reduced to living in filthy, degrading conditions. Nuns themselves did not work as nurses for a long time: when Gilbert of Sempringham provided, round his eleventh-century convent, homes for 'the poor, infirm, lepers and orphans', it was not the consecrated nuns who looked after them but the lay sisters, the poorer working half of the community.

But within the convents themselves there was a considerable amount of medical knowledge, as the twelfth-century writings of a German superior, Hildegard, show. Known as the 'Sybil of the Rhine', she was a well-born woman, put into the care of the nuns at Disibodenburg at seven, and professed at fourteen. She did not start writing till she was middle-aged, and most of it was about her visions. She was taken very seriously: her work was submitted to the Pope, with whom she corresponded. Archbishops, emperors, princes and dignitaries all wrote to her, often seeking advice on the most personal matters. She seems to have been a medieval sob sister. Two of her books are on medicine, and are quite remarkable for their age. One of them, *Physica*, is on the nature of man and the various elements of creatures and plants. It is an amalgam of sensible advice and primitive superstitition. She wrote about plants and fish, animals and birds, stones and metals. The mulberry tree is described, and she tells how a decoction of its leaves cures skin diseases. Prunes, she says, are good for a dry cough. Pork is indigestible and to be avoided in sickness. The properties of soda are described – and so are those of the unicorn. For gout, she recommends carrying about a dead frog. Drinking water from a cypress bowl rids one of devils. On the other hand, eating raven's flesh encourages thievery. Many of her remedies were for indigestion, coughs, fever, delusions and leprosy. She recommends bathing in various concoctions of leaves, which differ scarcely at all from current knowledge of the curative properties of herbs.

Convents already had formal rules for caring for the sick. The nuns of Syon had a document which reads: 'Often change their beds and clothes. Give them medicines, lay to

them plaisters and minister to them meat and drink, fire and
water, and all other necessaries night and day, as need
requires after the counsel of the physicians, and precept of
the sovereign; do not be squeamish in washing and wiping
them by avoiding them. Be not angry nor hasty nor impatient
though one have the vomit, another the flux, another the
frenzy and now sings, now cries, now laughs, now weeps,
now chides, now is frightened, now is wroth, for there be
some sickness vexing the sick so greatly and provoking them
to ire that the matter drawn up to the brain alienates the
mind. And therefore those in attendance should have much
patience with them, that thereby they may secure an everlasting crown.'

All this, of course, referred to nursing their own sick; all
nuns were still forbidden to leave their enclosures. The first
order able to undertake public nursing, to go to people's
homes and look after them, was Vincent de Paul's Daughters
of Charity. The peasant priest was horrified by the conditions
of the underprivileged in seventeenth-century France. There
was work to be done founding hospitals, sheltering abandoned
children and feeding the starving.

Early in the seventeenth century St Francis de Sales, the
Bishop of Geneva, and St Jane Frances de Chantal, a rich
widow, wanted to start a congregation to do similar work,
visiting the poor in their homes – hence their name, 'Our
Lady of the Visitation'. But the bishop of Lyons, where they
began, was a conservative man who argued that the presence
of unenclosed nuns in his town would lead to scandal and all
kinds of difficulties. Solemn vows and enclosure were the
inevitable result. But Vincent de Paul, with much the same
ambitions, exercised 'holy cunning' and won the battle. He
avoided the rigours of canon law by sheer diplomacy. He
called the institute a 'company' and the novitiate a 'seminary'.
Their residence was not a convent but a 'house' and he
appointed not a superior but a 'sister servant', while the
sisters were not called religious but 'daughters of the parish',
and dressed in grey serge like the common people.

Vincent de Paul and his Daughters of Charity made the
breakthrough from enclosure to a life in the world, an active

postolate. By the nineteenth century, ten Catholic Sisters of
Mercy from Bermondsey and eight Anglicans from Lydia
Sellon's Park Village Sisterhood, as well as five nuns of the
Company of the Faithful Virgin, went to Constantinople
with Florence Nightingale at a time when no decent woman
would nurse because of the reputation nurses had for being
both drunk and dirty. Yet these nuns not only braved the
sea journey but tended British troops suffering terrible
wounds from the battlefield of Balaclava, living in poor conditions to do so. Florence Nightingale, though she reckoned
them among the best of her nurses, did not find them easy
to get on with. The conduct of one, she wrote, 'has
been neither that of a Christian, a gentlewoman, or even a
woman'.

It is interesting that the areas of medicine in which religious
women today are particularly successful are not conventional
nursing at all, but coping with the diseases of our time:
addiction to alcohol and drugs.

The Maryknoll Sisters of St Dominic in New York started
helping hard-core heroin addicts in the 1960s. Three sisters
moved into a small apartment in Greenwich Village. They
were available at all hours of the day and night, and their
phone rang constantly. Between them, they had over 1000
addicts in treatment within two years, under the supervision
of an expert.

Working with addicts even earlier was the Anglican
Community of St Mary the Virgin, an English order started in
Berkshire in 1848, when the local vicar housed 'women of
the streets' in two cottages while he trained them to be
schoolteachers.

Spelthorne St Mary in Surrey is one of their houses, a
three-storeyed Georgian manor set in a landscaped park. The
box hedges are neatly trimmed, the azaleas flourish, and swans
decorate the willow-fringed lake. The cosy parlour has water-
colours on the walls and tulips in the vases. Creamy carpets
cover the highly polished floors. The whole house radiates
calm, which is undoubtedly one of the reasons for its success:

Spelthorne St Mary is rated Britain's most successful ur
for 'drying out' women alcoholics.

When it was opened, when nothing was being done to he
such women, no sympathy was given to alcoholics. Alcoholi
Anonymous did not exist. The Sisters of St Mary the Virg
recognized the need and responded to it: their work w
revolutionary. Soon they started admitting drug addict
In those days addiction was often to opium preparations whi
had been prescribed for medical relief. Addicts to morphi
and heroin purely for sensation did not appear in numb
until between the two World Wars, and when synthet
drugs began to flood the market in the 1950s, Spelthor
St Mary found its drug-addicted patients increasing. The
continue to increase, while the average age of the patien
falls.

If the sisters' work is less revolutionary now, it is no le
successful. Their high cure rate is due partly to the length
time for which they continue to supply help, and partly to th
warmth of atmosphere and family feeling which the siste
themselves provide. This, they feel, is vital for the recove
of their patients. It is not just the budgerigars chirping in th
windows, or the names on the doors of the sisters' rooms
STANDFAST, WELCOME, HOPE – but something the patien
feel. 'The sisters,' says a bleached-out blonde woman, 'real
give you a lot of themselves.'

Two-thirds of the patients there at any one time a
alcoholics. They are largely middle-aged women whose ma
riages have gone wrong and who found themselves drinki
too much sherry. The other third, the drug addicts, a
mostly middle-class too: the hospital nurse who under stre
started taking the patients' barbiturates; the twenty-yea
old girl whose parents live abroad and who needed 'help
grow up'; the eighteen-year-old who got involved with
drug group.

At lunch, taken at long tables, the patients sit quietly
their skirts and baggy cardigans, chatting about the coa
outing for that afternoon. One woman, younger, has a fix
stare and an aggressive manner. A pretty girl in a pi
flowered mini-dress shows dimpled knees. Next to her

fragile tousle-haired girl in tight cords remains aloof and silent. Later, in the corner of the large sitting-room, she shouts to herself, desperate, shrill cries.

A dark woman wearing pink earrings was a nurse herself. 'I'd been to six places before this. At first, I found it very hard to get through to the sisters. I found the habit a barrier. But possibly I didn't want to be helped at the beginning. Then I found they wait for you to talk to them. So when I get the craving I can tell them because I *want* to tell them. Before, nobody could make me talk.' She is particularly conscious that in hospital 'you're just a case number. And the case is more important than the person. Here, they really want to establish you as a person.' She believes she has a much better chance here than in the special unit of any hospital. 'Some places, they don't give you any dignity, but here they build you up again. They give you self pride.'

'They treat you,' confirmed another woman 'as an adult human being: they don't talk down to you.' Women who arrive at Spelthorne invariably need this more than anything. Quite a few come direct from Holloway, the women's prison in London, on probation, in which case the Home Office pays for their stay. Often they have stolen to pay for the drink or drugs they cannot afford to buy. These patients will usually have been withdrawn from drugs already, or detoxicated if they drank. But those who come on the recommendation of a doctor may not necessarily have gone through the period of withdrawal, and may face a difficult time. With-drawal effects can be very serious, and they may well have frequent fits. They will be automatically given a period of bed-rest in the infirmary for days, or weeks if necessary, and given an intensive course of Vitamin B to repair their damaged nerve-tissues.

As soon as possible the newcomers join the life of the house, and their time is filled up by the sisters. This is vital because, as the sister-matron points out, 'We meet with a lot of apathy: that's why a lot of these people have got into this state.' Partly for this reason, partly because patients must be protected from access to alcohol or drugs, the regime is strict. No one goes out for the first month except in the company of a sister. After that, patients can go home for weekends if they are progressing well.

Days start with eight o'clock breakfast, after which they join the 'Pill Queue' at the dispensary for prescriptions. Then the house sister organizes housework from nine-thirty, helping in the kitchen or garden before going to occupational therapy for an hour. After lunch and a cup of tea together everyone washes up, patients and sisters. In the afternoon there is recreation, when they are encouraged to take classes in pottery, singing or flower-arranging. In the craft room they paint, sew, or weave raffia baskets. They can go shopping with the sisters, use the library or the games room, play darts or watch TV.

There are usually twelve sisters at Spelthorne. Some are state-registered nurses, one a doctor, others have perhaps forty years' experience as club leaders. They are all considered suitable for the work they do by Dr Max Glatt of St Bernard's Hospital, Southall, one of Britain's leading authorities on the problems of addiction, and consultant at Spelthorne. Under him are the psychiatrists and specialists who visit regularly. There are also secular nurses and a full domestic staff.

The main aim of everyone at Spelthorne is to rehabilitate the 'whole person', to integrate her again into society. The sisters believe that the whole personality is damaged by alcoholic or drug excess, and that treatment must therefore be physical and mental, spiritual and social. Rehabilitation is going on all the time: the housework and the basket-weaving are all part of it. But there are more basic and concentrated efforts. The sisters give personal counselling to those who want it: 'It's really a question of getting to know them, so they feel they can really open up for us. We need this specific knowledge to know how to link them on when they leave us.' As one patient puts it, 'You might go on an outing and find you're sitting with one sister and, somehow, words come out.'

Another important feature of the rehabilitation process that relatives can come and stay for a night or two in the guest-house, which is a tremendous help in rebuilding family relationships. 'Reconciliations can take place far more easily says one of the sisters, 'in comfortable and neutral surroundings than in the emotion-charged atmosphere of the home, or even in Spelthorne with all its associations of illness and treatment.'

Each afternoon after tea there is group therapy. Some of the groups are taken by the doctor and the infirmarian, others by the sisters. It is an encounter, getting to know each other, getting to know people as a group and to coalesce as a group, getting the people to know themselves. The sisters generate all the gaiety they can. There are parties for every occasion. They have a large costume wardrobe, do a pantomime every Christmas, and, occasionally, a Victorian melodrama, with one elderly sister famous for her roles as gay young blades. They book a year ahead for films to show in the evenings. They do everything possible to get the patients through the day without despair: 'Depression is what may have started them off on an addiction.' And as soon as they are well enough, the sisters encourage them to take jobs in the nearby town of Staines, so that they can meet testing situations while still under care. Some work in department stores, others can learn shorthand and typing for office work. The sisters are anxious that the women shall be able to keep away from the 'dangerous' places of their past. But this comes during the last part of their stay at Spelthorne. The ideal length of time is a year, and they hope people will stay at least six months. 'We can't do very much with less than that.'

Leaving is probably the hardest part of the cure. 'A lot of people start producing symptoms when it's time to go because they're afraid of facing life outside.' But it is the older ones who are difficult to place when they leave. One middle-aged woman on drugs had a stroke and was severely paralysed. It took over a year to get her into a rehabilitation centre. It is partly this problem that prohibits the sisters from taking anyone over sixty-five, after which they feel it is not really possible to help. Many of their patients are private, but the fees are extremely realistic: there is no profit margin for the community.

It is quite impossible that Spelthorne St Mary could be anything but a religious institution. It has just the same soothing quality as the order's mother house in Wantage, Berkshire. There is no hint of the impersonal bustle of a hospital. But though the sisters 'try to get to the problem and sort it out' they 'don't in any sense thrust religion at people. We make no discrimination about a person's faith. We have Anglicans, Catholics, Methodists, Jews. They're completely free.'

There is, obviously, a formal religious side to the life, but only if the patients wish to take advantage of it. 'Unless you ask,' says one woman, 'the subject isn't brought up.' Patients can go to Mass at 7.30 each morning, joining the sisters who have started with Lauds at seven, and sometimes there are modern hymns accompanied by one of the sisters with a guitar. There are prayers again after breakfast for anyone who wants to attend. Sometimes, say the sisters, the patients 'become aware of a lack in their lives'. They do find that quite a few in fact 'take up' religion again as a result of their experiences at Spelthorne.

But perhaps the most vital part of the sisters' work is that they are a stable community to which patients can always return and know they will be welcomed. The sisters try hard to keep in touch with their former patients by letter, and they hold quarterly meetings for those who have left. 'We're always glad to see them for a meal or a short stay.' Both the alcoholic and the ex-drug-addict have to make a new start in a new environment, and often find themselves very lonely until they make new friends. 'It is,' says a sister, 'of the greatest value to them to know that they *can* come, that they *matter* to us.'

The work of this community concerns those who have fallen victim to the stresses of our society. But other orders work for those whom the law considers to be the aggressor. The Sisters of the Good Shepherd were founded in seventeenth-century France and specialize in social work with delinquent girls (who are brought 'back into the fold', hence the order's name), and run hostels for unmarried mothers. They also staff women's prisons in several countries. In Portugal, for example, they run the only prison for women, near Tires in the Estoril area, where few male guards are seen in the white-washed buildings with their red-tiled roofs. Discipline is left mainly to the nuns, who have few problems in this devoutly Catholic country: when the nuns enter one of the workrooms, the women rise and kiss their hands as a sign of devotion.

They have good cause. Thanks to the work of the Good Shepherd sisters, their lives are not wasted even though they are behind bars. The nuns train them to weave exquisite wool rugs, which they make so successfully that the demand for them cannot be met, and the prison has a three-year backlog of orders. The women earn good money for their work, some of which supports their families outside, and some of which they save. One prisoner recently left with $1500 saved.

Another French order was founded a century later specifically for prison work. In 1841 a Frenchwoman, Anne Quinin, began the order of the Sisters of Marie Joseph to combat the dreadful conditions. So desperately needed were her sisters that the government provided free accommodation for them, and before long they worked in Lyons, Montpellier, and the ancient prison of St Lazare in Paris. They moved into the Central prison and La Roquette, and by 1927 they were established in Fresnes, where it has now become customary for the French government to send women from any prison who are in need of special care and medical treatment.

From central Paris it takes a train and a bus to reach the prison of Fresnes, whose high grey walls loom forbiddingly over the Avenue de la Division Leclerc. Along the unpaved avenue, beyond the heavy iron gates, beyond the gendarmerie and its armed inhabitants, squat the apartment blocks which house the warders and their families. Among them, directly beneath the prison walls, is an ugly oblong house: the convent of the Sisters of Marie Joseph.

Sister Kathleen Mulvany is the superior of this house. Her face is ravaged by tiredness, there are dark shadows under eyes that are astonishingly, serenely blue. Sister Mulvany, as her name suggests, is Irish, and the traces are still there in her voice. But she has lived in France so long now that she has trouble with her English: she gestures with her hands, searching for the words she wants, and ends up with Franglais.

Sister Mulvany did not intend to work in Europe. She wanted to go on a mission, 'but my brother wouldn't hear of it'. One of five children, she eventually entered the order's English house, paying the cost not only of her dowry but of the voyage from Ireland to do so. She transferred to Paris as a very naïve twenty-two-year-old. 'Well, you know, I didn't understand a lot about life.' It was not long before that changed, and she chuckles at the thought. 'I often think of my mother. She didn't want me to go to the Good Shepherd order, she thought the nuns weren't nice. If she only knew what I know now – I hear more confessions in here than any of the priests in the churches.'

Sister Mulvany looks after women who are awaiting trial and those who are serving sentences. 'We have women here who've got twenty years. They've done horrible things. But we don't ask what they've done. Our duty is to care for them and try to get them well. They've been judged. You can't judge them again.' She brings to her work complete compassion. 'They don't need pity. They need to be respected, to be treated as human beings.' Nothing shocks or horrifies her, and those tired eyes have seen women at the very end of their tether. 'I see women in passion, and they're not themselves. Sometimes it is discouraging, trying to help people who don't want to be helped. I say to myself, you must always sow. Perhaps we'll reap in years to come.'

Sister Mulvany's work starts when she receives women into Fresnes. She waits in a little ante-room for them to be taken through the freezing formalities of entering: the fingerprinting, the body search, the shower. When they reach her, they see in the sister 'something else. They begin to cry. You let them cry a little, and ask, "Can I help you?" And little by little it all tumbles out. I have to spend a lot of time with people who arrive. It's one of the most dramatic moments in their lives – when they arrive and when they're judged.'

She attaches enormous importance to the care she can give

at such a time. 'When they come into prison, they're not
themselves. When they're tried a year afterwards, they're not
the same. They've had time to see the calamity they've
brought into their lives and the lives of their children, and
they only realize that little by little.' Because of the time this
realization takes, Sister Mulvany will spend hours comforting
and listening to them. 'I think our perseverance, being near
them at this time, is something they never forget. They must
never feel they're being judged by me. They talk, they say
words, I understand without having the details. I comfort
them and make them understand they have a possibility to do
otherwise, to revaluate their lives. I'm not here to convert:
you can't force yourself on anybody from the religious point
of view.'

One woman she particularly remembers was condemned to
death for the murder of one of her lovers. 'I was working in
the linen room and all the time I used to talk to her.' The
woman went, finally, to the Central prison for eighteen
years. 'One day she rang at the door and threw herself into
my arms. Her first visit on coming out was to see us.'

Sister Mulvany's understanding of their problems has a
practical value above the immediate help she can give. She
regularly goes before a board at Fresnes to discuss the women
with the social assistants and doctors. Their comments are
listened to and acted on by the director of Fresnes and the
commissioners who hear the applications for parole. Sister
Mulvany's great strength is that she can see past the horror of a
crime to the emotion which caused it. 'There was one lady
who killed her husband. He was not a nice man at all, he had
two other women. She loved him very much, and she couldn't
see him with these other women so – she made her choice and
she killed.' She shrugs her shoulders and holds out her hands
palm up. 'And he is hers now in death.'

That a nun should be involved in such work totally demolishes the idea that nuns are 'other-worldly'. 'We can't
be dead to the world,' Sister Mulvany exclaims, horror-struck
at the very idea. 'We live in the world. We're all human.
We're all women.'

Out of a prison holding over 2000 people, Sister Mulvany

and her sisters look after at least fifty women, and any men
who are sick. 'They are asthmatic, tubercular; they have skin
troubles, eczema. The women cry, but the men keep it
inside and suffer from stress conditions.' The sisters are all
trained nurses and there is also a midwife for the births:
there are always about a dozen women with babies. Most of
them are single and often they are very young. The sisters
help them through the pregnancy and the birth, and teach
them how to look after the child. These women have very
much more freedom than other inmates, and usually a very
much better time than they would have had outside, abandoned
without public assistance.

The sisters treat them with great affection and understanding.
'We have one girl, twenty-six, with a lovely little baby. This
woman had a friend, *un amant* – we know all about that, you
know. She was abandoned by her mother and brought up by a
grandmother. Now that explains a lot about her behaviour.'
Some of them, says Sister Mulvany, have to be taught how to
be mothers. And she laughs. 'I don't regret not having
babies – I have so many.' In the beige-tiled rooms, with
cream walls and turquoise bedspreads, and the cot in the
corner, the mothers stay for eighteen months with their
children. They have full medical care, and do most of the
work for the children themselves: cleaning the rooms,
washing the nappies, doing their own ironing. There is a
modern nursery, and they have the use of a private yard, full
of flowers and trees and birds. Of course the women are
subject to security regulations, but their doors are only
locked at certain times, and at night. Security is a matter of
which the sisters are very conscious. They each give their
number – Sister Mulvany's is 647 – on entering, and have their
own keys to the maternity wing. To enter the men's section
they ring a bell and the guard opens the door.

Apart from the medical and welfare work, and visiting both
men and women, Sister Mulvany is also responsible for such
odd duties as picking up the letters in the morning and
arranging with the accountant if a woman wants to buy
anything. 'They're allowed *maquillage* and presents for the
family. You must always remind them that inside they must

save for when they leave. Then we check that they have the money and arrange for it to be stopped until something is paid for.'

To get everything done, the sisters rise at six. Their bedrooms in the convent are cool and pleasant, and beside every bed stands a little plastic bottle of Lourdes water. After meditation they sing Lauds, then there is Mass. After breakfast which, like all their meals, they prepare themselves, they go straight into the prison. Other meals are not taken by the community together because of the demands of the work, and dinner is eaten in rotation. The sisters all work far too hard, seven days a week. The order simply does not have enough sisters to sustain its workload. They have four days' holiday in a year – not counting the time for the journey home. Sister Mulvany accumulated three years' holiday: 'That was fourteen days. But time flies, you know.' There is, she admits, 'physical despair from overwork, and sometimes spiritual despair from your own heart. But that might also be a trial from God. There is much misery around us, so we have to acquire, little by little, self-control. We must never be too cold or too warm. Each has to find her own measure.'

The women in Fresnes come to the sisters with all their troubles. '*Ma sœur, ma sœur, aidez-moi.*' The problems might be small – a row, a depression. Or they might be big. 'Sometimes a woman receives a letter that tells her everything is finished. That is terrible, in prison. Just imagine their state of mind. But, you know, the women get over it better. A man let down in prison won't get over it.'

Sister Mulvany has done a stint in La Roquette, the Paris prison which deals with special cases such as professional lesbians who even in prison try to collect girls for the street. 'One told me all about her life, it was something terrible. She had been born neither male nor female. I had terrible work with that girl: she turned one girl wild, so that when she was released she immediately got herself back inside so they could be together. But we visited her in hospital and, do you know, she still writes to me? She has great strength.'

Many of the women she deals with now are prostitutes.

'They are very humble in themselves. They know no one ha
respect for them, and they have none for themselves. There
is something very touching about them.' How does Sister
Mulvany help these women? 'Well, you try to convince them
they can do something else, to do social work with them.
Several have left after prison and buy themselves out. But
others say, "I have no profession, do you want me to earn
100 francs a week when I can earn that in an hour?" But I say,
"You earn so much but you're maltreating your body,
drinking a lot, and you haven't put any money aside." ' The
prostitutes generally put their children in nurseries outside
Paris. 'And for nothing in their life would they want their
children to know. So I say, "It's necessary your children
should be proud of you." Several have told me they feel real
horror at doing it every day, horror of themselves. And I say,
"You must not think like that. You have a body and a soul
that are God's all the same, and you can recover all that you
were." '

Many of the women prisoners are drug addicts. One of the
Marie Joseph sisters became particularly interested in the
case of a girl who as a result of her addiction was having
trouble with co-ordination, and had virtually lost the use of
her hands. The sister made her follow a course to educate
her hands, and literally forced her to type. When the girl
was sent to the Central prison, a letter followed her to the
sisters there to encourage her. 'Now,' says Sister Mulvany
with pardonable pride, 'she has a secretarial diploma and a
job, a very good position.'

She becomes most emotional when she hears from former
inmates. 'At Christmas we receive a lot of letters from those
who have gone. We have people who have been very un-
grateful and never sent a word. Some write a few times,
others never forget. Others write, and you're really astonished
to get a letter from them with thanks for such a word on
such a day. And you expected nothing.'

They lead strange lives, the Sisters of Marie Joseph, in the
grey shadow of Fresnes, hearing daily of crimes brought about
by passions they have never known. 'The prison,' says Sister
Mulvany, 'it is an inward world.'

Speaking of religious life, she says that it is not surprising a lot of people are afraid to enter, 'because they don't know how they're going to end up.' She pauses, and hunts for the right words. 'But for me — I'm full of hope.'

8

MISSIONARIES AND
MARTYRS

*We're glad that you did what you did — even if you sisters
made a bad job of it.*
AFRICAN BISHOP TO WHITE SISTERS

The woman who joins the missionary orders is of a special
breed. Tough enough to live the life of a navvy in Hong Kong,
and dedicated enough to 'show our religion to be perfectly
lovable before showing it to be perfectly true'. Tenacious
enough to travel thirty-six hours by motorbike to reach a
remote village in central Borneo, and gentle enough to win
the confidence of the inhabitants when she gets there.

There is among missionary sisters a spirit reminiscent of
the last century. They are the only group of people I have met
who still refer to 'Palestine' and talk wistfully of 'rejoining
the Home Front'. When they do go home, it's 'on furlough'.
They survive alarming hazards with a mixture of prayer and
practicality, like the sister who, caught in the middle of a
terrific African storm, prayed diligently for deliverance,
then put the feet of her metal bed into two pairs of rubber-
soled wellingtons for protection from lightning and went to
sleep.

Spending years at a time in remote corners of the world
hundreds of miles from medical help, they must be the only
women who not only consider it a positive advantage to be
minus their appendixes, but see it as 'an asset rather than a
handicap if one has the kind of teeth that come out at night'.
It is the three H's they value: Humour, Health and Holiness.
The Maryknoll Sisters of St Dominic consider the first so
important that 'any girl without a sense of humour should be
discouraged from considering our congregation. If she cannot

laugh at herself, cannot see the funny side of life's ups and downs, she will not be able to bear even the better times of missionary life.'

For the majority of missionary sisters, the life is rugged. They have to be adaptable and accessible, able to adjust to the most unlikely circumstances and acquire at least an inkling of the most difficult languages. They need a sense of responsibility and considerable emotional stability, for they often find themselves in dangerous situations. They need every skill they can acquire, from growing vegetables to carpentry. They must have initiative to face the emergencies, and something more with which to combat the loneliness.

If this is true now, it was even more so sixty years ago. Then, missionaries set out expecting to remain away for life: their communities had no money to bring them back for holidays – or even to die. Long before World War I, the Missionary Sisters of the Society of Mary in Massachusetts were going to the south-east Pacific. Of two sent to Fiji at that time, the first died within a year. The second, a small and frail woman, founded a native sisterhood which had a hundred members at the time of her diamond jubilee. She remained active to the end of her life, proud that she had only two possessions: her one tooth and her umbrella.

Incredibly enough, even strictly enclosed sisters did their part on the missions, though without ever infringing the rules of enclosure. Communities of teaching orders would be established in foreign countries, and the sisters would arrive draped in heavy veils, go into the convent, and never step outside again except to leave the country. Elizabeth D'Arcy, a sister of the Society of the Sacred Heart now well into her seventies, taught in Peru, high in the mountains of Lima. 'In eleven years, I never went out of the house.' Today, though, another member of the order has just spent two months travelling throughout the country.

It was a long time before this work was open to women. The first great missionaries were all men – Martin of Tours in central Gaul, Patrick the Apostle to Ireland, Augustine in Canterbury – sent out on the wave of Christianity after Constantine first granted toleration to Christians in Rome.

When, under his successors, it became the state religion, it was paganism that had to be suppressed. When the voyages of discovery between 1500 and 1750 showed a new world to Europeans, Catholicism became a world religion. Spain, Portugal and France had the responsibility of starting and continuing missions, and building churches in lands they ruled. Central and South America, the Congo, India and Ceylon, Japan, China and Indonesia were all affected. And in Rome in 1622 the Vatican set up the Sacred Congregation for the Propagation of the Faith to centralize the work and take responsibility and control over it. From there, territories were assigned and the work was directed and supported. Even so, missionary interest declined, until by 1815 it had almost ceased: wars disrupted the home bases of many orders, the Portuguese and Spanish empires were disintegrating.

Meanwhile, the Protestant Church had done little missionary work until in Germany the new Pietism movement began to spark interest. Some organizations had continued to act as missionaries – the Dutch East India Company, for instance, considered that its chaplains were obligated to baptize and confirm the people of south-east Asia. But little was being done for the pastoral care of Christians living in pagan countries – immigrants, soldiers, merchants and officials on government business. It was to print religious literature for use at home and abroad – chiefly in America – that the Society for Promoting Christian Knowledge was founded in 1698, and a Society for the Propagation of the Gospel in Foreign Parts opened later in London to send out missionaries. In the late eighteenth century missionary societies were founded in London and the Netherlands, but it was the nineteenth century which really saw great Christian expansion. As the European Protestant powers acquired greater territories, out went the missionaries, filled with zeal and charity. They were strongly backed at home: every village in England at that time had its weekly sewing party, with one woman reading aloud while the rest sewed Mother Hubbards for the heathen. Armed with these, the missionaries set off to conquer the ignorance, illiteracy and physical suffering which they knew belonged to Satan, and must be stamped out rigorously. With their bibles, school-books and medicine bags, they did their best. But it was not enough. For all their selfless ideals and genuine concern, they made a lot of mistakes: they did not realize that it was Christianity, not the potential converts, which had to adapt. The whole experience of Christianity we brought,' says a White Sister, 'was a Western experience: it's the only experience we knew. If we'd known more of Africa, we'd have done it differently.'

The nuns, like the lay missionaries, went out knowing virtually nothing of the countries where they would work. For many, such ignorance proved fatal. They thought mosquito nets were unnecessary fussiness – and died needlessly from malaria. An Anglican order sent out five sisters in the 1890s, all under thirty. They all died within a year, the last just as she arrived back home.

If their ignorance hurt the nuns, it also hurt those they were trying to help almost as much. They had no understanding at all of native cultures, and they imposed their own ideas and beliefs willy-nilly on people whose own culture and ritual they thus destroyed. The Presentation Sisters of South Dakota, for example, formed to work as they still do with the American Indians, admit now that when the Indians were forced to drop their 'pagan' beliefs, they lost much of their heritage that could well have been preserved. Sister Carol Quinn says: 'The Indian spirit of Thunderbird is our Holy Spirit. And they believe that to give is the most important thing. We didn't integrate with their beliefs, we made them give up their ways. And now among the South Dakota urban Indians, who are almost all Christianized, there is a movement by the more radical to go back to their native religion and give up Christianity.'

Much of what the nuns taught must have given their pupils' a feeling of inferiority. The orders took with them their European art forms – and their white Christ-child in a winter crib. 'We don't do that any more,' admits a missionary sister with some relief. 'Now He's black.' They took, too, European church music to which they added the native language, thereby helping to obliterate the native musical heritage in Africa, India and Indonesia. It is only now that the

nuns encourage the creation of hymns by people in their ow
language, with their own instruments and rhythms. At th
Carmelite convent in Kigali, Rwanda, where over half th
community is African under a Belgian prioress, the office
sung to African instruments while novices dance the *Magnific*
at Vespers. And at the Poor Clare monastery in Likuni th
service is in Chichewa, and the choir accompanied by Africa
instruments, while even the boldly-coloured vestments ar
African. This came as a great relief to people who found th
European prayer pattern quite unacceptable. 'We like t
use drums,' says an Ashanti bishop, 'to sing and pray togethe
The idea of someone standing up and preaching while all th
others are silent is totally foreign.'

Some of the innovations brought by the missionaries wer
deadly: natives bundled into Western clothes to hide thei
unseemly nakedness did not know how to keep them clean
and suffered from infection. They did not realize they mus
be dried when wet – and became ill and even died as a resul
of unaccustomed sickness.

But the nuns were only daughters of their time, an
missionary work was seen as part and parcel of the great tas
of empire building and expansion. Gradually the worl
influenced the cloister and now, as a Maryknoll sister says
'We don't believe in the melting-pot concept but in a ste
where each ingredient retains its own identity.' Wherea
in the past nuns related to people in formal roles – teache
religious, nurse – now they are involved in leisure situation
They go to family celebrations, to weddings and fiestas. The
are expert in the most esoteric languages – Céline Durnan,
Franciscan Missionary for Africa, even speaks Xhosa, th
curious 'click' dialect of the Lusikisiki district of Sout
Africa.

Missionary nuns have not only become more broadminded
when two Medical Mission sisters recently left a leprosariu
in Ghana they were given a farewell party at which the feti
priestess poured libations for them – but more honest. The
confess that they have more failures than successes. The
are well aware that now they are tolerated in many countri
only for the free welfare and education they provide. A

while they do not separate education and Christianization
('You inculcate Christianity through whatever you do'),
they see now that of the girls they educate, many wish to
become Christians because to do so confers a higher social
status. And others who genuinely seem to accept Christianity
often, says one Belgian sister, 'end up as third wives'.

For a long time those in the missionary field operated as
enthusiastic amateurs. They moved into areas where they
could help, but not sufficiently. They were faced by malaria
and cholera, smallpox and dysentery, TB and leprosy. They
saw children dying of malnutrition and disease sweeping
through shanty towns. And they could not really change the
situation. 'Unenlightened heroism,' as Pius XI said when he
reviewed the medical section of the Missionary Exposition
in the Vatican in 1925, 'is not enough.' Even when religious
orders began sending out trained nurses at the turn of this
century, they still faced problems. Four sisters of the Franciscan
Missionaries of Mary went to India to nurse at Rawalpindi but
had to engage a laywoman as a doctor, since priests and sisters
with public vows at that time were forbidden to do surgical
or obstetrical work, however desperate the need. The laywoman was a seventy-two-year-old Seventh-Day Adventist,
Dr Agnes McLaren, who returned from India convinced that
a religious community must be created of sisters trained to
fulfil all medical and surgical functions. Five times she went to
Rome to seek sanction for her plans, but with little success.

It was another woman doctor, Anna Dengel from the
Austrian Tyrol, who was finally to fulfil Dr McLaren's dream.
She visited India, realized the need for qualified women
workers, and in 1924 toured the United States to explain that
need. Within a year another woman doctor and two SRNs
had joined her and in a Washington house the Society of
Catholic Medical Missionaries became a reality. At first they
did not take vows but made 'promises'. They lived as though
they had made the normal vows, but continued to work as
doctors and nurses, to prove to Rome that the two vocations
were compatible. In India they staffed hospitals, opened

health centres, and trained local midwives and nun nurses
In one jungle area the verandahs of their new hospital wer
thronged with the sick before any medical supplies ha
arrived. 'What did you do before there was a hospital?' th
sisters asked the head of the village. The man replied, 'W
died.'

The sisters had much to learn about the ways of the peopl
they were serving. When a child was born in another nev
hospital, the relatives rushed to the astrologer to tell th
exact hour of its birth. Later the mother was found in tears
the baby pushed aside: it had been born at an unlucky hour
One of the sisters had the sense to say the hospital clock wa
fast, and the child was retrieved.

By 1932 the sisters had permission to take private vows, an
two years later adopted their grey and blue habit. And in 193
Dr McLaren was vindicated when the Vatican issued a decree
urging that congregations start special units for health worl
in the missions, and asking that because proper technical an
spiritual preparations were needed, 'the Sisters should obtair
certificates as doctors or nurses'. The Medical Mission Sister
now spread fast: they ran hospitals for black miners in Soutl
Africa, and they moved into Ghana. Four missions wer
opened in Indonesia, and the first South American hous
started in Venezuela. They went to the Mexican Indians an
the Spanish Americans of Santa Fé, as well as to the blacks o
Georgia.

Already, other orders had moved into the medical fiel
on a professional level, and it is almost impossible to overstres
the heroism of these women. They were the first people t
treat leprosy at a time when such work demanded rea
courage, years before medicine recognized the nature an
manner of contracting the disease. Even then they wer
prepared to share their living quarters with their patients. The
Anglican Sisters of the Community of the Sacred Passion, fo
instance, were founded by the Bishop of Zanzibar in 1911, and
much of their work has been to make leprosy an 'acceptable'
disease to the extent that sufferers will admit it in time fo
effective treatment. They now also staff one of the only two
leprosy hospitals in Britain: there are now about 350 cases

in the whole country, mostly immigrants or English people who have been living abroad.

Some of the hospitals founded by nuns in the early twentieth century now enjoy an international reputation, like the Leprosy Control Headquarters in Buluba, East Africa, founded in 1934 by Mother Kevin, foundress of the Franciscan Missionary Sisters for Africa: it is now the biggest and most modern leprosarium in Uganda.

Those women went to the new territories quite literally for life, knowing the outward journey would never be retraced. And formidable journeys they were. By truck and train, foot and caravan, they forged their way in full habit across Asia and Africa. The Franciscan Missionaries of the Divine Motherhood, travelling to Kasaba on the Bangweulu swamps in Zambia to take over a leper hospital on the death of a woman doctor from blackwater fever, travelled by truck for 200 miles. They then journeyed by bicycle when the road ended, following narrow paths across half-destroyed bridges until the swamp became so watery they had to travel by canoe. They completed the entire journey in full-length white habits with pith helmets stuck jauntily on top of their headdresses. Until 1930 the women who went to Africa travelled like this. Though the East African railway was built at the beginning of the century, they had to get to their missions from the railway on foot. And it was the 1920s before any supplies were sent from home. Then they arrived once a year. At one time the only way of reaching parts of Zambia was on the sawmills train on the bushtrack – which was said by missionaries to possess square wheels. Passengers paid no fare but were required to sign a declaration that they travelled entirely at their own risk. Today, sophisticated transport has made it possible for nuns to reach areas previously beyond them. A Franciscan missionary who lives in New Guinea and teaches medicine in pidgin English remembers that when her plane first landed at Aitape the people, who live and dress in leaves and feathers as their Stone Age forebears did, rushed out to feed the plane bananas. And with the coming of better and cheaper transport, the nuns started to go home after twenty-five years' service. Now orders give them, on average, three months' leave every five years, and the mother houses of the bigger orders are constantly greeting new arrivals. In one day the Franciscan Missionaries of the Divine Motherhood had their mini-coach shuttling flat out between London's Heathrow Airport and the convent as sisters arrived from all over the world – Rhodesia, Zambia, Singapore and Australia. Sisters now are able, as they never were before, to return home for refresher courses in their fields – particularly important for those involved in medicine.

It is the medical skill of the missionary sisters that is their greatest contribution to those they want to help. Often they are not merely dealing with sickness and casualties – which might be anything from gunshot wounds to crocodile bites – but actually uncovering illness. It was the Sacred Passion sisters, an Anglican community in Tanzania, who realized that children with polio were hidden in the villages. No one had realized the number who could not walk. The sisters started visiting them, got them into calipers and trained them to use their limbs again; now there is a special hostel for them, and local Africans are taught to make the calipers themselves.

The missionary nuns, though, do not confine themselves to medical and educational problems. They are increasingly anxious to improve the living conditions of the people they are helping. Mother Mary Martha, a Franciscan Missionary of the Divine Motherhood, works in a hospital in Zambia, 300 miles from the nearest town. Horrified by the lack of resistance to disease, she decided something had to be done about the chronic food shortage. Although soil near the mission was sandy and unsuitable, she discovered that a few miles away it was good enough to farm wheat. One July morning she set out with a group of villagers to start work on this land. 'I noticed,' she said, 'that the men got into the Land-Rover armed to the teeth with bows and arrows, axes and knives. I discreetly enquired as to their use, and the men very politely informed me that the villagers near where we planned to start our farm objected very strongly to our going there and were waiting to kill us.'

Another nun working in Africa, White Sister Monique

Vien, watched women walking miles for every drop of water for cooking, washing and drinking. With her none too fluent Dagarti, she took an intensive course in well-digging methods, travelling on her Honda to talk to experts. The local head-master became her project manager, but it was she who collected the equipment to build wells in ten villages. Almost immediately, they found water forty feet below the surface. After this proof that the task was possible, fifteen men worked on each well with hoes and hatchets, once the site had been chosen by the local bishop, conveniently skilled in water-divining. In three months, each village had a well.

Other nuns teach people trades at which they can earn, for the first time, a living. In Kenya, in the densely populated squatters' slum of Mathare Valley near Nairobi, a Maryknoll sister, Edith Fragola, runs tailoring and blockprinting work-shops, where cloth is printed with local designs before being made up. And in Sri Lanka, the Good Shepherd sisters, whose missionary work is mainly in schools, brought in subsidiary industry when the provincial Mother of Good Counsel sent sisters to Italy to learn silk weaving which was then taught to the native fishergirls. Not all the work they do is welfare: sometimes it is a more basic change they seek. The Maryknoll sisters in Peru, for instance, work hard for the liberation of women. Male 'machismo' there dictates that women be kept pregnant, if possible, and for the last eight years the Mary-knollers have been teaching that until this attitude is overcome the children are doomed to poverty and semi-starvation. So they have been forming groups of women, making them aware of their rights, and opening their eyes to the way they have been exploited: recently a group even picketed a new hotel in Lima where a beauty contest was being held.

If most of the changes in the lives of the natives are for the better — greater hygiene and improved eating habits, for instance, which means more children survive — the arrival of the nuns with their schools and their western values has also created problems. 'By coming into Africa and giving the people an education,' says Sister Marguerite of the White

Sisters, 'we created needs for them which they didn't have before — better homes, a watch, a bicycle. And to get these things, they have to change their way of life. They can't just live simply in the field, they want to go to the city and make money.' Although she herself approves, 'as long as they are not deformed needs, as long as they live a better life', she does admit that 'we improved their education and therefore changed the whole system, which is from birth to the grave. And that system, even if different, was very valid.' As a result of the breakdown in this system, the White Sisters, who have so far dealt mainly with bush people in country areas, are now moving sisters into the cities. They see their educated country girls going there for jobs and getting into trouble, and they hope that by having nuns working with students and office workers there, as they do now in hostels in Mombasa, many of their difficulties will be more easily resolved. This calamity, claims the Bishop of Kumasi, an Ashanti called Peter Sarpong, 'has been caused by the Christian condemnation of puberty rites. It was almost impossible for girls to have sex before the puberty rites, and usually, when they had completed them, they were earmarked for marriage.' The missionaries condemned out of hand this 'mechanism of social culture', with the result that some Christian schoolgirls become pregnant and abort, all because the Church has not worked through what already existed in the culture.

None the less, missionary sisters do take on work which no one else will tackle — including the government of the country involved. In Jordan, for instance, Franciscan sisters run clinics for the poor around Amman. These people are the refugees from border areas involved in the last three wars with Israel. No medical help is provided for them by any Arab government, and water supplies are so bad that babies suffer during the summer months from dehydration. The sisters themselves have found the money to open a rehydration centre at Nuzha.

Lack of money is a constant problem for missionaries. As countries have received independence, particularly in Africa, the missionary orders have found themselves faced with financial crises. While colonial government had helped subsidize buildings and salaries, independent governments do not have the money. The Zambians, for instance, allow 22½p a day for the sixty-four maternity beds and thirty-two TB beds of the Franciscan Missionaries of the Divine Mother-hood. Out of this comes food, hospital clothing, dressings and drugs, as well as domestic staff. So the aid of the charities – Caritas, Oxfam and Cafod – has become in-creasingly important. Even so, the nuns attempt to raise vast sums of money themselves to build and run hospitals. They not only use the traditional method, and beg, but they put on film and fashion shows, stage plays and operas: one order recently held a 'slave market' in the centre of Hamilton, New Zealand.

Missionary sisters are invariably overworked to the point of exhaustion. Mother Mary Luke is a Franciscan of the Divine Motherhood, and the only doctor in a bush territory in the Zambezi valley, which contains 20,000 people. She is responsible for the hospital in the town centre and the rural health centres staffed by medical assistants throughout the area. She travels on foot through forest and scrublands, and in summer goes by barge through the flood plains of the Zambezi.

Pamela Reynolds is a Medical Mission sister who works as a midwife in Kalimantan, Indonesia, where it takes her three days by motor scooter to get through the forests to the most distant of her patients. En route, she stops overnight with the people she is treating, sleeping in one room with the entire family. She keeps, for the benefit of the sisters back home in Osterley, Middlesex, a racy diary. Describing a trek to see a woman who had just given birth, she explains she had to travel over a Djalan Tickus, or mousepath, which could only be negotiated on foot. 'For three-quarters of an hour I followed the man up and down hills, over streams and rivers on two bamboo poles. I thought, if people could see me in slacks and a blouse following a man dressed only in briefs and a dagger further and further into the heart of the forest, they would never believe it . . .'

Many nuns work as part of a mobile group. In August 1972 two special teams of workers were established for a two-year

period in the Amazon area of Brazil. Each consisted of a
priest, a nun and a development specialist, travelling up and
down by boat to the twenty small communities in the interior.
They spent a week with each, and the nun cared for the women
and children, giving advice on cooking, hygiene and child
care. In the evenings, they held group meetings on religious
matters and the problems of developing the area. As soon as
this group finished its work stint, two Franciscans, Sister
Regina Wachowski, a medical technologist and nurse, and
Father Luke Tupper, a missionary, started travelling up and
down the Amazon on a two-deck ferryboat renamed *Esperança*,
Portuguese for hope, and fitted up with an operating room, two
dental clinics and a pharmacy. They reach people in isolated
villages, immunize them against illness, and thus raise the
survival rate, particularly of children.

Nuns and sisters far outnumber anyone else working in the
mission field. In Africa there are now nearly 28,000 sisters
from about ninety orders, as against 15,000 priests and 500
lay missionaries. In Asia, there are over 47,000 nuns and
sisters, while the numbers of priests and lay missionaries
remain the same as in Africa. Many of these women are
accounted for by the increasing number of native religious.
As early as 1858 a congregation of African religious women
was founded in West Africa by Mother Anne Maria Javouhey,
foundress of the Sisters of St Joseph of Cluny, who did all her
work among slaves. That was at Dakar in Senegal, but it was
half a century before there was any sign of religious life in the
rest of the continent. In 1899 the White Sisters arrived to
staff one of the first missions in Uganda, and eleven years later
a group of girls were clothed as Bannabikira, or Daughters of
Mary. Today there are more than 700 professed Bannabikira,
fifty novices, and forty postulants. Their forty-seven convents
run schools and dispensaries, and are one of the major orders
for African sisters.

The White Sisters – the name is a shortened version of the
Missionary Sisters of Our Lady of Africa – find the name 'not
too good actually, because people think it's racial'. The

originally started in North Africa in 1869 with just five sisters. They are now in fourteen African countries, and while the majority of the 3000 African sisters they have trained remain in Africa, they can if they wish join the main congregation. But the White Sisters see their main task as training Africans to take over the work of the European sisters, concentrating on preventive medicine in remote areas.

Originally, little effort was made to adapt the way of life in black communities to suit the African sisters. Everything was done according to the instructions for canonical institutes from Rome. There might be an adapted habit – but it certainly was not African. And the daily customs in the convents were very Western. It is only now that they are realizing that native sisters have different rhythms of life, different needs. So the Anglican Sisters of the Community of the Sacred Passion, whose black community in Tanganyika, the Community of St Mary at Nawala, was founded in 1946, now have a different routine for their forty native sisters and fifteen novices. The European sisters have longer hours for prayer while the native sisters do much of the heavy work, which the whites simply cannot handle in that climate. The White Sisters now encourage their native communities to sit on the floor instead of on chairs in the European manner, and the convents themselves are built and furnished along African lines. But it will be a long time before they 'invent' a religious life which is absolutely African.

Any African girl who does want to enter religion is usually bitterly opposed by her family. Parents who are not Christian themselves cannot understand such a life for their daughters. Many put their girls into missionary schools because the education they receive there will ensure a better bride-price when they are married. This money is lost to the family if a girl enters a convent. But more than that, they expect the custom of centuries to be followed, and their daughter to produce children for the clan. As a Zambian sister says, 'Something of me seemed to die. I saw that, for my father, it was as if his own life had been diminished, and my mother felt as though she were doomed to misfortune because I would not bear children.' She was ritually cursed by her father before his ancestors: 'Your companions will mock you, the hens, the goats will make fun of you. You are cursed wherever you go. All the village curses you. You no longer have any father or mother. We no longer think of you as our child – we shall perform the funeral rites for you as if you were dead.'

In the majority of African countries, the role of woman is to do most of the work and defer to the men, and this presents a major difficulty for African nuns who achieve any kind of authority. Sister Jacinta is a Tanzanian, a decisive and striking woman who is head of the mother house of the ninety Tanzanian Sisters of St Therese at Kashozi, on the banana-covered hills above Lake Victoria. She finds she is regarded with deep suspicion by men of her own race, not least because of the innovations she is making in the area: the nuns, all peasant women, are developing their hundred acres of land with a tractor and implements to grow crops never seen before in the area. Beans and bananas, maize and coffee were all grown by primitive methods, but now Sister Jacinta and her sisters work side by side with the local women, teaching them how to grow more nourishing foods.

Black sisterhoods are not confined to Africa. The Franciscan Handmaids of Mary were founded in 1917 in Savannah, Georgia, the deep South of America, by Mother Mary Theodore, because no white community would accept negro girls – a situation that did not change until the 1940s. She was forced to do so when a law was threatened that would forbid white sisters to teach black children. 'We serve all God's people,' says Mother Miriam, the quiet-voiced mother general. 'But we were founded to serve our own.' They do so now from St Mary's Convent on West 124th Street, New York, in the depths of Harlem, where children play in the spraying water from fire hydrants, and people sit in chairs on their front steps. The convent is a square building facing a dusty park. In the inner courtyard, shaded by high walls, a fat old woman talks and talks, while a sister in full habit holds her hand and listens sympathetically.

Ironically enough, a lot of the sisters, according to Mother Miriam, are afraid to go out at night. This is partly because they fear addicts desperate for money to buy drugs, but especially because of attacks by Black Nationalists. In an area where everything Afro is cultivated, where dance halls give lessons in ethnic music and black really. is beautiful, the sisters are scorned as following the white religion: windows have been broken, they have been jeered at in the streets. Even now, setting off for a nearby school in broad daylight, they walk in pairs. The sisters themselves have never been involved in black power. 'When the black movement started,' confides Mother Miriam, 'I couldn't get particularly interested in it.' There is a group of militant black sisters – including Sister Louise Marie Bryan who, arriving in Melbourne for the Eucharistic Congress in 1973, was photographed by all the newspapers making the clenched-fist salute and declaring, 'If the only way oppressed people can be freed is by violence, then the need for violence is justified.' But Mother Miriam does not agree with this at all. 'They got in touch with us and said they wanted to organize because black sisters in white convents are frustrated. We didn't join – we're not frustrated. We're all black in this order.' What particularly incensed Mother Miriam was that white women are excluded from the black sisters' group. Yet she herself regularly attends workshops and conferences with other major superiors, 'and I have never been segregated'. The first black sisters conference was held at the beginning of the 1970s, 'and a lot of sisters went back to their orders feeling bitter'.

The Franciscan Handmaids of Mary not only do much of their work with whites – in the Depression, the soup kitchen they ran served mainly Irishmen – but have had several white sisters. Even in the American South, integration is now to some extent a reality. 'The church is really Catholic, black and white running it together.' But in countries where apartheid is practised, mixed congregations have faced severe difficulties. In Rhodesia, five black nuns, members of the Congregation of the Little Children of Our Blessed Lady, went to take over domestic duties in the house of the Archbishop of Salisbury, which had previously been carried out by white sisters. The house was in the city's white area – and the

African Affairs Committee of the city council forbade them
to live there.

One missionary order that manages to avoid the difficulties
of apartheid is the Little Sisters of Jesus. In one country where
the laws of apartheid are enforced (they do not want it named
in case it hinders their work), the white sisters live in the
black quarter, which is absolutely forbidden. 'But we're so
poor and so few, they don't think we can do anything.'

The order is the inspiration of a woman who in 1939 went to
the Sahara to start, in Moslem surroundings, a sisterhood to
the Little Brothers of Jesus founded by Charles de Foucauld.
The community is so new that their constitutions were only
fully recognized during Vatican II, but they have expanded in
the thirty-odd years of their existence to become a completely
international order, many of whose sisters come from Italy
and Vietnam. There are now over a thousand of them in more
than fifty different countries. The foundress, Little Sister Mag-
deleine of Jesus, was for many years mother-general of the order;
now in her seventies, she has retired. 'I chose to be a Little
Sister to follow Jesus. I don't want to be the one in charge.'

The Little Sisters work as no other community does: they
try to become part of the group of people with whom they
live. They are not allowed to own property and, since they
cannot bring money into the community – no dowries are
allowed – they have no capital to do so. There are no convents,
and even their mother house in Rome is a collection of little
prefabs hurriedly erected on land lent them by Trappist
monks, while the chapel is in a cave. Instead, their homes
are those of the poor they want to reach. In the bay of Hong
Kong, three of them live on a sampan among hundreds of others
in the fish-scented floating village of the boat people. At Stes-
Maries-de-la-Mer, in the French Camargue, they have a trailer
in which they follow the caravans of the gypsies from place to
place. Two more sisters travel with a circus through Switzerland, Greece and Turkey to provide help for the immigrant
workers the circus attracts. And in the Sahara, they usually
live in a tent lent by the Arabs.

They live simply 'because we feel that's the way Jesus lived at Nazareth, so that's sufficient'. They do not rely on others: when they move in, one or two of the sisters will go out and look for a job to keep them all. And most of the work they do is manual. 'We want to be of the working class.' At the Tai Po Market in Hong Kong, where they have a house, there are eight nuns living together from Canada, China, Vietnam and France. One works in a glove factory, the others do manual work on building construction. This work is usually done by the women of the Hakka tribe, who support themselves by hard physical labour: a long bamboo pole across their shoulders has, suspended at each end, a heavy wicker basket in which they carry rocks and dirt. Like the Hakka women, the Little Sisters wear loose black jackets and baggy black pants — with the addition of a veil. Some do more skilled jobs. Two sisters from another Hong Kong house work in a plastics factory. In the Portuguese colony of Macão, forty miles away, one sister is a nurse in a hospital for the handicapped, while another works in a large fireworks factory. They generally take the jobs immediately available. In Leeds, one sister works in a clothing factory and another cleans offices.

The Little Sisters believe that 'it's possible to break down barriers by being little and approachable,' and to prove it they work among the half-caste Indians of Canada's Hudson Bay and in the fields of Kenya. They keep a flock of goats in the blinding heat of the Sahara, and live amongst the aborigines in Amoonguna near Alice Springs in Australia. They are invited into countries where other missionaries are forbidden: three of them were asked to work in the government hospital in Afghanistan. But when after three years the government asked for twenty more like them, they could not supply that number and asked the Medical Mission sisters to help.

They are not concerned with proselytizing. 'If a person becomes a better Moslem through having known us, that's fine.' But they do manage to improve conditions for many of the people they reach. They are the only women's order to be with the pygmies of Central Africa. When they arrived, the sisters found that the pygmies were regarded by the local villagers with real fear. 'They were hardly believed to be

human. When they wanted to sell skins for food, they left
them in a heap outside the village. We went off into the
bush as we always do, with nothing. We were dependent on
the pygmies to help us. One of the sisters actually learnt to
write the language and now they bring their children into the
village to school.'

The Little Sisters of Jesus believe there is missionary work
to be done everywhere, which is why they are also in London's
Hammersmith: 98 Brook Green is a minute house, with a
creaky front gate and a cross on the door. Sister Constance,
the superior, is a little over thirty, her heavy, quiet face
exposed by the blue denim cap that pulls back her hair, her
feet bare and sandalled even in March. When she visits the
order's other houses in Britain, she hitch-hikes. The Hammersmith house is as simple and unadorned as she: rush mats on
linoleum, cane stools and a little gas fire. 'We're really
contemplatives,' she says, sipping Nescafé out of a mug.
'We're just not enclosed.'

The order recently started a foundation in Dublin, to work
with itinerants there. 'We'd known about them for years,
but we didn't have any idea where to start,' says Sister
Constance. 'We just got permission from the archbishop to
go there, and two of us went with a couple of pounds and
stayed with friends.' They hoped to get a flat in the industrial
area, and spent their time talking to the people in the streets
and praying. Then they approached the city authorities to get a
prefab, one of a group meant for 'itinerants'. 'No one thought
we stood a chance. But we got it.' Someone rented them a
caravan which they use for a chapel, and soon afterwards the
sisters arrived with mattresses and haversacks on their backs.
'The people saw we had nothing to offer except friendship.
They're very proud, and we asked for their help, while most
people give them handouts. They watched us making our own
furniture, and when they saw we hadn't a table they brought
us one.'

Now they are well settled there. Of the four sisters, one is
in a printing factory and another a part-time cleaner in a
hospital. In Dublin as elsewhere they 'do what any other
neighbours would do. We aren't trained for counselling, but

e can listen and talk to people, and pray with them. There's
much poverty and misery and distress that we know we
an't do anything to alleviate it, but we hope in times of
rouble that we can influence people, perhaps to get in touch
ith a social worker.'

And perhaps their value lies simply in this lack of pro-
ssional qualifications. 'Sometimes,' as Sister Constance
ys, 'people don't want to go to officials. Then we're
meone to talk to.'

At the other end of the missionary scale from the Little
isters of Jesus are the Foreign Mission Sisters of St Dominic,
he Maryknolls, the biggest missionary order in America.
Intil World War I, America was a magnet for foreign
issionaries. In particular, Italian and Spanish orders flocked
to work with their own nation's immigrants. The first
merican citizen to be canonized was an Italian nun, Mother
abrini, who founded her Missionaries of the Sacred Heart in
880, and nine years later took the advice of Pope Leo XIII
'go west, not east'. Her work was with the neglected
alian immigrants, and by her death she had established
xty-seven houses, one for every year of her life. By the
me the War ended every major missionary order had a
ranch in America. But there were many new ones which
id been started by Americans.

The Foreign Mission Sisters of St Dominic have their
eadquarters at Ossining, a couple of hours from New York
ity. Their mother house, Maryknoll, is a huge, rambling
uilding set in landscaped gardens near the centre of the
aryknoll Fathers. The only other building approaching
eir size in Ossining is, as they like to point out, Sing-Sing.

At the very beginning of the twentieth century a plump
ish-American redhead was asked by her faculty at Smith
ollege in New England to start a mission study class. She
rote for advice to Father James Anthony Walsh, then director
r the Society for the Propagation of the Faith in Boston. He was
orking towards establishing a seminary to train young men
r foreign work, and Mollie Rogers joined him. She worked
one of a small group of secretaries, and gradually they all
lopted his name for her – Mary Joseph. He asked them to

draw their hair back in a simple style and wear a grey uniform
and by 1914 they were starting to live a community life. A
the end of 1921 there were over a hundred of them under th
leadership of Mollie Rogers, now Mother Mary Joseph, an
by the mid-1920s girls were entering not in fives an
sixes but in groups of thirty and forty. By 1940 there wer
forty-nine houses throughout the United States as well as i
China, Korea, Manchuria, the Hawaiian Islands and the Philip
pines.

When Japan attacked China in 1937, the sisters watche
the Chinese retreat, and they buried the dead and sheltere
women and children refugees. They became used to runnin
for refuge from bombs; they looked after the maimed; the
distributed food and clothing and ran food kitchens an
clinics for the refugees. The United States advised its national
to leave, but Mother Mary Joseph followed the general polic
of the Church, and her sisters stayed on. On December 8
1941, a few hours after Pearl Harbor, the Japanese attacke
the Philippines, where fifty-three Maryknoll Sisters worked
Japanese police and soldiers arrived at the doors of all th
Maryknoll missions throughout Korea and Manchuria. The
came to intern, imprison, interrogate. In Hong Kong an
Manila sisters were treated as interned enemy aliens. Tw
were suspected of passing messages and tortured constantly.

Nine years later it was the Chinese who were the oppressors
The superior of a hospital in Toishan, South China, wa
picked up by the police and charged with failing to provid
someone to clean the public streets or pay business taxes -
though the hospital treated all patients free of charge. Th
convent in Kowloon was taken over. Sisters in Laofuheo an
Wuchou were accused of possessing opium and imprisoned
while others were put under house arrest. Bishop Franci
Ford, a Maryknoll father, and Sister Joan Marie, who did hi
secretarial work, were seized in Kaying and imprisoned
After two years Sister Joan Marie was expelled from th
country, but Bishop Ford died in prison.

Other missionary sisters were attacked. In 1966 the las
remaining nuns were expelled from the country. Eigh
British Franciscans were taken from their convent in Peking

made to trample on the cross and sent to Hong Kong: thirteen Chinese nuns of the order were detained.

If other congregations can afford to be 'unworldly,' the missionary orders cannot. They need to follow international politics closely if only, as one Maryknoll sister puts it wryly, 'to know who is going to throw us out or lock us up next'. At Ossining there is a specialized research department to monitor political and economic information.

Internal political changes in a country can have sudden and dramatic effects. Many missionaries, for instance, left Uganda after General Idi Amin came to power. Today, almost a third of the world is closed to missionaries. Burma is completely sealed. Work permits are necessary for those who want to work in India and also parts of the Caribbean. Countries which already have their own religious orders but no longer find religion acceptable to their ideology, either close down all convents and churches, or bring in legislation which means the orders will not survive once their current members are dead. In Roumania, nuns under forty and lay sisters under fifty were told to leave the cloisters and devote themselves to 'a more socially useful activity'. The same system is adopted in Russia: the Pokrovsky convent in Kiev, which was said to have 300 nuns in 1967, including fifty young women, has apparently been forbidden novices since 1958. The nuns, who survived on sewing, icon work and bookbinding, were finally dispersed two years later when the Ukrainian authorities announced the closure of the convent. In 1962 the Mikhailovsky convent in Odessa, where the nuns had earned their meagre income from making vestments and altarcloths, was turned into a military hospital. But in other convents the nuns go out to work as ordinary citizens during the day, and return at night to continue their religious life. This happened at the Ovruch convent in the Ukraine, said to be one of the oldest in the Orthodox Church. It was reopened in 1947 after forty years of closure, and 140 nuns lived there. In 1961 they were ordered by the local town council to abandon the premises and work in the brick factory:

they had no right to a pension because they had not been engaged in productive work.

The World Council of Churches at present estimates there are ten convents and five monasteries still in Russia, but there seem to be others working secretly. In 1963 ten nuns were 'unearthed' working in local hospitals in Lvov. And where convents are closed, even the Russian authorities seem to feel the need to qualify their actions. When, in 1967, the Kuremyae monastery, the only convent for women in Estonia, was closed, life there was presented as gloomy and harmful, and the nuns were charged with feuding, amoral behaviour and mercenariness which would be a harmful influence upon the local people and pilgrims. Some of the religious are merely dismissed; others sent to forced labour camps. Last year a Russian, giving details of his ten years' imprisonment to a Washington security committee, spoke of hundreds of thousands of people, including Russian Orthodox nuns, having been committed to concentration camps for their religious beliefs.

In 1950 over 10,000 Czechoslavakian nuns were turned out of their convents; half died in prisons or camps. Others had been shipped out of the country, like the 365 members of the Sisters of the Holy Cross who were either German-speaking or of German origin, and who were taken in by their order in Bavaria. About 8000 nuns were allowed to pursue their vocations only in homes for the old, forbidden either to nurse or teach. But during the Dubček regime there was a thaw in Church-State relations, and many nuns quietly returned to parish work in the cities. The government was even said to be raising £100 million to compensate men and women in orders for their unjust loss of freedom and property. But in 1972 all nuns were removed by force from their parishes and returned to work out of sight in mental hospitals and on farms. Some are on state farms, others in 'concentration convents', as the factories where they work under forced labour conditions are known. The White Canons printed description said to have been furnished by one of these women about the life. 'Our nuns are being physically destroyed by the irregular meals and disturbed rest at night. The first shift leaves for work at four in the morning and returns at three in the afternoon. The second shift works from one in the morning and returns at six. They return pale and exhausted, famished, drenched with dirty water, especially those working in the wool-washing department. For the most part their health is ruined. Some have grown deaf through the din of the machines. Many are suffering from TB owing to undernourishment and lack of exercise and fresh air. Others show symptoms of nervous disease. Even the Communist press has admitted half of them are tubercular. Of course they do not mention this is the result of inhuman labour conditions but blame convent life which, they say, "is bad for the health".'

In other countries bizarre charges are brought against religious. In Jugoslavia Sister Slavka Nada Malic was sentenced to three months' imprisonment for spreading lies: she was heard to say that 'When the old disappear, the young take their place.' This was interpreted as a forecast that the present Jugoslav government would soon be dissolved.

Nuns in South America have had a worse time. In Brazil, the world's largest nominally Catholic country, priests and nuns suspected of 'leftist sympathizing' have been arrested and tortured. Brazilian bishops, tamed by the government, claim that the Church is being 'persecuted' by such people. In 1970 Mother Maurina Borges da Silveira, superior of an orphanage in southern Brazil, was flown to Mexico City in exchange for a Japanese diplomat. She had been arrested on the charge of allowing an opposition group to meet in her convent. Stripped and locked into a cell with a man, she was beaten up savagely and subjected to electric shocks. Her interrogators, both Catholics, were later excommunicated. Religious in Bolivia have been accused by the state of playing 'war games' and aiding members of the National Liberation Army there, an accusation admitted by the Archbishop of La Paz, who agreed that individual nuns and priests have indeed aided guerrilla members: 'You must consider, however, how many times this is done in the fervent desire to aid their people.' In 1972 one Mother Superior, Carolina Betancourt, was actually expelled from Bolivia with three of her nuns after a clash between troops and members of the National Liberation Army, who were found hiding in their convent sixty miles from La Paz. In Paraguay, too, nuns and priests have recently been beaten up by police dispersing a student demonstration, for which the chief of police was excommunicated.

All religious ceremonies have been prohibited in Albania since 1967, and all churches, monasteries and convents either destroyed, closed or converted for 'profane' purposes. In view of this, it is a fitting irony that perhaps the best known and best loved nun of our time should be an Albanian: Mother Teresa of Calcutta.

Calcutta is a city where the rich wrest fortunes from industry. But it belongs to the derelict and hopeless who inhabit its streets: it is the poorest city in the world. It holds over 8,000,000 people and the estimate of those destitute – not official, for they are uncountable, is as many as 4,000,000. At night every shop doorway, every verandah, is covered with sleepers. Huddled in their thin wrappings against the cold, coughing quietly, they lie on the strips of matting that are their homes.

Lower Circular Road is long and rambling. Trams rattle past the little workshops and thin cows. Crows scavenge in the gutter. No. 54a is the sparsely furnished home of Mother Teresa. She is acclaimed a modern saint and with good reason, for she has chosen to work in the slums of this city, and others like it. She has given her life to those who keep so little of life itself: to the dying and leprous, to the tiny abandoned babies her sisters find daily in the dustbins. And in return, the poor revere her. They kiss her passing feet and the hem of her sari that is made of the cheap white cotton edged with blue which all her sisters throughout the world wear. And it is with the poor that Mother Teresa and her Missionaries of Charity identify. The sisters live as the poor live, eat as they eat, suffer as they suffer. For, says Mother Teresa in her soft, accented voice, 'without our suffering our work would be just social work, very good and helpful, but it would not be the work of Jesus Christ, not part of the Redemption.'

She has taught high-caste Indian women, who only a few years ago would have considered themselves corrupted even to pass near an untouchable, that they must look on these people as being Christ. She teaches that the innocent are paying for the sins of the world, and that is why suffering exists. The Pope has called her 'a symbol of the discovery in which lies the secret of peace on earth which we are all seeking – the discovery that every man is our brother'. It is one of her greatest achievements that she has brought people of different religions together: few of those with whom she works are Christian, the majority being Hindus, Moslems and Parsees.

Agnes Gonxha Bojaxhiu, Mother Teresa, was born more than sixty years ago to an Albanian peasant family in Skopje, Jugoslavia. By the time she was twelve, she knew she had a vocation to the poor. Wanting to do missionary work, she joined the Loretto nuns and went with them to India, where she took her final vows in 1937. It was not until nine years later that she received what she refers to as 'a call within a call' and realized that God wanted her to work in the slums.

Then she started teaching illiterate children, working in the compound of a slum family. Five came that first day; the numbers grew, and women started to join her. The first were those same girls she had taught at the Loretto convent, and within three years the first home for dying destitutes was opened. It came about one morning when she found a woman lying in the drainpipe in an open sewer, her body half eaten away by rats and ants. Mother Teresa took the woman to hospital, where she was received only because of her rescuer's persistence. Later, she found the woman's body in the street, put out to make room for those not yet dead. Mother Teresa asked the municipality for a place where she could bring these people to die a decent death. The health officer suggested she use the empty temple of Kali, the Hindu goddess. Within twenty-four hours the Missionaries of Charity had started their work. 'I take people with leprosy and TB, but it is their inner suffering that I try to cure,' says Mother Teresa. 'I want to make them accept dying with peace of mind. That means they die beautifully, sure of the love of God.' But the care and love they receive means that many do not die, and

these people are helped back to life, and then given training
if they are capable. When she recently received the Pope
John XXIII Peace Prize of £10,000 ($25,000), she spent it on
building a rehabilitation village for lepers on land given by
the Indian government. When the present Pope visited her,
he gave his white ceremonial car to be raffled for the same
purpose. Receiving the £34,000 Templeton Prize for Progress
in Religion in 1973, Mother Teresa, the woman who started
her community with five rupees, said: 'Money is not enough.
Don't just give me money or things I can get for the asking.
My people need you to love them.'

All the sisters ascribe the success of the community completely to God. 'The Lord provides,' they say. 'The secret is
in the surrender to God and providence.' It may well be so,
but Mother Teresa's personality cannot be overlooked: she
has genuine charisma in an age in which the word has been
devalued. She is tiny and seemingly frail, but the black eyes
burn in her wrinkled face, and the energy that mobilizes
her is inexhaustible. Her nights are broken by the need to do
her own clerical work, but still she meets all the demands
made on her; the needs of her sisters for money or medicine,
the meetings with officials. She does so much that often she is
actually days rather than hours late for appointments. Her
order is not large: 700 sisters work with her in fifty houses.
The majority are in India, others are established in Venezuela,
Sri Lanka and Tanzania. She has sent Missionaries of Charity
into Gaza, part of Egypt which is now Israeli-occupied territory
where the inhabitants are isolated from both sides. Shortly
afterwards another group moved into the Yemen. Recently
they were given a convent in New York's black Harlem,
where they concentrate on trying to reach children between
nine and thirteen before they form criminal habits. And in
Fitzroy, one of the poorest areas of Melbourne, Australia,
they work among the neglected aborigines. Most recently, the
Pope invited her to open a home in Rome for the people of
Baracchi, the shanty town outside the walls where the poor from
the south squat in tin shacks. The Missionaries of Charity
acquired a similar shack where they look after young children,
while their mothers work in the houses of the wealthy.

It is, above all, the rejected and the desperate who interest Mother Teresa, and the brief 1971 Indo-Pakistani war left both in its wake. The Missionaries of Charity moved in to live with the stateless Bihari Moslems under appalling conditions, and Mother Teresa played the major role in transferring tons of food from warehouses across the border in India. She moved to Dacca two days after it was liberated by the Indian Army and went to the aid of 3000 East Bengali women who had been left in the Pakistani bunkers. Abducted by the troops, used for months as servants and whores, the majority were heavily pregnant and abandoned by their families because they had been violated. The Pakistanis had taken their honour and their saris, lest they hang themselves. When they were given saris, that is just what many of them did. Mother Teresa's first action was to find houses where these women could live, and offer them training in craftwork and typing so they could support themselves.

It seems surprising that the Missionaries of Charity, who work with the poorest of the poor, should find it necessary to open houses in England, home of the Welfare State, National Assistance and the pension book. It was when Mother Teresa went with the Simon Community round the bomb sites and railway stations of London, and saw the meths drinkers and the drug addicts, that she decided a house was needed. 'I have walked your streets at night and gone into your homes and found people dying unloved. Here you have a different kind of poverty. A poverty of spirit, of loneliness and being unwanted. And that is the worst disease in the world today; not tuberculosis or leprosy.' Each night, two sisters go out on the soup round with the St Mungo Community, a non-religious group which serves the itinerants of the capital, the forlorn people who sleep on benches and in churchyards. Some of these women will be housed by the missionaries in St Stephen's Gardens, one of a mostly derelict block in West Kensington, ugly as bad teeth, where the smell of rotting wood penetrates the boarded-up doors and windows. Despite the bleakness, the house is quiet. In the front room, close beside the oil stove which makes the air humid, a fat woman slumps in a chair, snoring loudly under a portrait of Mother

Teresa done entirely in white rice grains. There are not many women here at a time, usually about seven. Mother Teresa is not, after all, interested in big institutions: it is the individual who concerns her. The sisters wait until the women have a chance to recover themselves, then accompany them to the labour exchange: they can stay at the house afterwards until they are financially able to make a fresh start.

Not even Mother Teresa is successful in everything she undertakes. Against all advice, she took her Missionaries of Charity to the Ballymurphy area of Belfast in Northern Ireland, where she believed by their example the sisters could remind the Irish Catholics and Protestants of God, and thus unite them. They worked with families there, looking after children, running a crèche, teaching the women to type and knit. But in the face of constant criticism – that her presence was a reflection on the many communities of Ireland, that the Indian sisters were insufficiently qualified for the work they undertook – she left after a year, without a word of explanation from her or from the Church hierarchy.

Just as Mother Teresa never asks for money, so she never needs to ask for novices. In India 120 join each year; in the London house there are currently twelve novices.

Several superiors from other orders, who appear to regard Mother Teresa with less than total admiration, have pointed out that the Missionaries of Charity do in fact lose more entrants – and faster – than other orders. Certainly the process of selecting applicants is less stringent than that adopted by Western religious orders, and they are less concerned with training. The order has some highly qualified women – seven doctors, a lawyer – but it does not regard any professional qualifications as essential. Nor do the Brothers Mother Teresa started in 1963, to take care of the men in the Houses of the Dying, to look after the boys and do work in the docks and other areas where even the Missionaries of Charity cannot go. Their superior is a former Jesuit, Father Andrew, and under him the hundred-odd brothers live a life identical to that of the sisters.

Like the sisters, the brothers have taken a fourth vow in addition to those of poverty, chastity and obedience: to give service, wholehearted and free, to the poor. Nowhere is this better illustrated than in the chapels of the Missionaries of Charity. Throughout the world they are the same: simply a room of whatever house the sisters occupy, without seating so that the sisters crouch on the floor Indian-fashion. There is rush matting in warmer countries, and in Europe carpet — when it is donated. The altar is bare and wooden, the hymn numbers marked on a little board. Often, there are small coloured pictures of the saints on the walls. And always, dominating the chapel there is a crucified Christ with the words 'I THIRST' written beneath.

Mother Teresa was first introduced to the West by Malcolm Muggeridge, who made a television film, shown both in Europe and America, about her first house in Lower Circular Road, Calcutta. She is, he believes, 'one of the most remarkable people alive today; one of those figures born into the Church perhaps once a century, especially at times of great confusion, who go back to the pure heart of Christianity'.

She is named, not after Teresa of Avila, ('I am not big enough for the big Teresa'), but for the little Carmelite, Thérèse of Lisieux, who is the saint of missionaries — though never for a moment in her short life did she leave the cloister. It is perfect that Mother Teresa should be so named, though, as she herself says, 'We are not saints yet.'

For above all else, Mother Teresa loves God, and believes He wants His people to be happy, and to be holy. Her religion is everything to her: 'This, no one can take from me. This is something within me.'

And she smiles her rare and joyful smile. 'I behave always as if Christ were here in front of me.'

9

IMAGES: SACRED AND PROFANE

Religious have done a terrible disservice to themselves and the Church by being so damned humble.

SISTER OF HUMILITY OF MARY

Liz Thoman's battered white Mustang skids to a halt outside the Los Angeles Hilton. It is a stifling June evening and a thin layer of smog floats over the city. Although it is Sunday, Liz has half a dozen rollers in her hair. She is wearing a tiny flowered bra top, knee-length green Bermudas over an ample bottom, and flip-flops. Her toenails are painted, she wears pretty rings, and drives much too fast.

Liz is just thirty – which she hates – and lives with a girl-friend in a modern apartment block off Hollywood Boulevard, at the sleazy end where the hermaphrodite people gather in see-through blouses and sequined eye-lids. She is a professed sister, a member of the Sisters of Humility of Mary at Ottumwa Heights in Iowa, but it would be hard to glean this fact from anything in her life-style. It is unusual even in the most advanced and liberal community of sisters for a member to be employed in a creative and commercial business. Liz Thoman is extraordinary in that she has just started her own advertising agency, the Rainbow Word and Picture Company, of which she is both creative director and chief photographer. She has been on television several times, and is constantly flying to conferences and meetings. She has a great many men friends, says she falls in love at least once a year, and has had several marriage proposals.

Last year she won the Lulu, the award given by the Los Angeles advertising women for the best campaign. It was presented for what must be the most stunning piece of public relations put out by any religious order. A glossy white folder proclaims in black: WOMEN IN LOVE . . . WITH LIFE. With words and photographs, Liz has pictured the lives and aims of the sisters of her own order in a series of booklets: *Life-style*, *Spirit and Goals*, *Health Care*. She has designed, photographed and edited it with, as she points out, a little help and a lot of support from her friends.

Liz Thoman got her own training when she asked her community to let her work in a Minneapolis publishing house on a religious magazine. She became their director of advertising and sales promotion, in charge of ideas. 'I turned up at junior advertising clubs in a mini-dress and eyeshadow and they didn't know what to think. Few of them were Catholics, and they had a very bad image of sisters. I spent all the meetings counselling people. 'I'd say, "I'm Sister Elizabeth," and they'd say, *"Sister?"* ' Her first television appearance came when she went, complete with earrings and make-up, to photograph Steve Allen. 'He got me on the show, trying to find out what it was like to be a sister in a mini-skirt.'

Liz represents the first sign of the hard sell for the religious life. In Europe, public relations is confined to a couple of sisters visiting a school for talks, or a community placing ads in a Catholic newspaper. But Liz Thoman is something else again. The Rainbow Word and Picture Company is the first company of its kind set up to handle public relations for religious communities alone. In the past, several communities have employed professional public relations consultants, although few can afford to do so. As Liz says, 'The sisters have no money to pay a professional – and even if they had, how could he or she capture whatever it is that makes a religious without turning them into freaks?'

She cites the women's order which hired an agency to handle press relations, internal and external information, which costs them over $10,000 a year. This, to Liz Thoman, is not doing the important part of the job. 'What matters is image building. It's not just for the girls with vocations, but for the public: you don't want them to say, "Oh, you're a sister." But: "Hey, you guys are doing some really neat stuff.'' ' To that end, she thinks one of the first tasks is to stop religious communities from using what she calls 'wall to wall type' in their brochures. Liz also admits her way is smoothed by the fact that 'every nun I know who's talented ends up as a sculptor or something – but never in commercial work. People just flip when they see a nun in advertising.'

It is too soon yet to measure how effective her methods are in terms of attracting people into the communities: the Rainbow Word and Picture Company began only late in 1973. But what is certain is that, for the first time, the communities that hire Liz Thoman to represent them are being aggressive and sophisticated and these are amazing qualities in terms of women's religious life. Liz believes that many of the problems orders face today – particularly when it comes to recruitment – stem from their attitude to any kind of publicity. 'They won't talk about themselves: they just pray for years and years to someone like St Joseph to come and help, instead of telling the public just who they are and what they're all about. And this applies whether they want money or just psychological support.' Nothing, she says, annoys her more than communities which regard public relations as 'kind of a nasty thing. I get very provoked with them. Very few communities will in fact have anything to do with it, and I just don't know how they expect people to fathom what they're about if they won't tell.'

We talked in her apartment, with its great pile of brightly coloured floor cushions, the green carpet and the glass dining table which was once a shop door. She cooked a delicious spaghetti dinner out of a couple of packets and mince, and spent most of the evening making a dress for a conference she was flying to attend the next day. When I left after midnight she was only half way through, and spent most of the night working on the sewing-machine in her bedroom. After all the bleak, white-painted cells with a holy water stoup and a crucifix, Liz Thoman's room is refreshing: full of odds and ends, books, and jars of nail varnish.

Liz Thoman is far from typical, but there is no doubt that

she is right: the image of the nun needs burnishing. To the majority of people, they all seem to be middle-aged, rather prissy, unworldly women who are in convents because they never got asked. They get placed into two categories: either they are incapable of a successful career, human love or making a home – or else they are seen as superhuman 'saints' endowed with every virtue. This is part of the pious odour that hangs over religious life. A great many women's communities mix the really superb work they do with an unfortunate attitude towards those whom they are helping, and sometimes it is hard not to side with the woman who said angrily of her experience with nuns that she had never before come across so much 'sanctimonious smugness'.

The fact is that nuns and sisters all too often fail to see themselves as they appear to others, and do not bother to adapt their ways to the climate of the times. The convent of the Irish-founded Sisters of Mercy in London's East End is a typical example of women doing a superb job while presenting themselves badly. These sisters show their devotion to the more helpless part of humanity in a wide range of activities. Apart from their work in schools and hospitals, they provide low-cost accommodation for business girls – teachers, students and civil servants. There is a home for women who are unable to cope with living alone, where some inhabitants have been since they were girls. And there are flats where homeless families can live rent-free until they get on to their feet again.

There are several unmarried mothers, harassed girls who need time to plan their lives. And there are refugees. The first ones taken in by the Sisters of Mercy arrived after the Hungarian uprising in 1956. Now, there are families who have left their homes and fled from the bombs and threats of Ulster. These people arrive in London only to find that the borough councils have no room for them even in the condemned 'halfway' houses. The sisters claim never to turn away a family. But the major part of the East End work is the Night Refuge for down-and-outs, the destitute men and women whose only alternative accommodation is the streets. Each year 20,000 of them turn up at Crispin Street for a night's lodging and food, which costs them nothing.

By late afternoon two queues have already formed outside the black and sombre building. Inside the doorway of the men's entrance, a man at a desk signs in each name, while a habited sister watches. Each comes in silently, cap in hand. Each is asked if he has work. If not, has he tried to find any? What happened? Will he try again tomorrow?

For the Sisters of Mercy help only those who show they want to help themselves. If a man continually fails to find work, he will no longer be able to use the shelter. The sisters who never turn away a family in need will have no place for a lonely failure. 'After all,' says the superior, 'we're refusing men every day, we haven't got the space.' The men (the 'out-of-works', the sisters call them) eat in a dining-room downstairs, sitting in silence at neat tables, all facing the front like recalcitrant schoolchildren. Soup, meat, mashed potatoes, the same food as the women receive in the room upstairs. But the women's room at least has a bird chirruping, and plants, though the occupants scarcely look more cheerful. Carefully made-up, they sit, each isolated from the other by her troubles, before going up to the pink-painted dormitory, where rows of black iron beds stand in tight rows.

The Sisters of Mercy do not expect the women to get jobs. 'The majority of them are beyond redemption.' The sisters find working on the men's side more satisfying. 'They do get on their feet and come back and say thank you and give some little donation.' While the sisters do not encourage people to come regularly because 'we want to help everyone,' they do give those who reach them very real assistance. Those with a drinking problem will be recommended to Alcoholics Anonymous, and one sister was particularly delighted because she helped a man to save shillings until he had £100 to make a new start.

But all the time the sisters are trying, earnestly and conscientiously, to improve those who come to them in desperation. No one can stay in the Night Shelter during the day, and they have to be up and out painfully early. A shabby man stops on his way out and presses two shillings into a sister's hand. 'Will you buy a candle for me, Mother? It's me birthday, see.' 'Well,' she says, 'happy birthday. But don't take drink, will you?'

Intellectually, the image of the nun has suffered through enclosure. There, she was unable to read freely, to look at a newspaper, listen to a radio or – until relatively recently – receive higher education at a university. What one nun describes as her 'cultural deprivation' was a real barrier in her relations outside the convent. Today there are a great many orders which still do not allow indiscriminate reading material into their houses, like the English contemplatives who take only *Osservatore Romano*, the official Vatican newspaper. But others regard magazines and books as a useful window on the world. The well-stocked library of one small convent contains Agatha Christie, Georgette Heyer, Victoria Holt and Hammond Innes, as well as John Steinbeck, Gore Vidal, Evelyn Waugh and Iris Murdoch. They also boast Sartre, *The Last Days of Hitler* and *More Murder in the Nunnery*.

But if the religious communities have changed their ways, the public does not always realize this. Recently a group of American teenagers was asked why they were attracted or repelled by the religious life. A high percentage were repelled, because the sisters knew nothing of what was going on in the world.

They said this at a time when the educational level of nuns has never been higher and when sisters are tackling every field open to women: there are Ph.D.s working in the mountains of Peru. Sisters receive decorations for their services to science and education, they sit on consultative bodies and the boards of insurance companies. One sister is a lieutenant with the United States Air Force and another is an attorney general. One works for Ralph Nader and his consumer group, and another designs hospital theatres in Melbourne.

In one year, the Maryknoll sisters of New York earned sixty-five university and college awards, including twenty-nine bachelors' degrees, twenty-five masters' degrees, one Ph.D. and ten special diplomas. Five more won civic or church awards, one from the World Health Organization. Eleven more had articles or books published, and one sister had an art exhibition in Geneva.

Against this background, it seems ridiculous that, as on
nun says, 'People tend to think you're kind of frozen into a
attitude. They think of you as having a certain innocence,
certain protectedness. They never think of you as still goin
on, as any normal woman would, developing psychologicall
and emotionally.' And an Anglican sister feels: 'There's
certain image people have got of the religious life, and the wa
sisters behave, and you're a bit conditioned by this. The
think you're different – they think you're *better*. And a certai
kind of status has been assumed by religious who have accepte
this.' Recently this woman, who is university-educated
voluble and has a busy job working with students, was buyin
the drinks for a party her community was giving to thank
group of London dockers for their work in raising money fo
charity. 'I went to the pub for the drinks and the barmai
said, "Fancy seeing you here." And the dockers couldn'
believe it. "You didn't go into the White Swan by yoursel
did you?" '

Because they are seen as remote from life, it often take
longer for the nun to get through to the people she wants t
help. A fifteen-year-old girl, in a home for delinquen
children where she had been sent following an offence, say
that she did not know the facts of life 'and I didn't want t
talk about things like that to a sister, I thought they wer
just holy.' So it was months before the sister in charge of he
got her talking about the sexual misunderstandings whic
proved to be the basis of all her adolescent problems. '
never knew,' the girl said later, 'that sisters knew thing
like that. But they do, because it's important in their live
too.'

At various times in their history convents have been the scen
of many a juicy scandal. It would be odd if this were not so
standards of behaviour and morality which were perfectl
acceptable to society in the twelfth century are quite untenabl
today. And religious were only people of their times. But it i
undoubtedly true that at no time have monasteries an
convents been so free of corruption as they are now: for on

ning, they are no longer places where people unsuited for
ny sort of life can be housed.

Many of the facts on which 'anti-papists' and pornographers
eized with equal delight centuries later were not at all
xtraordinary in their day. It was said, for example, that
obert d'Arbrissel, the hermit who established the double
rder of Fontevrault in 1101 at Maine-et-Loire in France,
sed to sleep in the same bed with his nuns. But such methods
f mortifying the flesh by exposure to temptation were common
t the time, and the order enjoyed a high reputation.

Some of the early scandals came about because religious
ouses were much involved with politics due to the kingly
nks between many of the occupants. One such story is that
f Chrodield, daughter of a King Charibert, who was a nun
f the Holy Cross, the order founded late in the sixth century
y Radegund of Poitiers in France. When another woman was
ppointed abbess in 589, Chrodield objected: 'Not as
aughters of kings are we treated but as though we were lowly
orn.' She and forty other nuns went to her royal relatives
to inform them of the contumely we have experienced'.
They went to Tours to Bishop Gregory and left most of the
uns there, while Chrodield went to her uncle at Orleans;
vhen she returned many had disappeared and married. But
he said, 'We are queens and we shall not return to the
nonastery until the abbess is deposed,' and she took the
emnants to Poitiers where, says Bishop Gregory, they were
oined by murderers, adulterers, law-breakers, and other
vrongdoers. A body of bishops urged the nuns to obey under
ain of excommunication. But they continued to 'dwell in
pen revolt', and raided the Holy Cross convent at night with
words and lances, carrying off the abbess, firing and plundering
he monastery. Finally, armed bands attacked the women and
heir followers, causing 'some to be beaten down, others
truck down by spears, and those who made most strenuous
pposition to be cut down by the sword'. The revolt had
ontinued for two years before Chrodield was sent, after a
ong enquiry, to live in a house provided for her. The next
year, there was a similar outbreak at Tours where another
woman felt herself cheated of becoming abbess.

As time went on, the quality of religious life did not improve, and the Black Death, which began in 1348 and raged throughout Europe, struck particularly at the closed communities. The numbers of religious were so reduced – only about a third survived – that discipline almost disappeared, and religion was treated with indifference.

A poem usually attributed to William Langland, 'The Vision of Piers Ploughman', written about this time declares that in one convent:

> *Dame Johane was a bastard,*
> *And Dame Clarice a knight's daughter, a cuckold was her sire,*
> *And Dame Purnell a priest's concubine, she will never become prioress,*
> *For she had a child in cherry time, all our chapter it wist.*

In 1397, the Prioress Margaret Fairfax of Nun-Monkton in Yorkshire was censured by the Archbishop of York for allowing a John Munkton to dine in her chamber, where he was said to have dallied with her and been served with drink. She also allowed her nuns to receive gifts from friends to support them, and too readily received those who had disgraced their profession through *lapsus fornicatione*. At about the same date Agnes, a nun of Catesby, visiting Northampton in her capacity as receiver of the nunnery, spent two evenings in two different friaries, dancing and playing the lute till midnight.

The Black Death also brought poverty, though it would seem that mismanaging superiors aggravated it. In 1404 Prioress Juliana of Bromhall in Berkshire was found to have 'injured the convent and her own character in that she had converted to her nefarious use, alienated and wasted chalices, books, jewellery, the income and possessions of the priory'. Forty years later at Catesby – a Benedictine house – the prioress Agnes Terry was suspended from conducting business relating to the revenue of the house. At Eastbourne in 1441, the house was £40 in debt due to the 'costly expenses of the prioress, who frequently rides abroad, and pretends she does so on the common business of the house, though it is not so, with a train of attendants much too large, and tarries long abroad, and she feasts sumptuously but while she does so the members of the convent are made to work like hired work-women'. The prioress was ordered to sell her costly fur trimmings to pay the debts and content herself with four horses when next she went out.

Such behaviour did not go unremarked.

A satire on monastic life was published in 1430 called *The Land of Cockeyne*. It describes a monastery built of food and sweetmeats with a crystal cloister, and the nearby 'fair nunnery' where the nuns wear silk and bathe in a river of milk, disporting themselves together with the monks, throwing off all restraint. And at the same time a poem called 'Why I Cannot Be a Nun' has characters called Dame Hypocrite, Dame Sloth, Dame Lust and Dame Wanton, and says that while some nuns are devout and holy, others are 'lewd and forward'. Life was so luxurious and dissolute in the monasteries that in 1489 Archbishop Morton of Canterbury secured a papal bull enabling him to visit all those in his diocese. He was particularly worried about the nunnery of St Mary Pre, where a married woman had not only entered but been appointed prioress 'notwithstanding her husband was living and is alive now'. And several monks were said to have had access to her and to others elsewhere 'as to a brothel or house of ill fame'.

Gradually, churchmen began to take over poverty-stricken convents and turn them into schools for religious education. The nunnery at Bromhall, for instance, already accused of enormities, misgovernance and slanderous living, was granted to St John's College, Cambridge. The way was paved for the dissolution of the monasteries, and twelve years later Henry VIII decided to suppress all religious houses with an income of less than £200 annually – which meant all but the fifteen largest and richest. Their goods and lands, their houses and farms, their granaries and ornaments, were all to be 'enjoyed by the king and his heirs'.

As the dissolution progressed, there were more and more charges of immoral behaviour amongst the nuns. Such accusations of impropriety rendered it possible for Henry's men to acquire their land and goods 'lawfully', and such claims would have been hard even for totally innocent women to disprove against the word of the king's men. Then, too, much of the loose behaviour ascribed to nuns might well have been true of inmates of the convents who were not necessarily nuns: it was common practice at the time for women of the upper classes to take themselves off to convents temporarily as penance for past behaviour. It was all too easy to accuse a woman of immorality: even churchmen did so to gain their own ends. When Anne Boleyn wanted a friend made abbess at Wilton, a house under royal patronage, Cardinal Wolsey opposed the idea, having already planned that Isabel Jordan should have the post. However, he saw Anne's applicant and, as Henry later wrote to Anne, a Master Bell who was present 'certified to me that for a truth she has confessed herself to have had two children by sundry priests and further since has been kept by a servant of Lord Broke that was, and not long ago; wherefore I would not for all the world clog your conscience nor mine to make her ruler of a house who is of such ungodly demeanour, nor I trust you would not that neither for brother nor sister I should so strain mine honour and conscience.'

But some behaviour was undoubtedly due to the state of the religious houses. The nunnery at Lillichurch in Kent became so poor that numbers had dropped by 1521 to three or four nuns, notorious for neglect of their duties. The prioress was dead and the house frequented by clerics, and finally a public enquiry was made. Asked how this had happened, one of the sisters admitted yielding to temptation, but added sadly, 'And had I been happy I might have caused this thing to be unknown and hidden.'

As the dissolution got further under way, Thomas Cromwell, vice-regent in ecclesiastical matters, conferred power on laymen to visit the convents and monasteries. One common practice was to forbid the inhabitants ever to leave their enclosures, thus bringing certain ruin on houses which relied on farming for their living. All those under twenty-four were dismissed from convent life, even if they were solemnly professed. The richer convents attempted bribery, and payments into the royal exchequer usually guaranteed a measure of peace. Alice Fitzherbert, whose convent of Polesworth in Warwickshire had an excellent reputation, bought a reprieve for £50. Others paid enormous sums – one house, Pollesloe, with an income of £164 a year, paid £400. The choice of which convents survived seems quite arbitrary. At Catesby, for instance, the house was given an excellent character by the agent and commissioners who visited it for Cromwell and wrote: 'We found the house in very perfect order, the prioress a wise, discreet and religious woman with nine devout nuns under her as good as we have seen. The house stands where it is a relief to the poor.' They recommended that no house was 'more meet for the king's charity', but though the prioress offered the king 2000 marks, and Cromwell himself '100 marks of me to buy you a gelding', as well as her prayers, it was to no avail: the convent was dissolved.

The agents were usually ruthless men, eager for the spoils: vestments were seized, furniture and utensils sold, lead torn off churches and choirs, steeples and cloisters. Money, jewels and silver were reserved for the King's use, usually to be broken up and melted. Relics and pictures were burnt. The abbess of Godstow wrote to Cromwell complaining of London, most avid of the agents. Not only did he 'inveigle my sisters one by one otherwise than I ever heard tell that any of the king's subjects have been handled', but he 'here tarries and continues to my great cost and charge'.

Those whose convents were dissolved were supposed to be given pensions, but only a few ever received them. Then the amount depended on the wealth of the house in which they had lived: some got twenty shillings a year, others £133. Being thrown out of their homes must have been even worse for the women than for the monks and brothers. Francis Gasquet, writing his *Henry VIII and the Dissolution of the Monasteries*, remarks that few of the nuns were known to have married, and the French ambassador to England, Eustache Chapuys, writing in July 1536, four months after the dissolution began, thought that: 'It is a lamentable thing to see a legion of monks and nuns who have been chased from their monasteries wandering miserably hither and thither seeking

means to live; and several honest men have told me that what
with monks, nuns and persons dependent on the monasteries
suppressed, there were over 20,000 who knew not how to
live.'

What has primarily determined the image of the nun is the
social climate and the regard in which religion is held at the
time. On the Continent and in England, the idea that virginity
was pleasing to God was very much in the foreground until
the sixteenth century. But when the Protestant reformers
found their voice, they declared celibacy odious, in open
antagonism to monastic principles and the Church of Rome.
It was, they said, foolish and presumptuous to make a vow of
chastity. It was marriage, now, which was considered to be
the most acceptable state before God. The nun was either
attacked for her way of life or regarded with complete
indifference. One attacker was the Dutch philosopher
Desiderius Erasmus, who wrote of the lack of purpose in
convent life and the need to cultivate domestic qualities. In
The Penitent Virgin, he describes a seventeen-year-old who
wishes to become a nun. The man arguing with her points
out that if she wants to keep her maidenhood, she can live
with her parents and not turn herself from a free woman into a
slave. 'If you have a mind to read, pray or sing you can go
into your chamber as much and as often as you please. When
you have enough of retirement you can go to church, hear
anthems, prayers and sermons and if you see any matron or
virgin remarkable for piety . . . or any man who is endowed
with singular probity . . . you can have their conversation.
Once you are in the cloister,' he warns, 'all these things,
which are of great assistance in promoting piety, you lose at
once.' The girl goes into the convent, though – and after six
days she comes out, claiming she would rather die than remain.
Erasmus, while claiming to be 'by no means against the
monastic life', adds that he 'would undoubtedly caution all
young women, especially those of a generous temper, not to
precipitate themselves unadvisedly into that state from which
there is no getting out afterwards, and the more so because
their chastity is more in danger in the cloister than out of it,
and you may do whatever is done there as well at home.'

As it turned out, the Protestant Reformation completed what the Black Death, the Hundred Years' War and the Renaissance had begun: it swept away the monasteries of England, Scotland and Ireland, as well as those of Holland and Scandinavia. Most of those in Switzerland and Germany also vanished.

In Germany in the fourteenth century monasteries had drifted from being indifferent to being positively evil. This was due partly to the scattered provinces and, by the fifteenth century, to abuse of convent life which was said to be far greater than in England. The teaching of Luther – who himself married a former nun – helped kill the convent system: many nuns left the cloister, some married, others continued as Lutherans. Many nuns, though, held fast against the Lutheran preachers who attacked them. Wilibald Pirckheimer, humanist and writer, describes how 'the preachers scream, swear and storm, and do everything in their power to rouse the hatred of the masses against the poor nuns; they openly say that as words were of no avail, recourse should be had to force.' His sister, Charitas, was superior of a Poor Clare convent at Nuremberg where she and her nuns were, she says, continually harassed by 'powerful and evil-minded persons', who attempted to persuade them that the religious profession was 'a thing of evil and temptation'.

Charitas and her nuns were sworn at, pelted with stones and finally ordered home by the town council, who said they would be given money and dowries for those who married. But they were a devout community, and none wanted to leave. Finally three of the youngest nuns were dragged out in tears, their habits torn off, and they were bundled away. 'I and all my nuns,' wrote Charitas, 'are so distressed by all this that I have almost wept out my eyes . . . nothing ever so went to my heart.' After this they were left alone and, following her death in 1533, the nuns dwindled in number and eventually the house was closed.

Many other convents disappeared during the reform, some dissolved by the Pope because of their evil ways, others on the pretext of such behaviour as continually dining out. One Benedictine abbess, trying to reform her convent at Urspring, found her nuns – mainly of the nobility – so opposed to her plan that they barricaded themselves into the infirmary and the soldiers had to be called in. The soldiers were not much use, however, because 'religious dread' rendered them helpless, and finally the nuns had to be starved out.

It was not this kind of behaviour, however, that in later years was to do the image of religious life the greatest harm. Far more riveting were the stories about the much-maligned 'double communities', which provided a wealth of salacious ideas for early pornographers.

> *Tho some are Barren Does, yet others*
> *By Fryars help prove teeming Mothers,*
> *When all to such Lewdness run*
> *All's cover'd under Name of Nun.*

> *Th'Abbess, in Honour as She excels,*
> *Her Belly too, more often swells,*
> *If any She proves Barren still,*
> *Age is in fault, and not her will.*

This ditty refers to the Gilbertines, one of the most famous and austere of the double orders, and it was written by Gabriel d'Emilliane, who discussed them in a *Short History of Monastical Orders.* Here he claims: 'This Hermaphrodite order, made up of both Sexes, did very soon bring forth fruits worthy of itself; there holy virgins have got almost all of them big Bellies.' He did not allow the fact that he was writing in 1592 about an order which was founded in 1148 and had disappeared sixty years previously to hinder his flow of information in any way. 'These nuns,' he went on, 'to conceal from their world their infamous practices, made away secretly with their children, and this was the Reason why at the time of the Reformation so many Bones of Young Children were found buried in their Cloisters.'

Nor did d'Emilliane neglect the convents of his native Italy, claiming that: 'All the Debauched Youths of the City flocked to the Church of the Celestines at Milan, where these Nuns equally tickled their Ears and Fancies by the sweetness and

lasciviousness of their songs. The Scandal grew at last to that
Excess, that the Cardinal sent his Orders to have their
Church shut up, and absolutely forbade them to sing Musick
any more.' He also claims that the case of the Italian nuns at
Bresse 'made a great deal of noise in Italy'. There, he said,
'the Religious, finding themselves quite weary of keeping their
Vow of Chastity, agreed amongst themselves to admit their
Lovers into the Monastery, and having all bound themselves
in an Oath of Secrecy, they wrought hard to make a Passage
Underground, under the Walls of their Enclosure, and which
was to end in the House of a young Gentleman. Their Undertaking had so good a success that the Nuns enjoyed the Gallants
as often as they pleased.' As a result, he claimed, the nuns
would frequently undertake a retirement for six months
during which time they would not come to the grate 'in
order to hide the results of their behaviour'.

All these stories were merely salacious. But the nun is a
figure also found in pornography. 'The nun,' says one British
psychiatrist, 'is the woman above sex. She represents the
virgin mother, the mother who is asexual. So from the point
of view of someone being sadistic, and getting a kick out of
forbidden objects in sexual fantasies, she could come to
represent someone who could be used. And it's really a form
of blasphemy, this link between private fantasy and religious
practice. Swear words used privately in church, for instance,
or thinking of a nun while masturbating – these things deride
religion.'

Perhaps this explains why so much of the pornography of
the repressed Victorians refers to nuns. A curious document
called *Les Vestales de l'Église* describes the abbess administering
the discipline with '*un air lugubre*', while poems with titles
like 'The Pious Nun' describe flagellation in convents with
great enthusiasm. *Nunnery Dialogues* and *The Monk and the
Nuns: A Funny Tale* are fairly typical of English and German
literature of the time on the subject of convents, both much
concerned with the problems of young monks unable to
satisfy the demands made upon them.

Undoubtedly, though, plenty of the shocking tales of convent life were rooted in truth.

In France, in 1611, a Franciscan priest, a Provençal mystic called Louis Gauffridi, was burned alive on the charge of seducing two nuns. One, Louise Capeau, was only twelve years old. He then put her into an Ursuline convent to which he was confessor, in Saint-Baume. The convent was said to become possessed, and Louise reported to have three devils. She raged twice a day in front of an audience, confessing to monstrosities, and before an exorcist and an Inquisitor she screamed that her lover must be sent for trial and burned.

Louviers was another seventeenth-century convent where women were 'disturbed' – this time fifty-two of them. Yveilin, a surgeon who visited the convent, gave it as his opinion that they were suffering from 'extreme disturbances and derangements of the womb'. A novice there, Madeleine Bavant, claimed to have been used as 'altar and sacrifice' by the priest, a man called Picart, by whom she bore several children. She was sentenced to life imprisonment in the penitentiary of Evreux, and would apparently accuse people of witchcraft almost at random: the authorities found her most useful when they wished to rid themselves of people they found annoying.

This was a period when the decline in moral standards of some religious houses combined with the ignorance of the age to produce horrific results. Just after the Reformation both Catholic and Protestant countries were much concerned with mysticism and magic. In Europe women presumed to be witches were assiduously hounded throughout the sixteenth century, and many thousands of men and women were tried – and invariably found guilty, thus meriting terrible deaths. By the end of the seventeenth century, the American colonies were in the grip of the same hysteria, and the most famous witch trials, at Salem, Massachusetts, condemned nineteen to death. Possession of humans by evil demons, and influence on them by the devil, were completely acceptable ideas, remnants of the incubi and succubi of ancient European mythology: a succubus was a female demon, an incubus the male demon who preyed upon sleeping women. Nuns appear to have been uch troubled by their attentions during the Middle Ages.

Of all the stories of demonic possession, none is more
orrible than that of the nuns of the ancient Ursuline convent
f Loudun. The prioress there in the middle of the seventeenth
entury, Jeanne des Anges, was an intelligent but misplaced
voman with a deformed back and a vivid imagination. She
eard of Urbain Grandier, the new parish priest, and invited
im as chaplain to the convent. As the months went by,
he began to retail her sexual dreams of him to the sisters:
aany of the nuns developed obsessions and began to experience
octurnal visitations. What today would be seen as self-
nduced hysteria, an outlet for the pent-up sexual energies of
vomen who should not have been in religious life at all,
vas to prove fatal Grandier.

Sister Jeanne des Anges describes how she 'tore off all my
eils and those of any of my sisters I could lay hands on . . . I
rampled them and cursed the hour when I took my vows . . .
vhen I received the host at communion, when I had half wet
: between my lips, the devil took it and flung it back into the
riest's face.' She was said to speak in seven different diabolic
oices, and described how the devil arched her body until her
ead nearly touched her heels, and shouted obscenities out of
er mouth which it shocked her to hear. Before long, almost
ll in the convent were 'possessed', and the public flocked in
heir thousands to the convent to witness the shouting and
xcitement. It was reported that three of the exorcists called
n to release the nuns later died from terror and exhaustion.
Cardinal Richelieu, anxious to bring Loudun under his own
olitical control and fearing Grandier as a freethinker,
rdered that the malice of Sister Jeanne be exploited, and on
er evidence Grandier was sent to the stake. But naturally the
possessions' did not end with his death: Sister Jeanne was
xorcized finally by a Jesuit called Jean-Joseph Surin, which
eft him subject to pathological symptoms for the rest of his
ife.

Another French convent which caused a major scandal –
hough of a very different kind – was that of Port-Royale. This
Cistercian house, whose nuns were said to be 'as pure as
ngels and as proud as devils', provided one of the great

sensations of the reign of Louis XIV. Attacked by the Jesuits, defended by Racine, the nuns were finally removed forcibly by soldiers, 'as though,' wrote the diarist, the Duc de Saint-Simon, 'they were whores arrested in a bawdy house.'

Nothing stands now on the site of the famous convent but a round grey stone tower and a few outbuildings, isolated in the green Chevreuse valley twelve miles from Paris, and guarded by a cross old man with snarling Alsatians. Its history stretches back into the beginning of the thirteenth century when a married woman, Mathilde de Garlande, started a Cistercian abbey there. By the end of the sixteenth century the discipline had deteriorated and only twelve nuns were left. In 1602 a ten-year-old girl was received as abbess. The daughter of a Paris lawyer who lavished money on the house, she was to become Mère Angélique, restoring the abbey to its Cistercian strictness and refusing to allow her family to enter the cloister. Francis de Sales was her spiritual director, and the nuns wore a white habit emblazoned with a scarlet cross.

Port-Royale was an extraordinary place. Rigorously penitential, it was said to harbour miracles, and a niece of Pascal was supposedly instantly cured there by the miracle of the Holy Thorn. The abbey accepted the doctrine of Jansenism, which claimed that man, in order to achieve salvation, must have received the grace of God through predestination. This brought them into direct conflict with the Pope, Louis XIV — who saw it as republicanism — and the Jesuits, all of whom tried to get them to admit their heresy. There was never any proof of misbehaviour on the part of the nuns. When the surgeon Maréchal was asked to attend a woman there whose leg needed amputating, he later told the king that he had never visited a convent where the saintliness and piety impressed him more. Nowhere, he said, was the king more fervently prayed for.

In an attempt to starve the nuns out their funds were withheld; they were not allowed novices, and were denied the sacraments. Finally they were arrested by detachments of the French and Swiss guards and their subsequent treatment in prison was so bad it aroused a public outcry.

The abbey was razed to the ground, 'chapel, outhouses, everything,' recorded Saint-Simon, 'exactly as they serve the dwellings of kings' assassins. At the end no stone was left standing. All the building materials were sold, and the site was ploughed and sown with grass. In very truth, no compunction was shown, they were quite ruthless. The scandal was extreme even at Rome.' Three years later, by a papal bull, the nuns were permanently condemned.

The public has always relished scandals about nuns and convents, whether real or imagined. They have been the subject-matter of a plethora of books, often far from flattering. Among the most delightful is the *Decameron* by the fourteenth-century Neapolitan writer Boccaccio, whose nuns and monks pursue their unholy ends with bawdy charm. And Balzac's nuns and novices in *Droll Tales from the Abbeys of Touraine* were equally wanton – and equally winning. This was social satire but done with great good humour, which cannot be said of one of the best-known books about convent life: *La Religieuse* is a scathing attack by the eighteenth-century French satirical writer Denis Diderot. The image of religious life was not helped by books which purported to have been written by nuns. One of the most famous of these is the seventeenth-century *Letters of a Portuguese Nun*; supposedly five letters from a cloistered nun to the French officer who had seduced and deserted her. They are now usually ascribed to a French author and diplomat, Gabriel de LaVergne, Vicomte de Guilleragues.

But of all the fabrications concerning convents the *Awful Disclosures of Maria Monk* regarding a nunnery in Montreal occasioned the loudest uproar: in nineteenth-century America and Canada there was bitter controversy over the case, and in England the House of Lords attempted to bring monastic establishments under closer surveillance.

The story broke in 1836 with the publication of the book which immediately sold 250,000 copies. It claims to be 'a narrative of her suffering during a residence of five years as a novice and two years as a black nun in the Hôtel Dieu Nunnery at Montreal' – to which is added 'Notes, Affidavits, Confirmations and Facts of the present day, wherein Maria

Monk's disclosures are fully proved and the hideous nature o
the conventual system exposed'.

The frontispiece is a picture of Miss Monk holding a baby,
which she claims was fathered by one Father Phelan, priest of
parish church in Montreal. When she entered, she had been
told by the superior that 'one of my greatest duties was to
obey the priests in all things; and this I soon learnt, to my
utter astonishment and horror, was to live in the practice o
criminal intercourse with them'. That very afternoon, she
claims, she was taken to a private apartment by one of the
Fathers; 'I feared what was his intention but I dared no
disobey. He treated me in a brutal manner.' The priests, she
avers, had total control over the nuns. 'To name all the work
of shame of which they are guilty in that retreat would
require much time and space.'

The story grows more dramatic. 'The superior of the
seminary would sometimes come and inform us that he had
received orders from the Pope to request that those nun
who possessed the greatest devotion and faith should be
requested to perform some particular deed, which he named
or described in our presence, but of which no decent or
moral person would ever endure to speak.' She describes in
horrid detail the murder of twin babies, 'the children o
Sister Catherine', smothered by one of the old nuns with the
utmost indifference and then thrown in a cellar and covered
with lime. The accusations continued with descriptions o
underground passages between the convent and the priests
seminary next door.

Published in periodicals as well as in book form, it was
discussed at public meetings. And Maria Monk – who
'escaped' from her convent in 1833 – seems to have been
received by society in New York for her curiosity value
Reading her book now, it is hard to believe how seriously it
absurdities were taken. The inaccuracies – the five years as a
novice, for instance – did not seem to render it any les
believable to a lot of people. Even when Maria was unmasked
as a prostitute from Montreal, the total ignorance abou
religious life at the time was such that the story continued to
be believed. It was a tasty morsel of anti-Catholic propaganda

l even the assertions of many Protestants that the whole
ng was a fake failed to silence it. *Refutations* was published –
be met by further *Disclosures* answering them. Maria Monk
ered to go before a court of justice to swear to the truth
the accusations. She asked to be taken through the convent
th spectators, so that her account of the building could be
npared with the place itself. And the very fact that she
s not taken up on these offers added fuel to the fire.

By the end of the nineteenth century there was a good deal
doubtful literature published about nuns, some by former
igious and others quite clearly by women with severe
ntal problems. A former religious was Margaret Cusack –
e Nun of Kenmare' – an Irish Poor Clare at the turn of the
tury who had originally entered an Anglican community
the sudden death of her fiancé. After publishing over
enty books of pious fiction, she wrote a famous attack on the
ival of Anglican communities in Britain, called *Five Years in
Protestant Sisterhood and Ten Years in a Catholic Convent*. Ten
rs later she was lecturing in America and England on the
vin evils of Romanism and Ritualism'.

A similar writer was Edith O'Gorman, who claimed to
ve been a Sister of Charity in New Jersey, and who wrote
nvent Life Unveiled – the Escaped and Converted Nun* published
1871 in New York. This tract is now in its forty-second
inting. It is published – like the Maria Monk booklet –
the Protestant Truth Society, a rabidly anti-Catholic
ganization operating in England and Canada. *Convent Life
veiled* is full of all the clichés. Edith O'Gorman says she
s forced to hold her hands in lime because she was too
ud of them; the orphans in the charge of the nuns were
rminous and half-starved; she herself was made to bite
' the head of a live mouse at which she had screamed. It
st have been quite a community: Miss O'Gorman became
perior less than five years after entering, when she was only
enty-five. She reported the treatment meted out to nuns
o refused the advances of priests: they were thrown
o rat-infested dungeons until they went mad. She herself
t after similar advances. 'I fled in mid-winter out into
e world, without shelter, without protection; but better

than the abode of vipers and a life of sin.' Amazing even
were to follow. ('Suspicion that I had been ensnared to
maison d'infamie crossed my mind and paralysed my sens
with unspeakable horror'), but finally our heroine decid
she will lecture on her past. 'I was amazed at my own word
Lecture! Impossible. I, a weak, timid woman and natural
retiring, could never face assembled multitudes in order
teach the world the bitter lesson Rome had taught me.' Sl
did, though, choosing as her subject 'the Romish priesthooc
and at well over eighty she was still delivering two lectures
day all over the world. She married, too, one . Willia
Auffray. 'All the unspeakable delights of newly-wedded lo
are up to the present realized by us.'

When, in the latter half of the nineteenth century, Cathol
nuns began quietly to reappear in Britain, these stories
persecutions had an unfortunate effect. Sometimes con
munities found it politic to buy houses in the name of
individual, since owners often would not sell if nuns we
buying. The Sisters of the Cross and Passion, arriving
Lochgelly in Scotland to staff a primary school, found a lar
crowd gathered outside the convent one evening shouti
'Release the sister,' and 'Sister Mary Anne.' It turned out th
the white lamp swinging in the church porch looked like
nun in a guimpe hanging from a rope, and the people we
eager to believe the worst.

When Anglican communities first appeared in Englan
they too were regarded with great alarm, and attacked
tracts with such titles as *Sister of Mercy*, *Sisters of Misery*. Tl
feeling in Wales was particularly strong, the Welsh being
the main nonconformists. One man from a village ne
Swansea swears that as a child he was drawn indoors by l
grandmother, who with trembling fingers locked all the doc
and windows. 'What's wrong, Mamgu?' he asked. 'They'
coming,' she replied, her voice shaking. 'The nuns!'

In the United Sates, there were similar reactions. Whe
in the 1800s, communities arrived from Poland and Jugoslav
and Italy they mostly went to the East Coast, to New Yo

d Detroit. For a long time Maryland was the only Catholic
province in America. People were suspicious of Catholics,
who lived in isolated ghetto communities, educating their
children in their own schools, staffed by their own nuns,
united and segregated.

The nineteenth-century writings leant heavily for their
effect on the misinterpretation of certain monastic practices.
This is just as true today: 'nuns' are favourite performers in
nipclubs, particularly in London and Berlin; for some curious
reason they are usually menacing bored and prostrate 'school-
girls' with whips. And publications such as *Die Perverse Nonnen*,
which sells at £4 on the porn black-market, show 'nuns' in
various stages of undress, but complete with crucifixes,
whipping a tied and naked man.

Religious penitential practices have always held a morbid
fascination for the public. Most such pornographic material
is based on garbled half-knowledge. It also has to be admitted
that self-torture, though undertaken for religious reasons,
frequently produced sexual pleasure – although the nuns
themselves did not recognize it for what it was.

Extreme physical penance is now rare and it is certainly
no longer obligatory. But individual nuns do still inflict
considerable pain on themselves. It has been a real enough part
of religious life to have developed its own terrifying gadgetry.
Women in religious orders justify penance very much as did
Bernard of Clairvaux, ascetic abbot of that most ascetic of
orders, the Cistercians: 'The body of Christ is crushed, let us
learn how to subdue our bodies . . . our bodies must be
conformed to the likeness of Our Lord's wounded body.' Until
recently the Cistercians continued to take the discipline
daily. Now it will be whenever the individual feels it necessary,
perhaps once a month. Even so, plenty of women consider
such mitigation of the rule a mistake. A Cistercian abbess told
me: 'I'm a traditionalist. I don't like any change, and if I had
my way the discipline would continue to be used regularly.'

It is with the discipline, the traditional thrashing-cord of
the monastery, that religious wage war upon the natural
desires and inclinations of the body. As Christ was scourged, so
generations of men and women have submitted to the twelve-

inch-long whip of thin waxed cord with five or six knott
tails. Another version is formed of a small metal ring wi
five chains suspended from it, each chain ending in a hoo
The discipline is used on specified days, perhaps Wednesd:
and Fridays, for a period of time laid down in the regulatio
and only on certain parts of the body – back, legs and buttoc
while the nun recites prayers. The pain suffered is offered
for the sins of the nun and the world. 'It was a method,' sa
a young American, 'of disciplining the imagination and t
memory, and thus constantly keeping out of touch wi
certain feelings.' 'We felt,' explains an English Sacred He:
sister, 'that we were really following Our Lord who h
himself had a painful life. That helps you.'

As the novice continues in the life, so the number
permitted strokes increases – though at no time should
draw blood. But the pain inflicted is considerable, and tl
caused by the metal discipline, with its snake-like tails,
greater. When not in use, the discipline is kept in the cell
the black cover sewn by the owner and for many, that its
is painful: 'The anticipation is the worst part.' Many wome
indeed, have found it almost too much for them. 'The fi
time I used it,' a Carmelite told me, 'I almost went off :
head in the cell.'

The connection between sexual pleasure and pain
particularly close for women. This is true even when the p:
is self-inflicted. One elderly sister of the Society of the Sacr
Heart remembers that the discipline became 'one of :
major troubles. Not because of the pain, but for some peop
such pain can give trouble in the sexual line. It upset me
that way. I knew it was arousing me in that direction
nothing else had done. It even got into my dreams.'

It was, she says, 'sheer fervour' which made her continu
That, and the fact that 'we girls were incredibly ignora:
and it was so difficult to find out. It was a long time befor
got to know what those physical emotions were.' Things we
not helped by the mistress of novices, who herself could :
understand it. 'We went to Rome – and not one of th
women understood it either.'

Nuns are less innocent now. 'We aren't as naïve as '

were,' remarks one superior. 'We can see the correlation between the discipline and sexuality.'

There are other instruments of penance. The hairshirt is one. Made out of horsehair, roughly knotted with as many ends as possible left loose to prickle the wearer, it can either be worn as a long sleeveless tunic or as a wide belt round the loins. Or there are linked metal bands to go round arms or legs, designed so that the points with which they are studded press into the flesh with sudden movement. Chain girdles can be used with the same effect, though, like the discipline, they are not intended to draw blood.

Another penitential object is the small wooden cross studded with blunt nails worn under the clothes against the skin. Pressed on the shoulder beneath a heavy mantle this produces almost excruciating pain. Hedgehog skins serve the same purpose.

The penances fulfilled a real function in the context of religious life. 'When wisely practised they produced remarkable results,' says Monica Baldwin, the English ex-nun, in her book *I Leap Over the Wall*. 'They do a very great deal to bring about that subjection of the body to the spirit without which the highest adventures in the spiritual life can never be achieved.'

It was very much part of the formalized tradition of religious life; even so, physical penance has lost favour. Younger and more sophisticated superiors, the teachings of Freud and the impact of Vatican II have had their effect. But if physical penance is not obligatory on the individual in most orders, it is certainly not forbidden. The extent to which it is still practised will depend largely upon the attitude of the country. At one time, for instance, the Carmelites derived much of their income from making their own instruments of penance. In Paris this was 'quite profitable,' but when they arrived in London at the beginning of the twentieth century they decided that 'this was not likely to be so in England,' and turned to baking altar breads instead. And in Spain today, where ordinary men and women make pilgrimages on their knees, extreme physical penance is still usual for those in religious orders.

At particularly penitential times, such as Lent, most nuns and monks probably adopt some form of self-torture. Few, though, would go as far as St Rose of Lima, a South American nun who, out of 'love for the crucified Saviour', wore a spiked iron band round her head and carried a heavy cross for hours on shoulders already bleeding from the discipline. She was also given to sleeping on a bed of pointed stones and is said to have spent whole nights suspended on a cross.

Another penitent was the seventeenth-century Sister Margaret Mary, who was so determined to make a complete gift of herself to the Sacred Heart that she carved 'Jesus' in her breast with a knife. Not satisfied with that, she burned the letters in with a lighted candle.

These cases are clearly extreme – not to say pathological – but some religious women do still regularly stay up all night in penance, arms outstretched for hours. There are other ways, too, of practising physical penance. A Carmelite nun now in England, who used to live in the French convent at Meaux, recalls the sacristan, a woman who did beautiful silverwork. One day she fell off a ladder and twisted her neck. She never did anything about it, despite constant pain. When asked why she did not see the doctor she replied, '*Pourquoi*? The good God has sent me this.'

The public image of the nun as a submissive spinster is so strong that the Franciscan Communications Centre in Los Angeles, a public relations organization for religion, does not ever use nuns in their films or advertising because they are regarded as so off-putting.

At best they are seen as meek and docile, encased in wimples and innocence, as in *The Sound of Music*. Some are not averse to exploiting this fact, like the Belgian Sister Luc-Gabrielle who topped the record charts in 1963 with a shrewd combination of the monastic habit and a bouncy tune called 'Dominique'. But most nuns and sisters are becoming increasingly irate at the way in which they consider they are being inaccurately portrayed by the media. Current films and plays, claims one American sister, 'perpetuate the medieval myths and present a distorted image'. Nuns are shown in one of two ways. they are either loveless authoritarians, such as the novice mistress in *The Song of Bernadette*, or highly romanticized, unreal women — Ingrid Bergman playing opposite Bing Crosby in *The Bells of St Mary's*. Even more unlikely is the central figure in one of the most successful American ABC comedy half-hours of recent years. In *The Flying Nun* a round-faced Sally Field zooms around the sky in full habit and a huge white cornet headdress, and the schmaltzy situations include a Jewish wedding in the convent garden and raising money for the neighbourhood kids.

A recent gem of the cinema is *A Change of Habit*, starring Mary Tyler Moore and Elvis Presley. A young doctor working with a woman out of her habit in a city clinic does not realize that she is a nun. He buys her ice-cream and tries to hold her hand, but never gets really rebuffed, which leads to the exquisite dialogue when she finally appears before him coiffed and starched and says, 'You know I have a vow of chastity?' To which he asks, 'Wouldn't a vow of honesty be better?' The whole thing ends with Mary Tyler Moore on her knees in the chapel trying to decide between religious life and Presley.

The Weekend Nun is an American offering which has already appeared twice on British television. Starring a pained Joanna Pettet, it is based on the autobiography of a former nun, Joyce Duco. The film opens with Sister Damian leaving her New Orleans convent to buy her first dress for her new job as a probation officer, then returning to the convent and the habit each night. Her superior warns her not to let the job interfere with her religious life, and cautions her against working on reports late at night. She is given the case of a fifteen-year-old prostitute and establishes enough rapport with the girl for her to turn up at the convent for help. But Sister Damian has been ordered to a retreat by the superior, and the girl, rushing to find her, is knocked down and killed. Forced to choose between her life as a nun and her 'other' work, Sister Damian leaves the convent.

When this film was first shown in the States in 1972 it would be an understatement to say that nuns did not like what they saw. Members of the National Association of Women Religious 'just couldn't believe it'. They objected particularly to the suggestion that religious life could not integrate with a woman's work. 'When the mother superior says, "Remember that the convent is a spiritual sanctuary," we just about hit the roof. We don't see it that way.' They, no less than other people, can be over-sensitive about the difference between the way they see themselves and the way others present them. In this case, they did perhaps over-react.

The NAWR sisters immediately launched a storm of protest to the president of the American Broadcasting Company, and all the showbusiness magazines, pointing out that the film with its insistence on the dominance of the mother superior, the naïve belief that the resort to prayer was a panacea for all problems, and its supposition that religious life does not allow initiative, hinders the struggle of 'the contemporary American sister for recognition as a competent professional'. They got a front-page story in *Variety*, a radio interview, and fifteen minutes on Ralph Story's show. Since then, Liz Thoman has started a campaign offering NAWR members as consultants on religious life to the entire American entertainment industry.

There are currently numerous films and plays about nuns — quite apart from such offerings as *Sex Life in a Convent* and *Le Couvent des Femmes*. Two major films, a West End play, and an opera appeared in Britain alone in 1973. Franco Zeffirelli made *Brother Sun, Sister Moon* about the young Francis of Assisi and Sister Clare, foundress of the Poor Clares. There was a film about Pope Joan with the Scandinavian actress Liv Ullman playing the woman who is supposed to have occupied the Holy See in the mid-ninth century for a short time, between Leo IV and Benedict III. She was a nun who is said to have died when the crowd trampled her to death in indignation after she gave birth on the steps of St Peter's.

In London's West End there was the premiere of John Kerr's play, *Mistress of Novices*, about Bernadette of Lourdes, and the Paris Opéra staged a new production of Francis Poulenc's *Dialogues des Carmélites*. This was inspired by the deaths of the entire household of Carmelites at Compiègne, who were sent to the guillotine during the French Revolution.

Much of the literature about life in convents is written by nuns themselves, invariably after they have left their orders. Titles like *Out of the Curtained World* and *The Buried Life* abound, but the picture they present is as biased as a divorcée talking about marriage. Outsiders manage to invoke the women and their world far more vividly, as authoress Rumer Godden does in her book about the peaceful Benedictines, *In This House of Brede*. Showing a less attractive aspect of the dedicated life is *The Nun's Story* by Kathryn Hulme. A bestseller, which was filmed with Audrey Hepburn and Peter Finch, it tells of the Belgian Sister Luke, who leaves her missionary nursing order because the strictness of the rule demands that she put the bells calling her to prayer before the needs of her patients. Antonia White's novel, *Frost in May*, is also about conformity in convent life, describing Fernanda Gray's education at the Convent of the Five Wounds, where the girls are subjected to discipline only a little less rigid than are the nuns themselves.

Much of the poetry inspired by the religious life is exquisite, like that of the Jesuit priest Gerard Manley Hopkins. He described the cloistered life in 'The Habit of Perfection':

> Elected Silence, sing to me
> And beat upon my whorlèd ear,
> Pipe me to pastures still, and be
> The music that I care to hear.
>
> Shape nothing, lips; be lovely-dumb;
> It is the shut, the curfew sent
> From there where all surrenders come
> Which only makes you eloquent.

Most poetry idealized religious women, like Wordsworth's nuns who 'fret not at their convent's narrow room'. Alexander Pope, the eighteenth-century Catholic, wrote *Eloisa to Abelard* when England was rabidly anti-Catholic. He describes the blameless vestal and her

Desires compos'd, affections ever ev'n;
Tears that delight, and sighs that waft to heav'n.
Grace shines around her with serenest beams,
And whisp'ring Angels prompt her golden dreams.
For her th'unfading rose of Eden blooms,
And wings of Seraphs shed divine perfumes,
For her the Spouse prepares the bridal ring,
For her white virgins Hymeneaals sing;
To sounds of heav'nly harps she dies away,
And melts in visions of eternal day.

Other poets took a more worldly view, like James Henry Leigh Hunt in 'The Nun':

> *If you become a nun, dear,*
> *A friar I will be,*
> *In any cell you run, dear,*
> *Pray look behind for me.*

One of the oddest poems is anonymous. Entitled 'I'm the Daddy of a Nun', it was given to me by a Catholic sister whose father – like many others – carries it around with a photograph of his daughter on the back. Published in Italy but sounding faintly Irish, it is illustrated with the Pope's hand raised in a blessing:

> *Sure my daughter has been vested*
> *And my joy I cannot hide,*
> *For I've watched her from the cradle*
> *With a father's honest pride.*

> *Since to err is only human*
> *There's a whole lot on the slate*
> *That I'll have to make account for*
> *When I reach the golden gate.*

> *But then I'm not a-worrying*
> *About the deeds I've done,*
> *I'll just whisper to St Peter:*
> *'I'm the daddy of a nun.'*

IMAGES: SACRED AND PROFANE

It is partly the traditional view of the nun's role – held not only by the public but by some of those within religious life – which explains the furious reaction to the work of Sister Corita Kent. An American sister of the Immaculate Heart of Mary order in California, she is a tiny, graceful woman whose work shocked the religious establishment. Hating the simpering plaster statues that lurk in the corners of Catholic convents, she has produced work completely against the grain of conventional 'religious' art. Her asymmetrical Christs and elongated madonnas were at first greeted with floods of letters, many abusive and anonymous – the more so because she was a nun. Within the convent, opinion on her work was divided, and she was blamed when some of the young sisters she had taught left the order.

Corita Kent is now recognized as one of the great contemporary printmakers. Her serigraphs – streaks of brilliant colour accompanied by quotations from e. e. cummings, Ugo Betti and Bertolt Brecht – hang in the New York Museum of Modern Art and London's Victoria and Albert. She is one of the few artists of real stature to emerge from the chrysalis of the convent to worldwide acclaim, and that she has done so is a hopeful sign. In the past, superiors would have considered it their duty to suppress any particular gift, to humble the person 'lest it take away from God'. It is an attitude that St Benedict summed up in his rule, saying: 'If there be craftsmen in the monastery, let them practise their craft with all humility, providing the abbot give permission, but if one of them be puffed up because of his skill in his craft, supposing that he is conferring a benefit on the monastery, let him be removed from his work and not returned to it, unless he have humbled himself and the abbot entrust it to him again.'

Even under such a rule, there were nuns whose talent could not be stifled. Mother Geneviève was one. A French Benedictine, she produced drawings, engravings and painted glass windows, and a recent sale of her work in Paris received wide publicity. She drew priests on bicycles and old women walking in the rain, and the power and vigour with which she did so caused critics to liken her to Daumier and Toulouse-Lautrec. She saw the world with a mixture of pity and biting wit:

one of her drawings is called '*Le Feu à la Communauté*' and shows a nun poking a fire above a caption reading: 'The more you poke the better it burns and shines: You see, O my soul, you need just that.' But it needed a woman of determination, as well as extraordinary skills, to retain and develop her art in the convent.

There must have been many more — admittedly slighter — talents which were lost for ever under the system. Since the softening of the rules following Vatican II, enough women of genuine artistic merit have appeared within religious orders to demonstrate that they must always have been there. It is only in the last few years, for example, that the poems of Sister Mary Agnes, an enclosed Poor Clare nun, have been published: they have been likened to those of Emily Brontë. The Goanese sister, Teresa d'Cruz of the Ladies of Mary, has exhibited her batiks — pictures made on silk with dyes and hot wax — in both London and Paris. Her order permits her to wear secular dress and live in a Left Bank apartment.

Nothing is better calculated to change the image of the nun than the emergence of such women. But a convent is by its very nature not an easy place in which to foster individual talent. Corita Kent has left the religious life. It remains to be seen whether orders can, in the future, contain her successors.

10

CAN CONVENTS
SURVIVE?

*The Church knows all the rules. But it doesn't know what goes
on in a single human heart.*
GRAHAM GREENE: THE HEART OF THE MATTER

Religious life has always had a one-way traffic in personnel –
into its convents and monasteries. Today the traffic is still
largely one-way, but it is beginning to turn and head over-
whelmingly in the opposite direction.

The future of religious communities of women is threatened
by two facts. Fewer and fewer girls are entering religious
life. And, every year, more and more sisters are leaving.

It is a malaise that has been increasing noticeably over the
last thirty years, but it has reached dangerous proportions only
since the beginning of the 1950s. Articles and books have
appeared in the religious press on the 'vocation crisis' and the
'sister shortage'; conferences are held to discuss the problem;
seminars convened on survival strategy; prayers are offered.

But all over Europe the situation has deteriorated. Convents
are closing as orders amalgamate under-staffed houses.
Schools are abandoned because there are not enough sisters to
run them; convalescent homes are being sold; hospitals are
handed over to local government. The needs are still there,
but the nuns are not. Small communities have chosen to
band with others who follow a similar life-style: in England,
for instance, the Sisters of Perpetual Adoration merged with
the Religious of the Eucharist, and the Sisters of the Faithful
Virgin with the Congregation of Our Lady of Fidelity. Many
others, however, have simply closed down houses and re-
treated. Within the few years it took to assemble this book,

several of the houses I visited disappeared, including two
schools, a home for mentally defective women, another for
disturbed adolescents, and a hostel for orphaned girls.

Communities with novitiates built to house fifty now think
themselves lucky to have five; even more communities have
found themselves with none at all. As recently as five years ago,
the Sisters of Mercy, an Irish-founded order, expected to
have forty novices at a time. In September 1972 they had
nine – and four of these left within the year. The Augustinian
Sisters of Meaux in London attracted seven novices between
1965 and 1974, but only three remained. The Maryknoll
order had nearly fifty entrants in 1962. In 1966 the number
was down to twenty and by the mid 1970s three or four was
considered a respectable number.

Of those who enter, a larger proportion than ever is likely
to drop out before reaching final profession.

Orders can chart the fall in entrants. The Carmelites
remember a 'tide of vocations' which started in 1905 and
went on for thirty years. Every year there were dozens of
ceremonies – clothings, professions, the giving of the black
veil. Today, they too are amalgamating their small houses. The
Dominican Sisters of Bethany is a Dutch order which runs
foster homes for parentless girls. In 1901 it was strong enough
to send twenty-three sisters to Chicago, where the order
speedily acquired eight novices. In 1973 it made plans to give
up its work. 'We had to' said the superior, 'there just weren't
enough of us to do it. To look after eight girls only, we need
two nuns – and we're down to six sisters.' Now, the Sisters
of Bethany are working individually in hospitals. 'We might
as well go home and do something there.'

It is hard to believe that once there were so many new orders
being formed that it was finally forbidden to found one unless
it was based on a recognized rule. Yet the sales slogan for the
religious life is superb. 'Everyone that hath left house or
brethren or sisters or father or mother or wife or children or
lands, for My Name's sake, shall receive a hundredfold and
shall possess life everlasting.' Why, then, do so few follow?

The reasons are many and complex, but one overrides all
others: opportunity. There was no lack of entrants in the

past because, often, there was no other life a single woman could decently lead. Until Florence Nightingale, even nursing was considered to be coarse and degrading. An unmarried lady could be a governess if she had to earn her living, or a housekeeper, or even a dressmaker. But she had no vote, no chance to hold any kind of public post. She could do neither welfare nor administrative work unless her qualifications were exceptional, and this was unlikely since universities were closed to her. In Catholic countries, the same tradition that kept religion strong, kept her down just as strongly. Even much more recently the possibilities open to women remained restricted, and the respectable girl who was neither married nor a nun was an old maid. There was just one way she could begin to free herself: by joining a religious community. There she could teach or nurse, or work with prisoners, or in hospitals, or with deprived children. She could travel the world as a missionary. She had a busy life, was part of a loving community, and was sure of a home in her old age. At its very worst, it was a better fate than many.

But today, to be single is no longer considered pitiable: the woman living alone is as likely to be envied as not. She can spend her time how and as she wishes, tackle almost any job for which she is fitted, and she needs no veil to do so respectably. If she feels she needs a community, a group of people with whom to share her life, she can look around and find a growing number of alternatives to a convent. Quite apart from the trend towards commune living, there are groups of all shades and tones of religious belief, from the Jesus hippies to the lay communities. That is, of course, if she wishes to remain single. Today, ninety per cent of the population in Britain can expect to be married by middle age, against seventy-five per cent in the last century – another nail in the coffin of religious life. Yet another is increased employ-ment and financial prosperity in poor Catholic communities. The richer a country, the fewer its vocations. It is in times of crisis that there are plenty of recruits: during the Depression years in America there was a vocations boom. With money comes increased sophistication – and the spread of birth control. And with financial security, attitudes change. 'Then there's very little emphasis on sacrifice in family life today,' according to the superior of one affected order.

The falling-off of vocations is not a fact in isolation but part of the general tide against the Church throughout Europe. Fewer people are baptized in church, fewer are married there. Attendances have fallen drastically, particularly in the last ten years. Even in Italy, the increased secularization of society has greatly affected vocations. Italy has about 160,000 nuns in its huge collection of different orders and convents, and many there have either closed or are on the brink of doing so through lack of recruits. Sister Lorenzina Guidetti of the Daughters of St Paul says with some sadness that in the past, 'a vocation was always considered a blessing, especially in the southern regions, in Lombardy and Emilia.' Those days are ending.

A French sister observes: 'Vocations don't seem to exist in France,' and names several orders which have one or no postulants. She believes women's orders are suffering from the phase of *aggiornamento* following Vatican II, and that uncertainty over the direction religious life is taking inhibits many girls from entering. At the end of the 1960s a group of sociologists examined monastic life, and their findings indicated that in Austria the contemplative communities of women are doomed to disappear soon, except for perhaps three or four convents. Out of nineteen houses, fourteen have had few or no entrants for many years. The sociologists found the same situation to be true in North America, Britain and much of Europe. The Daughters of Charity of St Vincent de Paul confirm this. They have found a lowering of vocations in almost every country – with an exception, interestingly, in those countries where, because of the political situation, a nun can most expect to be persecuted by the state. The majority come from the Philippines and Jugoslavia, as well as Vietnam, Indonesia and Japan. 'Once sisters were sent out from Europe to these countries,' observes Sister Agnes, secretary general at the Paris house. 'Now they're springing up there.' Meanwhile, vocations continue to decline in Great Britain, Germany, Holland and Belgium. And in America, according to a superior there, 'religious life has such a bad

ame right now that the really live American girl, who twenty-
ive years ago would have joined Maryknoll, just wouldn't go
here today.'

Sisters do their best to understand and explain what is
happening. They suggest all sorts of reasons, from the unhappy
example of overworked and harassed teaching sisters to the
debasing effects of mass media entertainment'. Bertrande
Meyers, an American sister, blames the 'deplorable practice
of steady dating begun in the too-early teens' and the softness
of American youth, while the Pope thinks the vow of obedience
is too much for the modern young woman to take.

The majority of women are philosophical about the shortage.
I think we shall get through this,' believes Anglican superior
Sister Thomasina of the Sacred Passion sisters. 'Once or
twice before, we've had a bad patch. If we die out, it shows
the work God has given us has come to an end.' Sister Marissa
of the Poor Servants of the Mother of God is not concerned
about her postulants, although she has only two. 'We live in
hope. There's so much glamour for young people. But if
they have a vocation they'll come, no matter about the
glamour.' At the same time, they realize the necessity of
catching the public eye, although they find this hard. One
contemplative community recently took part in a television
programme. After much heart-searching they allowed a whole
film crew inside the enclosure – all men except the continuity
girl. For two weeks their lives were disrupted, but they felt it
was worth while for two reasons. They wanted to give the
outside world a chance to see just what a life of prayer meant.
And they admit they hoped it would attract girls to their
life. The film was shown in Britain, Australia and South
Africa. The response was tremendous, and they received
letters, gifts and a great deal of admiration – but not one girl
came forward as a novice.

In the past priests and nuns toured schools seeking young
recruits for orders. They still visit but now, as one vocational
director put it, 'We do so to persuade people to become
Christians.' The vocations industry has had to become increasingly high-powered, and many American orders now have
a mediator or recruiter who does nothing but encourage

vocations by publicizing community efforts to reach suitable people. Shortage of entrants is just as acute among men's orders but none of the women's communities has yet reached the point of the American Trinitarians who advertised for brothers and priests in *Playboy*. European communities concentrate on a softer sell. In Britain, for example, there is a full-time vocations director in almost every diocese. He will be a member of the National Conference of Diocesan Directors of Vocations – a body which meets only twice a year. Prayer is a far more popular method of encouraging entrants, and the Vocation Sisters even organized a group of sixty to go to Lourdes and pray for them from there. In 1972, nuns from ninety-five convents gathered for a one-day 'pray in' for vocations. Five hundred of them, with guitars and the culinary assistance of the Army Catering Corps, descended on a Surrey seminary to 'dispel the everything-is-rotten-in-the-state-of-Denmark feeling conveyed by the press reporting the drop in vocations.'

Then there are 'convent weekends' and working holidays to which girls are invited to learn more about nuns, with conferences and discussions. And there are 'vocations weeks', when a team of religious men and women spend their mornings in a diocese, visiting the schools and the sick, and their evenings celebrating Mass in different houses in the parish – all in an effort to increase interest in religious life. Occasionally there are massive religious exhibitions, where perhaps a hundred different orders and societies will show films and arrange exhibits to describe their work. Missionary fathers give concerts on native drums, and sisters model their modernized habits as 'the most exclusive fashions in the world'.

Despite all the doleful omens and convent closures, some new orders have begun in the last twenty years and survived. But as Mary Garson, an English psychologist who founded the Sisters of Our Lady of Grace and Compassion in 1954, says, 'It is battling against the tide at the moment.' She decided to look after old people, not because it was work she particularly wanted to do – she would rather work with children – but because she saw the need. Now fifty-one, she is energetic and youthful, always travelling between the nineteen houses she runs in this country and the mother house in Sussex, a Victorian folly which looks like a Bavarian schloss escaped from its native hills.

During the first few years, 'people came and went. They served a purpose.' It was not until 1959 that any stayed, and only two of her present sisters date from that time. There are thirty-three at the moment and this can go up to forty. There are also four novices and two postulants. 'But we could have many more in the community if we hadn't decided to become more exacting.' Those who do enter come mainly in answer to advertisements. Sister Mary Garson was the first sister in Britain to advertise her order regularly in the Catholic press. 'We had to do it – if you're new, nobody knows you.' She finds that about two girls a month are sufficiently interested by the ads to come and try the life, and five actually enter each year. 'One year they might all stay, the next they might all go.' Last year she decided to make an extra effort to attract vocations and lay workers: apart from going to churches and leaving literature, she visited schools with slides, and made a film strip about the order. 'But personally, I don't feel that vocations are picking up.'

Now advertisements, hundreds of them, are used by almost all orders. 'Come, give yourself to God,' urge the Sisters of St Paul. 'There is work for you to do in the Ecumenical vineyard,' claim the Swedish Bridgettines. 'Searching for fulfilment?' ask the Handmaids of the Sacred Heart. 'If you are courageous enough to accept the CHALLENGE of no geographical boundaries, of no limit to your dedication to Christ through Mary,' write to the Marist Sisters. If, on the other hand, you feel that 'Our Lord is calling you to consecrate your life to him in the service of souls by teaching, nursing, youth work, child-care, housekeeping, catering or secretarial work,' then contact the Sisters of Providence. You can spread the Good News with the Dominicans, or work with Christ for the salvation of souls with the Sisters of the Convent of St Lucy.

The contemplatives advertise too, rather more gently. The Olivetan Benedictines welcome enquiries from 'ladies wishing to try their vocation,' and the Benedictines of Stanbrook Abbey, Worcester, promise: 'Prayer, Serenity, Wisdom.'

What does seem to be happening is that more and more enquiries are coming from women in their forties and fifties. The Vocations Sisters, who pass on enquiries to suitable orders, say that the number of women in this age group has 'greatly increased'. Such entrants are described tactfully as 'adult', rather than 'late', vocations. But the orders are less than enthusiastic about them, for ageing communities are already a problem. In many orders, nearly half the sisters are over sixty-five and only a tiny percentage under thirty, which bodes ill for the future. Then, too, older people find adjustment to convent life more difficult, and many orders do in fact refuse to accept entrants over forty-five.

The sisters say, resignedly, that every age in history produces its own apostolates. And it is probably true that the high standard demanded of entrants now, both educationally and emotionally, has something to do with the small numbers entering.

Even in the early and most enthusiastic days of convent life, there seems to have been no shortage of literature designed to lure reluctant virgins. Herrad, twelfth-century abbess of the convent of Hohenburg in Alsace, was a painter and in pictures and text she put together a work called *The Garden of Delights* which begins: 'Hail, cohort of Hohenburg Virgins, white as the lily,' and goes on to tell them of the pleasures they may expect from religious life. 'Delights await you, riches are destined for you, the court of heaven proffers you countless joys. Christ prepares espousals wondrous in delights, and you may look for this prince if you preserve your chastity.'

By the middle of the thirteenth century there was much material written in English for nuns, mostly spiritual love songs with titles like 'The Wooing of Our Lord'. One of these was 'Love Rune' by Thomas de Hales of Gloucestershire, which describes the happiness waiting for women who accept Christ as their spouse and keep bright for Him the jewel of maidenhood:

A maid of Christ bade me earnestly to make her a lovesong,
That she might best learn how to take a faithful lover,
Most faithful of all, and best suited to a free woman;
I will not refuse her, but direct her as best I can.

Maiden, thou must understand that this world's love is rare,
In many ways fickle, worthless, weak, deceiving,
Men that are bold here pass away as the winds blow;
Under the earth they lie cold, fallen away as meadow grass.

Ah sweet, if thou knewest but this one's virtues.
He is fair and bright, of glad cheer, mild of mood.
Lovely through joy, true of trust, free of heart, full of wisdom;
Never wouldst thou regret it if once thou wert given into his care.
He is the richest man in the land as far as men have power of speech,
All is given into his hand east, west, north and south.
Henry the king holds of him and bows to him.
Maiden, to thee he sends the message that he would be beloved by thee.

Another offering of the period was *Holy Maidenhood*, which shows signs of early Women's Lib: the unknown author, upholding the superiority of the free maiden over the one tied to family life, encourages girls to become nuns to escape the troubles of the world. 'And how, I ask, though it may seem odious, how does the wife stand who when she comes in, hears her child scream, sees the cat at the flitch, and the hound at the hide? Her cake is burning on the stone hearth, her calf is sucking up the milk, the earthen pot is overflowing into the fire and the churl is scolding. Though it be an odious tale it ought, maiden, to deter thee more strongly from marriage, for it does not seem easy to her who has tried it. Thou, happy maiden, who has fully removed thyself out of that servitude as a free daughter of God and as His Son's spouse, need not suffer anything of the kind.'

Somewhat less subtle methods of approach were used to attract convent entrants in the 1960s. 'The Scandal of the Nun-Runners' screamed the newspapers, but it was churchmen themselves who described the 'twentieth-century slave traffic', as they accused convents of 'buying' young girls from the poverty-stricken southern Indian state of Kerala. So great was the worldwide publicity, so horrified the outcry, that the Vatican was forced to hold a public investigation. Sad to relate, the traffic appears to be continuing.

It seems to have begun early in 1960, when girls from parts of Asia began arriving in increasing numbers to enter European convents. The 'trade' appeared to be a charitable effort to help the daughters of poor families to achieve a better standard of living and at the same time to assist the convents of Europe during their vocations crisis. As such, it received the blessing of many ecclesiastical authorities in India and Europe. The problem was that in reality these girls had motives for entering which were hardly religious. The majority came from families where food was scarce and the standard of living near poverty. The chance for these girls to escape to Europe and learn a foreign language and new ways was tempting. And for some, the convent was a way of continuing their studies when their families could not afford to support them. Still others entered because their families had no money for the dowry without which they could not marry.

In 1964 ugly rumours of the condition of these girls began to circulate. Many of the girls were minors (the youngest was only fourteen) and it was said that they were not becoming nuns at all but were being trained by the orders in the work they did, usually nursing or medical work, and used for menial tasks. Several had breakdowns. But the real scandal lay in the profit being made by a small number of Indian priests who supplied the girls to the European convents. The nuns paid up to £300 for each girl, which they believed went partly on the plane fare and partly to the girl's parents. At the same time the parents were also paying out money they could barely scrape together, believing they were contributing to the girl's keep: one priest was later said to have received what he called 'donations' of about £31,000 from European convents alone, which he claimed was used to build a recruitment and training centre.

The Vatican finally undertook a full-scale enquiry and, while it refuted allegations of 'nun-running,' it did admit defects in the recruiting system. The number of girls involved was said to be 1571, although people who had been concerned over the girls put the figure at several thousand. However, no girls were to be sent from India to foreign convents, and a committee was set up in 1972 to supervise the work of recruiting, training, and sending girls abroad for religious life.

There is no doubt that the convents took the girls in good faith, believing that they had already professed to a vocation. Their mistake lay in their naïvety and the fact that they were simply not curious enough.

It is significant that it was nursing orders, desperate for vocations, which brought the Indian girls over. It is the active orders, those teaching and nursing in particular, who are suffering most from lack of entrants. Over the past few years an odd pattern has developed; more and more young people seem drawn to the contemplative orders, and in many cases it is these communities which have grown in numbers and strength, most notably since World War II. Mother Mary Joseph who runs the Vocation Sisters, finds that girls say to her: 'I want to go the whole way.'

The Sisters of the Good Shepherd is an order with a wide appeal to the woman with a social conscience: 'Get lost in God as a Good Shepherd sister by helping troubled teenagers, unsupported mothers, maladjusted children, alcoholics and drug addicts.' The order is active in four of the five continents and altogether boasts over 10,000 sisters. They have, like some other congregations, their own contemplative branch, the Sisters of the Cross of the Good Shepherd: there are 2000 of them. The huge London convent, with room for thirty in the novitiate, has at present five novices and one postulant. The much smaller contemplative branch in Ascot, where there are just thirty-five sisters, also has five novices.

There is an increasing tendency for sisters in active orders to move to contemplative houses. It was happening in sufficient numbers by the early 1950s for religious women to start asking themselves whether it was a providential development or a romantic attitude of contemporary life, and for the Pope to point out that the members of an active community have the means of sanctity just as do those in the contemplative life.

'Stay where you are; you can be a saint in your own community.'

Cardinal Suenens, more recently, has pointed out that though there are differences – contemplatives seek the love of God and salvation for the world, and active religious work through speech and the direct transmission of God – 'the impulse of love is the same. The silence of one gives power to the words of the other; those on their knees give strength to those who march.'

It is hard to forecast what will happen in the future. Superiors themselves are convinced that vocations will reappear. Individual orders point to an increasing intake after the slack period during the late 1960s and early 1970s, and the religious press insists that 'there can be no question of decline when the quality of vocations is observably higher than it has ever been.' But even if vocations reappear at the pre-Vatican II level, it is doubtful whether the numbers will be sufficient to balance those leaving.

Leaving the convent without permission used to be a crime punishable by excommunication – and this is still the theoretical penalty in an enclosed order. But the penalty does not seem always to have been applied: the Holy Cross nun who escaped from her Poitiers convent in the sixth century by climbing down a rope and then regretted it was permitted to return – the only condition being that she had to use the same rope to do so.

Today literally thousands of nuns are leaving their convents every year. There are no accurate figures available, partly because it is not a tally anyone cares to keep, partly because it is hard to keep track of those who have actually left, or who have taken a year's leave of absence to consider their future, or who, as one superior put it, 'are just dithering'. But a conservative estimate suggests that in the last seven years more than 30,000 women have left American convents alone, while a more accurate one is likely to be that in one year alone 10,000 walked out. In 1975 the Vatican confirmed that the sharpest drop in the number of nuns had occurred in the

United States and Canada. Its own estimate was that over the previous four years the number of Catholic nuns in the world had fallen by 24.6 per cent to 609,369.

Leaving used to be the ultimate disgrace. 'Changing your mind about religious life was absolutely unforgivable,' remembers a former sister. 'I had a terrible sense of failure,' confesses another. But now, suggests an Anglican superior, 'leaving is more common than it was in exactly the same way divorce is more common. We're much more permissive, you know. We're not really so isolated. What goes on in the world goes on here, too.' She believes that the attitude of people towards their religious vows has changed, just as in the world the attitude has altered towards the marriage vow. 'The feeling of being bound by a vow has lessened. It doesn't mean the vow has any the less value; if you aim for the highest, you're bound to fail at times.'

Other women echo this feeling. As an American sister put it: 'It's ridiculous to talk about this once-and-for-all call to God — He may be calling you to something else.' Evelyn Whitehead, a former member of the Glenmary sisters, remembers that 'in the past, the vows were formalized, we understood that vocation was a lifetime thing. God had called you and to retract was to repudiate an invitation.' Which explains why the idea of leaving religious life used to be just about impossible. All the circumstances which conspired to put a woman into the convent — the lack of opportunity for single women, the prejudice against such women in the eyes of the world — conspired to keep her there. The result was that many women remained in convents who should not have done so. Monica Baldwin, who wrote *I Leap Over the Wall* in the 1940s, was the first woman to leave with so much publicity. She admits that she discovered it was not the life for her, but even a 'dreadful, tragic mistake' hardly seemed sufficient reason for 'backing out of what one had taken on'. And so she remained in the convent for eighteen more years with that knowledge. Others stayed even longer. A Sacred Heart superior remembers 'one person who really should have gone. She didn't, she stayed till her death: she just couldn't face the feeling that she'd disgraced herself.'

Some remained because they could not face the repercussions on their families, and even now this is a very real
problem. Catholic parents, happy to give their daughters
to religious life, are often horror-struck when they leave.
One Belgian nun described how her sister had left the convent
for a year to try and decide about the life. 'Our parents have
a small farm, they struggled to give us an education. My
mother prays desperately that she'll go back at the end of the
year. The fact that here she is, thirty almost, and not married,
is a terrible worry to them – and they were ashamed to tell
the neighbours.' Another woman says sadly: 'When I left it
nearly killed my mother. It broke her heart.' A former sister
explains: 'In Ireland, it is still considered a frightful disgrace,
a terrible failure, for a daughter to return home from the
convent. My mother didn't know how to show her face to the
neighbours.'

There are women who remain in their convents because
of other fears. Says a superior: 'It does so depend on a person's
relationship with her superior. If she feels she will be understood, well and good. But suppose you've got the sort of
superior who simply couldn't put herself in the situation:
there could be difficulties.' A woman now out of religious
life believes that 'many women would have left long ago, but
the superior would say, "I'm sure this is just a temptation,
I'm sure you've got a vocation." And if they did go, before
Vatican II, they were treated like traitors.' But even if they
did not leave, many considered doing so, and freely admit it.
This is a Sacred Heart sister in her late seventies: 'I've had
one or two real crises, and sometimes I've known that if
I'd had a home to return to, I might have given way.' Mary
Garson, foundress and psychologist, has found that 'every
religious has a very big problem at some time or other when
things are exceptionally difficult. Then she asks whether she
should be there and it's a test of whether she sticks it out or
whether she doesn't – like marriage.'

Before Vatican II, if a man or woman left religious life, it
was assumed that he or she did so because they could not live
it any longer due to some personal inadequacy. Even today it is
still sometimes considered – if not actually spelt out – that

leaving is a form of faithlessness. Yet after Vatican II there was a dramatic increase in the numbers of those leaving. These women claimed that the opposite was true, that it was because they wanted a really religious life that they were going. 'I had to leave the convent,' says one such woman, 'to do what I entered to do – live for others.'

Some superiors feel that these women are merely reflecting the restlessness in society. 'Individuals entering religious orders come from this unstable environment,' says an Anglican superior, Mother Joanna of the Deaconess Community of St Andrew. 'They themselves are bound to be influenced by it, and will bring some of the causes of instability with them.' Such people, she believes, expect change of circumstances, and even of vocation. They expect, too, immediate and perfect fulfilment. There is also, she thinks, an inability to accept and use difficulties in a constructive way, which may result in a desire to escape from the religious life, 'or in neuroticism which springs from prolonged repression'.

In medieval days depression, boredom and despair were acknowledged enemies of the soul, and nuns were solemnly warned to be occupied 'in profitable and honest travails' so that such emotions should be 'scared away and eschewed', as the Franciscan Minoresses' thirteenth-century rule explained. The melancholy and sadness peculiar to nuns even had its own name: 'L'accidie', or accidia, as spiritual torpor was known. Teresa of Avila knew about it, and wrote a whole chapter on this 'grave malady' in her *Book of the Foundations*. She believed this 'subtle disease' was an instrument of Satan. 'The matter is dangerous,' she wrote, 'and one sister in this state is enough to disquiet a monastery.' She charged the prioresses to have recourse to penance: 'if one month's imprisonment be not enough, let them be shut up for four; you cannot do their souls a greater service.'

'Some,' she wrote, 'waste away in weeping . . . It is very necessary at times to correct the peccant humours by the use of medicines to make them tolerable.' Diet was important. 'Care must be taken that they eat fish but rarely, and it is necessary also that they should not fast as much as the others.' She apologized for 'giving so much advice about this evil,

and none about any other', but explained she did so because
whereas in other illnesses the patient either recovers or dies
in this case they do neither but 'lose all sense, and that is
death which kills all others. They carry about within them
selves a cruel death of sorrows, fancies and scruples.'

Psychologists find that today's equivalents of accidia are the
psychosomatic troubles from which an increasing number of
religious women suffer. Mary Garson believes that in man
cases it is a sign of rebellion particularly common in young
sisters. 'In the early days, I used to come out in a rash, which
was probably frustrated aggression, and I'm sure that's what
Teresa of Avila's illnesses were.' The commonest example
suggests an American nun, another psychologist, is painful
periods. A sister suffering these may well be pushing her
yearning for physical love and children back into her sub
conscious, and will neither admit nor discuss them. But at
the same time the pain is regular proof that her body is able
to hold a baby, so in a way it is welcomed.

One woman, who suffered from severe psychosomatic
illness because of her unhappiness in convent life, was diag
nosed twice as having multiple sclerosis, and at different time
went blind in both eyes. 'I could not see because I did not
want to see.' She left her community in 1966, a year when an
estimated 3600 nuns left convents in the United States alone.

The nun, Midge Turk, can laugh about it now, but she
remembers with mixed feelings how she felt when, after
eighteen years as Sister Agnes Marie of the American Immac
ulate Heart of Mary community, she left religious life. 'I
hadn't any clothes and I hadn't any small talk. People would
ask me, "Have you been in prison?" ' That was eight years
ago. Today she is college editor of *Glamour* magazine in New
York, and looks every inch the part – streaky blonde hair
expensive scarlet suit, modern jewellery. But the transfor
mation was not easy.

Agnes Turk came from a devout Catholic family and, though
it was never actually said by her parents, a life given to God was
considered the best one possible. After high school she
attended Immaculate Heart College, staffed by nuns of the
community. She had a steady boy-friend. 'I was not the nun

type.' Yet she decided she ought to enter with the IHM community while she was still at college, feeling 'if I did not enter the convent I would have to live a life of agonizing penance.'

At first the life was trying for an eighteen-year-old: 'I wondered if God really cared whether or not we completely stripped and remade our beds from scratch every morning.' Then she found her first taste of teaching and mission life completely fulfilling, and took her first vows for a year. She hesitated – and took them for the second year. Then: 'I finally stopped floundering. I would be a nun, and I would – try to be a good one.'

By 1964 she was experiencing periods of depression and illness. One morning in 1965 she awoke to find she was blind in her right eye. It turned out to be a nervous condition, and was cured. Therapy followed, but six months later the sight went in her left eye, and again was cured. This time she heeded the warning, and in 1966 was granted a dispensation from her vows. She was nearly thirty-six. 'I was so secure, all my friends were there. Leaving was a terrible thing, the thought of having to go out and do it all over again.' She had no job, no self-confidence: 'I'd had two nervous breakdowns, I couldn't keep my health, I felt I couldn't do much of anything.' She went to New York and through friends landed a job in a school theatre department.

She met a man and began a hectic social life, but 'I could *not* tell anyone my background. I spent the first few months without telling anyone, and my friends say now they couldn't believe anyone could be so naïve. They'd ask, "Are you really thirty-six?" ' On one occasion she sat next to comedian Alan King, one of the most televised men in America. 'I said, "And what do you do?" He asked the man who brought me where he'd found me, and I just blushed.

'A day didn't go by when I didn't make a boo-boo. I'd say a lot of wrong things. I didn't wear make-up because I was so inept with it, and I'd wash my hair and dry it in the oven and singe it.' Although she still considers herself a Catholic, she does not go to church any more. 'I honestly don't have any guilt feelings.'

Midge Turk finally exorcized convent life by writing a book about it. *The Buried Life* appeared in 1971, and 'the greatest therapy for me was having to think about it.' It brought her considerable fame – or perhaps notoriety is a better word. There was an article about her in *Time* magazine, and a film on NBC. She appeared twice on the Dick Cavett show, and was deluged with letters saying she had no business to be out enjoying herself, she should be committed to the poor and back there working for them. But not for a moment does she regret those eighteen years. She sips her martini reflectively amid the palms in the Waldorf-Astoria Hotel and says that not only did she enjoy that time, but 'I wouldn't be where I am now if I hadn't done that. I'd have been married at eighteen, have five kids and be living in the suburbs running car pools.' She does not want to marry, although she has been living with the same man for several years.

Clearly, her present way of life suits her. She says with some satisfaction: 'I went to Charlotte Ford's wedding party. I know a lot of big names; I consider them my friends.' There is no doubt that today she is a very different person from the uncertain woman who walked out of her convent eight years ago. 'But when I entered, I did what I thought I had to do.'

Anita Caspary, Midge Turk's mother general towards the end of her religious life, says: 'We've lost a great number of creative and talented people. It isn't that they're upset, we keep in touch, they come back, help us raise funds. Like Sister Corita Kent. She's with us in spirit, but *we've* lost.' Not only does the community lose women who joined during the old days, but more recent arrivals, too, 'very attractive, intelligent, independent girls who have had their own cars, their trips to Europe. They've been given privileges by the community, and many have kept up strong bonds of friendship and even continue to teach for us.' Anita Caspary is sure that: 'We have to ask, why does a twentieth-century woman enter the religious community, particularly the more independent, the post-post-Victorian girls, especially those who came from highly affluent backgrounds? Was it the idea of a nun, built up in the Catholic home and school, that brought them in?

Whatever it was, until we get at that, we won't know why she's leaving now.'

For some time religious orders have realized that the reasons given by those leaving have not been causes but symptoms. But it is only now that an attempt is being made to discover why nuns, monks and priests abandon their vocations. In May 1972 the Pontifical Gregorian University in Rome took an unprecedented step and began a detailed study. The man in charge is a fifty-year-old Jesuit, Father Luigi Rulla, head of the university's psychology institute. The depth analysis methods he uses were pioneered by Freud – although as recently as 1950 Catholic clergy were officially warned against practising or submitting to Freudian psychoanalysis.

Even before the results of the study are known, some causes have been admitted. A Jesuit priest, who has worked closely with many women's communities, discovered to his surprise that a major factor is loneliness. 'Often they are unable to communicate with their fellows at a time or in a place that makes for fellowship. Living in proximity does not make for community.'

He is not the only one who thinks this way. Several novice mistresses suggest that the development of personal relationships has been neglected for too long by religious communities. They feel that the number of nuns who have to seek professional medical help confirms this view. Not only is there an increase in mental breakdowns but also, to a lesser extent, of physical ones as well. The novice mistresses put forward 'lack of communication, disintegration and isolation' as some of the causes, and an Anglican novice mistress points out that once a sister becomes isolated, 'the life is no longer dynamic but a gradual decay into bitterness with nothing but a frustrated old age and a long-delayed death at the end.' Which exactly echoes the emotions of the woman who left in her early thirties because, as she explained to me, 'Being in a convent is great when you're young. But I looked at the older sisters and started to wonder how long it would take me to become as bitter as some of them.'

The conviction inside the convent that those who wish to leave are failures has given rise to harsh treatment. This is perhaps less extreme than it was a few years ago, but it is still true that those who leave are often regarded by their sisters as pariahs. A former missionary sister (who left because she was horrified when she was allowed, during a training course, to visit a patient dying of cancer, but forbidden to do so once her course was finished and she was again under strict enclosure) says: 'The minute I'd asked for my dispensation I was taken out of the school where I'd been teaching with no chance even to say goodbye to the pupils.' Nor did the sisters discuss among themselves the fact that someone was leaving. Even when novices were sent home as unsuitable, the others were never told reasons, or even that they had gone. Margaret McConnell describes the departure as 'like a slaughter at a prisoner-of-war camp. The loss was swift and unexpected and no explanation was ever given.' The normal goodbyes were not even said, and the leaver's last night is often still spent in a guest-room well apart from her sisters.

A sister may, of course, leave her order freely if she does so at a time when she would normally have renewed her temporary vows. If she wants to go sooner, her major superior will give the necessary dispensation. Whatever the cause of her leaving, the measures which must be taken should always be carried out with 'justice, charity and kindness'.

After talking to her superior, the sister who chooses to leave normally talks to the provincial of the order, who then sends for the papers. These are signed and processed – the apostolic delegate sending them to the Holy See. If the reasons are considered sound, a 'rescript' is granted, and the nun is released from her vows and the obligations to religious life and restored to her secular state. The sheer machinery of extricating themselves was complicated enough to inhibit many from going: 'I couldn't face all that to-do filling in forms, endless visitations.' But those who stayed for such a negative reason, comments an American novice mistress, should not have been allowed to do so. 'I'm not saying they were bad nuns – they weren't as keen as they should have been, and this had repercussions on the others.' It could take as long as six months before the rescript arrived – three copies, for the nun, the convent and the papal archives, declaring her 'reduced to secular state'. Now, however, the answer often comes inside two weeks and carries no official stigma: the recipient of a rescript is still a full member of the Church, and she can marry in church if she wishes.

In fact, the system has changed so much that according to Sister Honor Basset, 'All sorts of *extraordinary* things are happening, which take us by surprise. I even heard of one person who decided she didn't like the people who were responsible for governing. She wrote the papers out herself, didn't tell her superior at all, and simply announced to her friends that she was going: she did it all back to front.'

Despite the changes, a woman is still apt to find a huge rift between her and those who remain behind. To a degree, this is understandable. When a nun leaves it does affect the whole convent: 'It leaves a sadness, a feeling that someone who's been really dear has gone. We're a family, and what happens to one happens to everyone.' But more than that, it inevitably must seem to those remaining that the departing sister has found the life they are living second-best. Perhaps that is why some religious take a degree of comfort from the difficulties of those who go. 'They have their little regrets,' comments an American sister. 'Those who have left,' says another, 'write and tell us how lonely they are.' But some women feel genuine anger at their going: 'When people left, I felt aggrieved.'

This attitude may help to explain the appalling difficulties many women face as they go. This was particularly true in the 1950s when leaving was still a very unusual event. At that time convents seemed genuinely not to know just how difficult was the transition to secular life. And they did not trouble to find out. It was not callousness, merely ignorance: a fact which can have been of little help to the nun who slept in Grand Central Station for nine nights, existing on a tin of Metrecal a day, before she found help. Things have now changed to a degree. A woman of fifty-seven, shortlisted as provincial superior, was given on leaving a car and 'a good deal' of money. On the other hand, in 1971 a nun from Virginia was given her ticket to New York – one way – and $5. She was sixty years old. And it is only within the last three or four years that convents have allowed people to stay on until they get a job and some security before leaving.

The woman leaving convent life is faced with a question of sheer survival. As one woman said: 'If I could not survive here, where would I survive?' For many the answer is all too plain – a one-room apartment, a clockwork job and an emotional desert. But over the years the number of nuns – and monks and priests – leaving their orders has reached such epic proportions that organizations have mushroomed to cope with their difficulties. Most are in the United States, but there are some in Britain and even Italy. The largest of these organizations is Bearings for Re-establishment, Inc., which operates out of a brownstone on New York's East 49th Street, and has a sign in the reception room: 'CAUTION. Human beings here. Handle with care.'

Bearings was started in 1965 by a former priest. Bill Restivo wanted to fill the void into which religious fell on leaving their orders, and also to give them small loans to tide them over 'while they got their bearings'. In those early days Bearings provided the men and women who came to the office with food, clothing, and somewhere to live while they looked for work. The organization was often the only recourse for people who found themselves without friends or money, and with no wish to ask their orders for help – even if it might have been forthcoming. 'People used to turn up on the doorstep with a suitcase,' remembers a member of staff, 'and say, "Here I am, help me."' Some of the people who came to them had been in their community twenty or thirty years, and had entered straight from high school. 'Half a life time of chastity, poverty and obedience is no ticket to success in a competitive consumer society.' Often, these people could get no references from 'previous employers' and therefore had to look for the type of jobs where none were needed.

Bearings never asks anyone why they left – 'We don't want

people to cry on our shoulder.' It is in no sense a clinic, but to help people through the early part of what they call the 'transitional process'. The organization has found that men and women respond best to group therapy. 'It's a quest for identity.' And, although quite a lot of religious do want therapy, it is more a problem of reorientation they face than anything else. Very rarely do they feel bitter. In fact, says a psychiatrist, 'very few have deep-seated problems – certainly no more than anyone else.'

Finding work is hard. Used only to the non-competitive religious world, unused to handling money, these 'formers', as Restivo calls them, find themselves at a total disadvantage when they try to resume normal life. Then, too, they have to contend with the public image of someone who has 'failed' in religious life. Bearings warns them not to hide this fact, since many 'formers' have actually lost their jobs when it eventually came to light. One sister to whom this happened said she simply could not believe it. 'It was as if they'd found out I was a habitual criminal.' And a former priest, who held a job for four months before revealing his 'past', was then asked to leave because he was felt to be 'unstable'. Bearings overcomes the question partly by tact – referring to former religious as 'people who have left professional church occupations', and partly by common sense: the advice they give to job-hunters is full of the most basic information, such as go to interviews alone, be on time, do not try to show anyone that you are a swinger yet.

Their 'pre-employment counselling' gives what is so desperately needed – an idea of the sort of work the former religious might do. Bearings can advise on anything and everything, from counselling at alcoholic clinics to working in a store, an important service for people who may never before in their lives have made such choice for themselves of what work to do. Over the years, Bearings has built up a reputation among personnel officers for 'good' people who are prepared to start at low salaries just to gain experience. They are single, able to move around freely, and conscientious.

Bearings reckons to see around a hundred people a month, of whom half are women, and although it is hard to be sure without accurate statistics, thinks it probably sees less than twenty per cent of all the people who leave. The organization now has offices throughout the States. Nor is it the only such organization. There is Contact Centre in Philadelphia and Next Step in San Francisco, both doing similar work, and there is clearly a need for yet more — Bearings has letters from nuns and priests as far away as India and the Philippines. Increasingly, Bearings has found its role changing. More recently, the need for the original emergency function has slackened slightly. People are now planning their leaving more carefully. Many have friends who have left before them to whom they can turn for advice; some of those contemplating leaving contact Bearings well in advance, or are advised to by their superiors, in order to plan properly and lessen the 'transition' problems.

Bearings has begun to see yet another form of transition, a sort of dropping out from within. Some religious, unsatisfied with their jobs inside religious communities, were leaving without seeing what alternatives might be available to them within the general framework of religious life. So Bearings received a foundation grant to start the Manhattan Career Centre to counsel such people. There was, for instance, the case of a women's order obliged to close a school which was no longer economic. Twenty women, who had taught there for between five and twenty-five years, were without work. The Career Centre ran a special group counselling for them, and they moved into child care, drug counselling, and teaching black people.

The other need which Bearings and similar organizations fulfil is social. The typical sister who uses Bearings is thirty-four years old, with a BS in education, part of an MS or MA, and with teaching experience. She is more concerned with her social life than with her career, whereas her male counterpart is career-conscious. She may want to live on her own, particularly if she is above thirty-four, because she has lived with women for years. She is usually in desperate need of a social circle, and if she is lucky enough to live in or near New York, or one of the other cities with a similar organization, she can join its social club with a $2 membership

Bearings has a social director who organizes theatre visits, socials, hikes and house parties. Those who live too far away for such activities are advised by Bearings to join 'community things – we suggest political clubs, chess groups'. The social-club newsletter invariably contains a list of engagements, with an asterisk for those who met through Bearings. And this pinpoints another major motive for women leaving religious orders: attitudes towards celibacy have altered radically in the religious lifetime of many women. They entered genuinely believing that this was indeed the way of perfection – and found themselves trapped when current thinking put forward the view that neither men nor women can develop normally and happily cut off entirely from any relationship with the other sex: that man is closer to God in contact with his fellows than he is apart from them; and that a life without deep personal relationships is less than complete. So religious who leave are often anxious to marry, and while it would appear that priests often have a specific person in mind when they leave, nuns rarely do.

The majority of women who leave convents do so between the ages of thirty and thirty-eight, whereas men tend to leave a few years later. This is connected very strongly with a woman's biological role. Between eighteen and twenty-two, celibacy is acceptable to most women. Adolescence is over and energies are channelled into university or some other training for a career. It is at this time that a girl usually enters and takes her vows. Afterwards the structure of the life involves her completely: 'I didn't have time to think,' says a young Italian woman. 'There was so much to achieve, there were so many goals to reach.' Nor was there any personal romantic involvement to hasten adult sexuality, so it was often not until the late twenties or thirties – or even forties – when the sister had achieved many of these goals, that she had time to think about any dissatisfaction she might feel. In any case, a healthy woman's physical sexuality is stronger at thirty than at eighteen. To cap all this, 'The menopause,' according to American sister-psychologist Judith Tate, 'carries a very special emotional pain for the celibate woman. Not only did she never have marital love and children – but now she never can.'

There are, of course, many women who leave religious life and make a great success of subsequent marriage.

Oak Avenue, Twickenham, is a neat London suburban street, and No. 60 looks trim and secure. Inside, a man is busy painting the hallway pale blue, while in the garden a sturdy three-year-old shouts and romps and a blonde woman cuddles a fat baby on her knee.

Therese McVeigh works full-time as the head of the English department at a boys' school, and relishes the holidays when she can spend more time with her family. She is thirty-nine now and started her family late. But few of her friends, and none of her colleagues, know that this is because she spent eighteen years as a nun.

Therese effectively entered at fourteen. She and her elder sister left their secondary school in Ireland to join the Good Shepherd sisters as school postulants. When they arrived at the London convent each was handed a black dress and a black net veil.

Even at fourteen, Therese and the forty-nine other young girls began to learn the rudiments of religious life: Mass every morning at 6.30; meditation for half an hour every weekend; keeping silent for two hours a week. They were not watched, but a reasonable degree of perfection was expected. 'The novice mistress sat by the door and you knelt down beside her and kissed the floor and admitted what you'd done wrong and she would give you three Hail Marys to say.' The girls were treated as mature adults. 'The fact that we said we had a vocation made them assume we had that kind of maturity, but we were only well-intentioned school-girls. They treated us as people prepared to sacrifice ourselves, and it knocked a lot of the courage out of us.'

Looking back, she feels that the worst part of those first years in the convent was that when she and her sister had entered, they had been promised they would return home, 'so I wasn't leaving for good.' In fact, she was not allowed to go home for fourteen years. 'The novice mistress said it would disturb me, and my parents accepted her judgement.'

At sixteen Therese went into the novitiate. 'I wasn't at that time very spiritual but I was beginning to absorb the atmosphere.' But once she was actually teaching and living the full convent life, 'I just wasn't happy. I had no deep human relationships because nuns are expected to live for the love of God alone.' She emphasizes that 'it wasn't that I needed a sexual relationship. In fact, I never did feel the need for it: I was very young for my age. It was just that I didn't feel I mattered very much to anyone.' By the time she was thirty-two she was conscious that 'I was getting older and I had this unfulfilled feeling. I decided to go. It was a hard decision, because I had great friends and in the convent they emphasized night and day that we had an obligation to stay. But the long littleness of life got me down.'

The reason for her leaving was given as incompatibility of temperament and bad health and in less than a week the papers were processed through Rome and she had six months' dispensation. It would be a year before she was fully dispensed from her vows, so she could try life in the world and decide whether or not to return. 'I left with dignity – none of this dressing me up in frumpish clothes. The mother superior gave me £150 and took me to the station, and my sister met me at the other end with clothes she'd bought.

'I decided I would get married within a year. I couldn't see any future for myself as a single woman teacher, I felt I'd develop mannerisms and oddities. The second vocation in life is marriage, and it never occurred to me that I'd have any difficulty.' She started off by going to a cosmetician in Bond Street. 'They really had a go at me – plucked my eyebrows and did me up. I'd cut my hair at my sister's and it looked desperate, because for all those years I'd worn a bonnet round my face. Then I bought some clothes and gradually got used to things – I found false eyelashes helped me. Then one day a lorry tooted three times and I knew I'd arrived.' She began going to dances as the only way to meet men. 'I took great risks. Not knowing the moral standards of the day, I didn't know the kind of man that was trying to pick me up, as an ordinary girl would.'

She need not have worried. She had seven proposals, 'which I took entirely for granted'. Looking back, she feels she led people on. 'But I was protected by my own innocence – and I was trying to live all my youth in two years.' She had left the convent in February. In April she met the man she later married, who was teaching at the same school as herself. 'I was still a nun when we met, but I wouldn't tell him,' partly because he is a complete agnostic, partly because she was still fully bound by her vows. 'But I thought I could get to know him without canoodling.'

Therese says she is incredibly lucky in her husband. 'He's a terrific husband, he really is ideal. It took me a long time to enjoy sex after marriage. You're trained to repress any thought of it, to cast it out of your mind, and so you don't come to terms with it. But my husband was delighted I was a virgin and he was marvellous.' There are still odd hang-ups from the convent, attitudes that have spilled over into her married life. Food is one of them. 'If you said something was nice, you were told it was very worldly to be a gourmet. And when I came out, I never said whether anything was nice or not. But my husband says I'm the worst cook in Britain, and he once went out to buy fish and chips in the middle of one of my meals. I was amazed – I expected him to eat what I put in front of him.'

They hoped for children straight away, 'so there would be more richness to life,' but waited three years for their family. Therese adores her children, but admits that 'I still have tremendous admiration for the religious life, and I got great fulfilment from it. It gave me a rock certainty in the existence of God and an afterlife. I've thought if I were faced with tremendous sorrow that maybe I would come to terms with it quicker. But I still feel there are parts of religious life I'd love to have kept – that tremendous friendliness in community life. If my husband died, I'd like to go back in my old age. The children are marvellous, of course, but I could hand them over: I've kept that detachment. But my husband's happiness is in my hands.'

*

It is an unkind irony that the most liberal and forward-moving orders have lost the most members – and were the first to do so. This explains the great numbers who left communities in America's Midwest early in the 1960s. The first nun to appear in mufti on an American university campus; the theologian whose books on renewal became standard textbooks for changing communities; Corita Kent of the startling lithographs – these are the women who have left their orders. At a time when the Church has in many ways never been so exciting, never offered so many possibilities to its sisters, never been so free, so open to ideas, the women who leave are some of the best and most adventurous. Recently Bearings and Next Step, as well as Human Resource Developers – a private consultant firm that places former American priests – have noted the increasingly high calibre of those going. Records show them to be even better qualified and more creative than their predecessors, and a growing number have left after holding positions of authority.

These women are leaving because they find the change too great. *Aggiornamento* brought with it uncertainty and restlessness, and the lack of clarity about the life and what it is meant to be has not yet resolved itself. As an American put it, 'The women religious I see are adapting and adapting and adapting until there's nothing left.' In the mid-1960s, after their chapter discussed and planned change, over one hundred Italian Daughters of St Paul left out of 3000.

It does happen that changes within a community drive out members who would otherwise not have dreamt of leaving. One young American, a former Glenmary sister, was 'really happy' as a nun: 'I might well have been a mother general when I was forty.' But her order disagreed with the hierarchy over the increasingly restricted life they were forced to lead, and she joined the non-canonical group, who continued to work amongst the poor of Appalachia and accepted married couples and non-Catholics as members. Eventually, she broke away completely.

Dr Corinne Hart was an Immaculate Heart of Mary sister in

Los Angeles, and went with the group which became non-canonical. After nearly three years, she decided to leave altogether. Now in her forties, she has spent a lifetime in the order, but 'what's holding us together is the past. For me, I have no sense of what the future is for this group. I don't see the vision of ours working any more: there is nothing I can do as an Immaculate Heart that I couldn't do as an individual.' Dr Hart is a businesslike, slightly brusque woman who works in Los Angeles at the Franciscan Communications Centre making religious films. She lives in one room over a garage, 'and it's lovely to get home alone'. Even while she feels that 'it was security, and not wanting to hurt the older sisters that kept me this long,' she deeply regrets the final step. For her, there was real pride in being an IHM. 'But now I find the freedom of life-style we're experiencing incompatible with maintaining an institution.'

Others go because the changes are not enough, and they feel their communities have not taken the cultural leap that is necessary for survival. They see religious life as irrelevant to the church today, an anachronism surviving into the twentieth century by virtue of tradition and reverence rather than need. Some, like the Reverend Mother Mary Clare, mother general of the Anglican order of the Sisters of the Love of God, find this not only understandable but blame the community, which they believe is responsible for the loss. She sees genuine cause for frustration in 'conditions which are outdated or outmoded,' and in regulations which deny them 'right and proper channels for growth in initiative and responsibility'. Women who find their ideas in conflict with those of their community very ocasionally move to an order they find more congenial. But most of these seem to find it hard to adapt to their new order.

It is far more common for dissatisfied sisters to leave. One sister now planning this step has no idea where she will go or what she will do, 'but it's no longer possible for me to live and work in such an intransigent structure.' Another found: 'It wasn't a place where I could function, so I moved on.' A third insists that her leaving 'wasn't a question of turning my back on Christ, I simply had to have the freedom to make mistakes'. And a fourth felt: 'I'd given up my freedom. I just woke up and said, I can't take any more.' Some rationalize their feelings even further, and admit they left because they could no longer stand living in a male-dominated society. This is true mainly of American women like Maryellen Muckenhirn. 'I left because I could no longer go on with women who wanted to continue being put upon by men – and foreign men at that – who don't understand our life-style at all.' Maryellen Muckenhirn is in her early fifties, and now teaches the philosophy of religion at Chicago's Marillac College. She is the best-known woman theologian in the United States – and she used to be Sister Charles Borromeo of the Holy Cross at Notre Dame.

'I was twenty when I entered and I loved it: I never had an unhappy day, and I was in the community for twenty-three years.' She believes she was really suited for religious life. 'I just wanted to teach and read, I wasn't interested in clothes and marriage.' But, over the years, she became conscious that she was with 'a very conservative group'. For a long time this did not matter since she was always on her own within the community because of her work: 'I've never lived in convents.' Finally, she became aware that 'if you change and develop and alter your ideas, you suddenly find you're not acceptable.' And when she left in her mid-forties, she realized that 'I had outgrown the life.'

Maryellen Muckenhirn feels neither regret nor guilt at leaving Sister Charles Borromeo so far behind her, and when she receives letters asking if she plans to start a new community, 'I go up the wall. To gather together with a group of middle-aged women? I don't *want* to.' What she does want is 'to live like a free human being. I'm interested in trying to really shake off the convent.'

She did so by leaving. But even those who remain are beginning to agitate for the end of dependence on the physical institutions of convents. As Sister Lillanna Kopp, the American sociologist and author insists, 'marble mother houses are what destroyed the old orders.' The feeling now is that massive convents, as much as the way of life within them, provide artificial insulation against the harsh realities of the world.

Growing numbers of nuns, like radicals throughout the
Church, are highly critical of the wealth of that Church.
They dislike being women of property despite their vows of
poverty. They see it as scandalous that they live in half-empty
convents while the homeless sleep in doorways. One young
English sister who raised this with her superiors was accused
of 'wanting to lower our standards', and told: 'We must
preserve our calm and our interior life.' She sees such talk
as a sign of spiritual bankruptcy and considers that the
standards are middle-class rather than Christian. And a young
American, a Sister of St Joseph of Carondelet, insists: 'We
must rekindle the Church. And we won't do it by living in
big houses with the rich.' Another American nun has even
suggested that new institutes should write 'self-destruct'
clauses into their constitutions so they would have to start
again every twenty or thirty years, thus avoiding a 'shoring
up of possessions'. Even the most successful of the 'old' orders
acknowledge now that change must come. Honor Basset, a
superior in the Sacred Heart order, believes 'we are at a
transition stage where many things are forcing a new type of
religious out, and it hasn't come yet.' She feels that 'something quite new will emerge and sweep the field for a time –
I can feel it coming. I can see a stage where religious orders
become more like regiments in an army, each regiment with
its own characteristics and its own spirit and so on, but all
doing more or less the same work.'

The most interesting new communities are not growing up
in the old way. In the past, a community would take on some
particular task – hospitals, schools, perhaps houses in slum
areas. But now there is a totally different approach. In a world
of increasing knowledge, the specialist is king, and as religious
women are leaving their houses to follow their own interests
and work while still remaining part of the community, they
are getting together with people of similar interests to work
jointly on projects. During the winter of 1961, a group of
nuns from Chicago decided they must co-ordinate their
resources to meet the needs of the people. They called

themselves the Urban Apostolate of the Sisters, and more than eight hundred from five areas work for education, communication and action, co-ordinating the work, assisting the white, Spanish and Negro communities. They were so successful that a similar inner city venture, Caritas House, was started in Washington, concentrating more heavily on basic education for families.

Such projects have had the effect of radically changing the concept of community. 'Community' used to be something ready-made into which the entrant walked: she was expected to be another community sister, not in any way singular, not different from the others. Community was seen in geographical terms: everyone was in the same place at the same time — in chapel, in the community room, in refectory. But so far has this sense of community lessened that it is not so much the sisters of an individual order which constitute community, but the bond of a particular work or cause. Sisters are realizing, as Eileen Gielty of Notre Dame says, that 'community is the sense of belonging, doing what you do with the strength and support that comes from belonging to that group.' And to an American sister student spending the summer with a health group for itinerant farmworkers, community 'is the sisters I am living with'.

Nuns are now beginning to talk of members of various communities joining permanently to form centres where some particular work would be pursued. Such groups would be alike enough in taste and temperament to be able to work and live together on a semi-permanent basis, and there would be no such thing as a Dominican, a Franciscan, a Maryknoll: they would all be part of one Christian community. One such project is already under way. In September 1973 the World Justice and Peace office opened on North Third Street in Milwaukee, Wisconsin. 'This will be a model for inter-community action,' promised Pat Drydyk, a dark and gentle girl and one of the first members. There are eight other sisters from five different communities working with her, and 'when we work together,' claims Pat, 'there's a beautiful interaction. This is the first place I've worked where the impetus really comes from everybody.'

N.—N

The first thing they did was to gather together a hundred 'key' Americans including two leading nuns, Sister Margaret Traxler of NAWR and Sister Luke Tobin, superior of the Sisters of Loretto at the Foot of the Cross and the only American nun present at Vatican II, and to take them in a chartered plane to the Coachella Valley, where they joined the picket lines against the Teamsters. The Justice and Peace team spend much of their time doing research into social injustice such as poverty and discrimination, and organize their own communities to take the most effective action.

Pat, a Franciscan sister, long ago moved out of any regular convent life, and in Los Angeles shared an apartment with a Victory Knoll sister. In Milwaukee, she lives with ten other sisters in a group ranging in number from twenty-five to sixty-five, but she feels this is too large, and hopes soon to move into a smaller group, preferably composed of the people with whom she works. This could mean sharing a community life with sisters from different orders, with varying constitutions and life-styles. 'It's not,' admits Pat, 'community in the sense of a structured setting – but it's community for me.' She believes it unlikely that the present convent system will be around in twenty years. 'It may evolve into a more open structure that would allow for different kinds of life-style.' Like all the women I met living away from their communities, Pat is anxious not to cut herself off in any way. When she was working in Los Angeles she telephoned regularly and ex-changed long letters, just as would the member of any close family. And she does in fact worry that, as increasing numbers of young women work away from their communities – and this is happening in such numbers that many orders have now opened their own personnel offices to help the sisters find suitable jobs – the older sisters must do without the young and enthusiastic workers.

Many European communities for whom such moves are still unthinkable are undertaking experiments which are nevertheless radical in their terms, and which they hope will help define for them the pattern of their future.

In the polished entrance hall of a large girls' boarding-school

n a leafy road near Tunbridge Wells, an elderly nun, stooped
n her black and white, sits in a small reception booth. A
ousled girl in jeans and a baggy sweater dashes in, jangling
ar keys. They smile at each other. 'Hallo, Sister.'

Both women are members of the Society of the Sacred
Heart. Although they live in the same house, they each have a
lifferent superior, separate living quarters, and a totally
lifferent life-style. They are involved in an experiment which
hey believe will help their order develop in the best way
possible. It began in the summer of 1971, when Sister Honor
Basset was superior of the house. The time had come to plan
renewal, but it was hard to know in which direction to go.
The problem was that the community fell naturally into
two halves: the younger sisters, active in teaching, with their
lives before them, and the considerable number of older
women.

After much discussion, they decided to form two groups,
divided more or less on an age basis, which meant that the
younger people had both their youth and involvement in their
work in common. The older community of eighteen took the
name Wells ('because still waters run deep') and Honor
Basset continued as superior. Life there goes on much as it
always did. Many are still in the full habit, though others,
like Sister Basset, wear a dark suit and white blouse with a
short veil, which is optional. The formal hours of prayer –
though these have been amended in recent years – continue
in the tranquil chapel. Once strictly enclosed, they now go
out, though still not casually.

The younger group of thirteen has become 'Bridge'
('they're the bridge to the new') and chose as superior Sister
Russell, headmistress of the school, though she insists that
'we have yet to work out the role of superior'. Their life-
style has changed drastically.

The older sisters find the breakaway group easier to understand than do the middle-aged. Mother Stuart is in her eighties,
a frail bedridden woman: 'The younger people are moving
away from our form of life. Nothing we can do will stop it.
I feel that something very good and new will emerge. It
may not be what we knew when we were young – but I'm

not frightened.' On the other hand, Sister Hilda Mason, teacher in her early forties, decided to stay with the olde group: 'I would hate to see religious life split into generations. She regrets the split deeply. 'We were one family and nov we're torn in two.' She finds that 'being organized is ver satisfactory. Also I like silence, I think it's strengthening. She sees good in both methods, but is convinced that 'if went further and we went into little houses, I'd apply to th bishops and join an order who've kept big houses – I think community based on compatibility is asking for the moon. But Sister Honor Basset sees no alternative. 'At the moment we let people have what they feel they need, knowing i won't be going on for ever. One knows that with anothe generation there won't be many of the things we're used to and the living will change.'

Certainly for the Bridge Community the rigidity tha characterized the life of their order until so recently ha gone. Sister Russell is particularly conscious that 'the youn; lay tremendous stress on reality. Any custom that is artificial they ask, why keep it?' They wear the clothes they choose putting on trousers, or jumpers and skirts. They can us discreet make-up, and curl their hair. They play tennis an swim in the grounds, and in the summer go youth hostellin; with the children in their care. They do not go to the cinema not because they are not allowed to, but because it cost more than they can afford. All decisions are made as a group But perhaps the most important change in the little Bridg group is that previously the concept of community wa strictly tied to the order of day – rising at 5.20, doing every thing by the clock, retiring at 10.10. Work was not the prim thing; the life was. Now, their work in the school is a fa: stronger link between them. They go to bed when they fee like it; they go for walks when they choose to. In fact, they are no more restricted than most teachers in boarding-schools In the eyes of the Wells community, their greatest change i: in the way they pray. Some days they join the Wells com munity in chapel, at other times they group in their crowded community room. Someone reads from the scriptures, they might sing a psalm; then, after minutes of silent prayer, they will talk rather like Quakers in Meeting. This, to some of the older sisters, is anathema.

Whatever the outside reaction to their community, the Bridge sisters believe that 'unless we have a change in our community life, there'll be no future in the twenty-first century, because young people of calibre won't enter. You're looking for something, either in marriage or convent life, where you can continue to grow. One wants that situation that makes a more complete human being.'

These Sacred Heart sisters are taking what they hope will be a successful path to complete renewal.

In the United States, changes within the old community structures are seen mostly in orders like this, particularly those located in the Midwest. The old, traditional, family-shaped convent has to accept the new urban life with its stresses and problems, its speed and facelessness. Those orders which have not adapted have either disappeared or shrunk to the point where they will soon do so. 'The end of many smaller institutes is in sight,' warns the American psychologist Sister Annette Walters, 'a chilling reminder that what God has given he could also take away.'

There is, however, a counter-movement: from about 1960, groups with a new concept began to spring up. They multiplied rapidly after the impetus of Vatican II, and now a regular yearly register is sent out to incorporate information about them. At least a hundred of these little experimental communities have appeared in America alone, though some disperse because their members decide they would prefer marriage or careers as secular single women. Despite this evidence of attrition, there are well over fifty flourishing at the moment, some with a membership of 300 or so women. Most of them are not subject to the Sacred Congregation for Religious and Secular Institutes, since they are too small — some have only three members. Nor are they bound by special promises of obedience to any bishop, though most are formed with the approval of their local bishop. They are operating in quite a different way from the old communities, virtually as lay groups in a commune situation, sharing a home, dividing duties, regarding their income as common to all. There are no plans to claim for them official recognition which would, they think, merely hamper their work. They are constantly changing and evolving, but the members are no less dedicated than the religious of the formal structures which they found so deadening. Their aim is to follow the spirit of Vatican II, and they feel that to do this it is essential to bypass the outdated rules and antiquated customs that still govern so many sisters. In fact, many of them are actually women who have left religious communities after many years of devoted work.

The largest of these groups was founded in 1970 by Lillanna Kopp of Portland, Oregon, to 'experiment and pioneer new forms of religious life for the twenty-first century'. Sisters for a Christian Community (SFCC) are spread over thirty-two American states as well as Canada and England. There is no mother general, no mother house. Each sister makes her own home, which she might share with one or two other members. She chooses her own work, pays her own taxes. No formal vows are taken, but she will write her own commitment to Christ. She need wear no habit, but she will probably, like Sister Kopp, wear a crucifix. Other groups are tiny, like the Fides community of San Jose, California, where five sisters of Notre Dame de Namur decided, in 1966, that they should explore a life more suited to the needs of a contemporary Church. Their work is wide-ranging, from giving theology courses at the local college to helping overworked young mothers. The parish of St Teresa pays them a salary for this work. And in Nanaimo, Canada, live five former religious in a little house in Newcastle Avenue. This group is headed by Margaret Rowe, the Carmelite who spoke out from her Welsh convent against the male hierarchy, and who left her order shortly afterwards. She is now conducting what is really a three-year experiment in contemplative living in the modern world, trying out private and communal prayer, co-responsibility, and shared decision-making. The group earns its own living and undertakes voluntary work for the department of Indian Affairs and the mental health organization, visiting the lonely and neglected people not reached by official charities.

Many of these groups are solely for former religious – the Society of Mary Immaculate in New York, for instance, which does not ask members to leave their homes to join; the Sisters of Mount Thabor in Detroit, who are contemplatives, living in a convent which they leave only when necessary. Others combine lay and religious, like the Contemplatives of the Sacred Heart, founded in 1964 by Madeleine O'Connell, who went straight into a convent from high school at seventeen, and left in her mid-thirties. One other member of her group is a former religious, the rest are college girls and factory workers, hospital attendants and lawyers, dancing teachers and hotel maids. The purpose of the group is to help its members live a contemplative life in the world and, while they are expected to work for at least four hours a day, beyond that they do not leave the house in Kingston, New York, except to do charitable work.

What these groups are doing is blurring even further the already fine distinction between religious communities and secular institutes like the Grail, whose members may observe poverty, chastity and obedience but who remain lay people. It is the secular institutes which many see as an alternative to traditional religious life which, they consider, has outlived its *raison d'être*. Even Cardinal Suenens has conceded that there is a feeling that secular institutes are better fitted for modern life than traditional convents. As Honor Basset admits: 'Many young people today feel they can do more good outside than they could in a convent,' although she does feel this is because 'they don't understand the wonderful experience of living closely with people who are all contemplating God.'

The best-known of the Protestant communes is German: Imshausen was founded in the 1930s by Vera von Trott, and what began as a shelter for orphans and refugees has developed into a stable community of ten women and five men, who live in the ancestral home of the von Trotts under the monastic vows of poverty, chastity and obedience. From all over the world visitors come to them, not only lay people but professed religious; some stay briefly, others may spend months with the community.

That lay apostolates attract people in the numbers they do proves the need for the kind of commitment they ask. The major difference between them and religious communities does not any longer lie in the style of life they adopt: both wear secular dress; neither need live in a formal community setting; both observe chastity. But it is here that the crux of the matter lies. Nuns, once past their temporary vows, promise chastity for life, lay people promise celibacy only for the time they are with their group. And while with many this does indeed cover a lifetime, it need not do so.

It is beginning to look as though the attitude of the churches towards chastity – that the consecrated virgin, the woman in vows, is set apart and her every act made sacred because of that consecration – might eventually change. Fewer men or women are prepared to put themselves for life into a condition of celibacy. They may be happy to experience this state for several years, but not indefinitely, as the number of those leaving the priesthood and the convent for marriage shows. So does the increasing number of older married couples who desire to enter religious life after their children are grown. Indeed, Rome itself has spoken of the possibility of a community of such couples in Italy.

It is against this background that suggestions are now being heard proposing short-term vocations as an acceptable part of religious life. Celibacy would be regarded differently – not as a lifetime decision, but as a temporary one, necessary for a particular task. Such vocations, it is claimed, are a perfectly logical and workable proposition, whereby a person could spend perhaps ten years in full-time dedication to the religious life, and then leave it for whatever lifestyle he or she chooses.

Increasingly, established religious orders – or individual branches of them – are beginning to accept that some of their communities may be made up of lay people who join them with a limited commitment. Not limited emotionally, but by availability. Such people would not be sisters, but members of the community for a number of years, while carrying on their own lives. It is a totally new concept of community and one which may be the pattern of the future. More and more adventurous groups are taking in, fully, people who are bound to them not by vows but by a moral contract.

Some of these, as we have seen, are non-canonical – the Californian IHMs for instance, and the former Glenmary sisters whose splinter group accepts married couples and non-Catholic members. Yet conventional orders have also taken this step. The Servants of Mary in Ladysmith, Wisconsin, have made some changes to encourage the personal growth of their sisters, such as allowing them to choose their own clothes and assignments. They followed this up by reopening the community to those sisters who had left before such changes were made. At the same time they decided to allow members of other orders to join them – and as a final touch ruled that outsiders may join the order for a limited time.

Other groups are attempting change within the Church structure. In a Dominican monastery of pinkish stone at Sainte-Baume, Provence, live several Dominican priests, a group of contemplative Dominican nuns – and five married couples with ten children between them. Father Maillard, the priest in charge, explains that the idea is that the community should 'enlarge horizons' for its members. The lay people, he explains, 'have come with a desire for spiritual renewal. They no longer felt at ease in the traditional forms of the Church, and they saw coming here as a means of going forward.'

The community decides together who they will accept. Anyone wishing to join to resolve personal problems would be rejected. 'Psychological balance and a stable married life are necessary qualifications.' The couples include an American dancer and his wife, and their small daughter who was born at Sainte-Baume; an engineer who directs the retreat centre with his wife, the family of a former mechanic on a Trans-atlantic liner who handles all the community's maintenance work, and the former director of a metalworks with his wife and child who manage the guest house which accommodates more than 200 people. For the community runs a cultural and spiritual centre where groups come for discussions on anything from psychology and sociology to religion, and take part in all sorts of activities – painting, yoga, ceramics. There are retreats, weekends of reflection, handwork sessions, and amateur dramatics.

The priests, nuns and married couples all live in separate quarters but eat together at midday with any guests who might be visiting them, though the evenings are 'family' occasions. There is a common treasury, and all goods and decisions are shared. The whole community is present for daily Mass, though other parts of the Divine Office – the Church's official prayers – are recited by the priests and nuns. 'In this way we want to create a true community.'

One experiment which has been violently criticized by Rome still continues in a small abbey in the rich lands of Brittany's Côtes du Nord. Boquen consists of a twelfth-century church, a monastic house and a few farm buildings – the classic Cistercian set-up. But the half-dozen brothers there have abandoned almost all the traditional forms of Cistercian life. They have left off their monastic robes and no longer observe monastic silence in special places or at special times. And they have opened the monastery to all who wish to enter: at the gate a notice invites anyone who passes to share their quest for truth and unity in brotherly love. By this they do not mean a chance to walk round or join in an occasional service. These brothers of Boquen have opened their whole community life to outsiders.

The community now consists of up to sixty people, men and women of all nationalities. Many are themselves religious, of different communities. Others are lay people, single and married. They go to share the heavy Breton bread of the brothers not only in the refectory but in the eucharist. They work in the house and garden, help with the meals, share discussions every evening, and the primitive dormitory accommodation for visitors. Some live permanently with the brotherhood. Others are attached more loosely, living away from Boquen and carrying on their professional life, but spending their free time there and taking on responsibilities. This – by Cistercian standards – incredible situation has

been going on since 1966. It was the inspiration of Dom Alexis
Presse, an extraordinary man who felt, after being abbot of
La Trappe, that a more primitive and simple monastic life
should be the aim. He established Boquen on stones razed
by the French Revolution, but having established a community
there he felt it was not enough to return to the original
austere spirit of the order. 'We have either to vegetate or
adapt,' he told his ten brothers. And it was the successor he
appointed, Dom Bernard Besret, 'who created the new
community. A Breton in his mid-thirties, a doctor of theology
and professor of philosophy, he was involved in Vatican II
as an expert on religious life. He believed the isolated monastic
life was a contradiction of what Christianity should be, that
everyone should be the same, that barriers of sex, age or
condition were artificial. His experiment was regarded with
deep suspicion by the superiors in Rome, and he was eventually
deposed. But so many thousands of people – friends, students,
Frenchmen and foreigners – flocked to the monastery to attend
the last service he would give there and to pay tribute to
his inspiration, that six months later Rome was forced to
acknowledge the feeling for him and to allow him to return –
though as a monk, not as prior. The monastery is still in a
state of suspension, their experiment under threat of suppression. But Boquen has shown what can be done with the
most rigid of structures and perhaps it will still become, as
one sister involved puts it, 'the centre of a critical, lyrical
and political Christianity'.

All these rethought forms of community life – the admittance
of lay and married people, the mixing of orders within
one group, the new double communities – are appearing
as viable alternatives to the formal religious order. Those who
continue to live within the old framework face almost
insoluble problems. On the one hand, they realize they
must look for new ways; on the other, they see all too
clearly that they can be crushed and suppressed if those in
authority lose their nerve in the face of innovation.

The only orders not affected are the established contem-

platives. It is surely inconceivable that the Cistercians and the
Carmelites, the Benedictines and the Poor Clares will ever
change. They are too entrenched, they have survived too
much. The basic essentials of contemplative life are as relevant
today as they have ever been: prayer is timeless. There is
evidence of increased vocations to such orders, for there will
always be those enviable fanatics for whom only complete
immolation is enough. Even so, contemplatives make up only
six per cent of all nuns.

The other survivors of the present orders will be those
active communities which have moved into vital work and
found a life-style to match. Mother Teresa and her Missionaries
of Charity, the Good Shepherd sisters, the Maryknolls, the
Daughters of Charity of St Vincent de Paul – if their intake is
smaller than it was, it is still there. Their work is geared
totally to present needs: poverty, delinquency, nursing,
developing underprivileged areas. They deserve success.

But there are many thousands of sisters who fit into neither
category. They are those who believe that formal, institu-
tionalized religious life will cease to matter once the present
generation of sisters in it disappears. The young are not
interested in institutions and anyway, as one American sister
points out, 'religious institutes are means, not ends.'

It is becoming increasingly difficult to define the borderline
between Christian laywomen dedicating their lives to others,
and those sisters who, to all intents and purposes, live and
behave in a similar way. These nuns do not lead a formal
religious life in any sense. They pray when they want to, dress
as they choose. They tend to live away from their communities and work with people who may or may not be
members of religious orders.

If nuns are to survive in any large numbers, then these new
groups which are springing up – small, autonomous, without
written constitutions or even figures of authority – must be
allowed to live and work as they wish with the recognition
of the Churches. They must be allowed to exist officially as
part of the religious life.

Before that happens, there will have to be radical re-
thinking by the Churches. How will they define a nun?

Should the vow of chastity be the criterion? But celibacy is already a feature of the lay communities. What of stability, another essential qualification? Surely, in our fluid society, this will have to be demoted. There will have to be an acceptance among churchmen – and women – that where the old ways do not have the strength to survive, it is better to allow change than to permit decay and disappearance. This cannot be a slow process: if the Church does not move fast, it need not bother to move at all. It may count time in centuries rather than decades, but the women in religious orders do not. Too many of them have been lost to religious life already. There just isn't any more time.

REQUIEM

We come to the monastery to seek God — and death is the shortest route to Him.

CISTERCIAN NUN

The life of a nun is dedicated to God, not for reward in this life, but in the next. It is a preparation and a waiting for death, and though the nuns know there will be purgatory, they know too that, like life, it is part of the redemptive work of Christ. 'Unless we are helping in the redemption, there are no bigger fools than we.'

It has been said that when a nun dies it is like breaking a pane of glass: you put in another. But the knowledge of the life to come does not preserve these women from sorrow for those they have lost, does not in any way lessen their mourning. Yet the ceremonial is joyful, as the early Christian burials were joyful. There is no death. Only a change of worlds.

In the Cistercian monastery of the Holy Cross of Our Lady of La Trappe in Dorset, when death approaches a nun, a wooden rattle is rung in the cloister, the signal for the commencement of ritual almost unchanged since 1098: the Cistercians of the Strict Observance follow the most primitive form of monastic life in the Western church.

All who can, answer that call, hurrying to kneel in the infirmary for the anointing by the chaplain, for the responses and the psalms. When they have prayed for the saints to intercede for her soul, when the priest has been summoned and the last prayers said, when the end has finally come, the body is left quiet for an hour so that the soul may go gently. And at the foot of the bed the great Paschal candle, Christian symbol of eternal light, burns in its wooden holder.

Then the infirmarian washes the body, and clothes the dead woman in her habit; the black scapular over the white cowl, the rough stockings and hand-made sandals. From the garden one of the nuns brings fresh flowers which she has woven into a crown, for 'this is part of life'.

When she is dressed and ready, six of the nuns carry her down to where the priest with his incense-burner receives her body. In procession after the juniors, and followed by the priest, she is borne into the church and placed on the white-sheeted bier facing the altar. She will not be left alone before her God. In their stalls by her side, two nuns recite psalms through the rest of the day, and on through the next night without cessation, while the Paschal candle flickers at her head.

Next afternoon the community assembles to sing the Requiem Mass, then she is carried through the cloister by the nuns singing their sombre Gregorian chant. Through the garden of the abbey she goes for the last time to the private walled cemetery, where even in death the nuns keep their enclosure. She is laid beside the grave dug by the lay brother and the nuns stand in two choirs on either side as the priest blesses the place and hallows it with incense.

Then the sisters, three and three, lower her carefully into the grave, supported on wide bands of linen. For Cistercians lie uncovered in the earth, buried without a coffin.

And before the last service they will perform for their sister, before two nuns start to drop soil softly on to her still body, before they return to the church to sing for her the psalms of penance, all kneel. They bow to the ground and touch it with their knuckles as only Cistercians do. And three times they beg that God may have mercy on her soul, their voices rising in that most plaintive and poignant chant of the church:

Domine miserere super peccatrice.
Domine miserere super peccatrice.
Domine miserere super peccatrice.

INDEX

Also available in Fount Paperbacks

The Divine Pity
GERALD VANN

Undoubtedly Gerald Vann's masterpiece. Many people have insisted that this book should not merely be read, but re-read constantly, for it becomes more valuable the more it is pondered upon.

The Founder of Christianity
C. H. DODD

A portrait of Jesus by the front-ranking New Testament scholar. 'A first-rate and fascinating book . . . this book is a theological event.'   *Times Literary Supplement*

Science and Christian Belief
C. A. COULSON

'Professor Coulson's book is one of the most profound studies of the relationship of science and religion that has yet been published.'   *Times Literary Supplement*

Something Beautiful for God
MALCOLM MUGGERIDGE

'For me, Mother Teresa of Calcutta embodies Christian love in action. Her face shines with the love of Christ on which her whole life is centred. *Something Beautiful for God* is about her and the religious order she has instituted.'   *Malcolm Muggeridge*

Jesus Rediscovered
MALCOLM MUGGERIDGE

'. . . one of the most beautifully written, perverse, infuriating, enjoyable and moving books of the year.'
David L. Edwards, Church Times

Also available in Fount Paperbacks

What is Real in Christianity?
DAVID L. EDWARDS

The author strips away the legends from Jesus to show the man who is real, relevant and still fascinating. A clear, confident statement of Christian faith taking account of all criticisms.

The First Christmas
H. J. RICHARDS

Can one really believe in the seventies in such improbable events as the Virgin Birth, the shepherds and the angels, the Magi and the star in the East? Are they just fables? This book suggests that they might be the wrong questions to ask, and may even prevent the reader from arriving at the deeper issues. What these deeper issues are is here explained with clarity, simplicity and honesty.

Wrestling with Christ
LUIGI SANTUCCI

'This is a most unusual book, a prolonged meditation of the life of Christ using many changing literary forms, dialogue, description, addresses to Christ, passages of self-communing. It is written by a Christian passionately concerned that everyone should know Jesus Christ.'   *Catholic Herald*

Journey for a Soul
GEORGE APPLETON

'Wherever you turn in this inexpensive but extraordinarily valuable paperback you will benefit from sharing this man's pilgrimage of the soul.'   *Methodist Recorder*

Also available in Fount Paperbacks

Prayer for the Day
WILF WILKINSON

A new collection of talks by one of the most popular religious broadcasters in Britain. Mr Wilkinson's introduction is entitled 'The Prayers of an Ordinary Man' and that is what they are – they come out of ordinary experiences, they face ordinary difficulties.

The True Wilderness
H. A. WILLIAMS

'I was moved by the plainness and lucidity of *The True Wilderness*. Mr Williams reminds us simply and eloquently of charity and the way in which "our intrinsic tenderness has been violated".'
John Osborne, The Observer

Into the New Age
STEPHEN VERNEY

This book is a declaration that now is the springtime of the Christian Church. As the human race faces the choice between catastrophe and an evolutionary leap forward in the realm of the spirit, Christianity is being profoundly renewed.

The Life of Jesus Christ
LORD LONGFORD

'It is an impressive piece of work and will help many. It will do much good, and as a devotional commentary on the life of Jesus it is excellent and will bear reading and re-reading. Many people will be glad Lord Longford wrote this book. It is a book of faith written by a man of faith.'
Bishop Nicholas Allenby, Daily Telegraph

Also available in Fount Paperbacks

Where the Action is
RITA SNOWDEN

Short sketches of interesting people from a wide variety of backgrounds: some famous and some who are not well known. At the end of each story Rita Snowden sums up the theme in a short prayer.

A Woman's Book of Prayers
RITA SNOWDEN

Covering the entire Christian year as well as a wide variety of special occasions, it provides a straightforward down-to-earth prayerbook for Christian women; as wives, as mothers, as workers.

Prayers for the Family
RITA SNOWDEN

'I have not the slightest doubt that this book would be of the greatest value in any home, not only as giving actual prayers to pray, but also as providing stimulation and inspiration for people to make their own prayers.'   *William Barclay*

A Book of Comfort
ELIZABETH GOUDGE

'A careful, sensitive anthology of the illuminations in prose and verse that have prevented the world from going wholly dark over the centuries.'   *The Sunday Times*

Also available in Fount Paperbacks

Bible Stories
DAVID KOSSOFF

'To my mind there is no doubt that these stories make the Bible come alive. Mr Kossoff is a born story-teller. He has the gift of making the old stories new.'   *William Barclay*

The Book of Witnesses
DAVID KOSSOFF

'The little stories are fascinating in the warm humanity they reveal. Right from the first one, the reader is enthralled . . . Bringing the drama of the New Testament into our daily lives with truly shattering impact.'   *Religious Book News*

The Bible Story
WILLIAM NEIL

'Like all his work it is hardly to be faulted, and I have never read so splendid a conspectus of the whole Bible. It will help a great many people to get their ideas sorted out. William Neil writes with such authority and lucidity that it can hardly fail.'   *J. B. Phillips*

The Plain Man Looks at the Bible
WILLIAM NEIL

This book is meant for the plain man who would like to know what to think about the Bible today. The first part deals with what the Bible is and what it is not. The second part shows that the Bible is also a record of certain things that happened.

Also available in Fount Paperbacks

Children with Special Needs in the Infants' School
LESLEY WEBB

'Throughout the book the observations and reports show a deep understanding of, and regard and sympathy for, the children.'
Teaching and Training

Prayers for Young People
WILLIAM BARCLAY

The book includes morning and evening prayers for every week of the year, designed to help young people to pray, and also a fine introductory chapter, 'You and Your Prayers'.

The Plain Man Looks at the Bible
WILLIAM BARCLAY

This book is meant for the plain man who would like to know what to think about the Bible today. The first part deals with what the Bible is and what it is not. The second part shows that the Bible is also a record of certain things that happened.

The Bible Story
WILLIAM NEIL

'Like all his work it is hardly to be faulted, and I have never read so splendid a conspectus of the whole Bible. It will help a great many people to get their ideas sorted out. William Neil writes with such authority and lucidity that it can hardly fail.'
J. B. Phillips

Also available in Fount Paperbacks

The Mind of St Paul
WILLIAM BARCLAY

'There is a deceptive simplicity about this fine exposition of Pauline thought at once popular and deeply theological. The Hebrew and Greek backgrounds are described and all the main themes are lightly but fully treated.'   *The Yorkshire Post*

The Plain Man Looks at the Beatitudes
WILLIAM BARCLAY

'. . . the author's easy style should render it . . . valuable and acceptable to the ordinary reader.'   *Church Times*

The Plain Man Looks at the Lord's Prayer
WILLIAM BARCLAY

Professor Barclay shows how this prayer that Jesus gave to his disciples is at once a summary of Christian teaching and a pattern for all prayers.

The Plain Man's Guide to Ethics
WILLIAM BARCLAY

The author demonstrates beyond all possible doubt that the Ten Commandments are the most relevant document in the world today and are totally related to mankind's capacity to live and make sense of it all within a Christian context.

Ethics in a Permissive Society
WILLIAM BARCLAY

How do we as Christians deal with such problems as drug taking, the 'pill', alcohol, morality of all kinds, in a society whose members are often ignorant of the Church's teaching? Professor Barclay approaches a difficult and vexed question with his usual humanity and clarity, asking what Christ himself would say or do in our world today.